MASTERS OF THE UNIVERSE
REVELATION ™

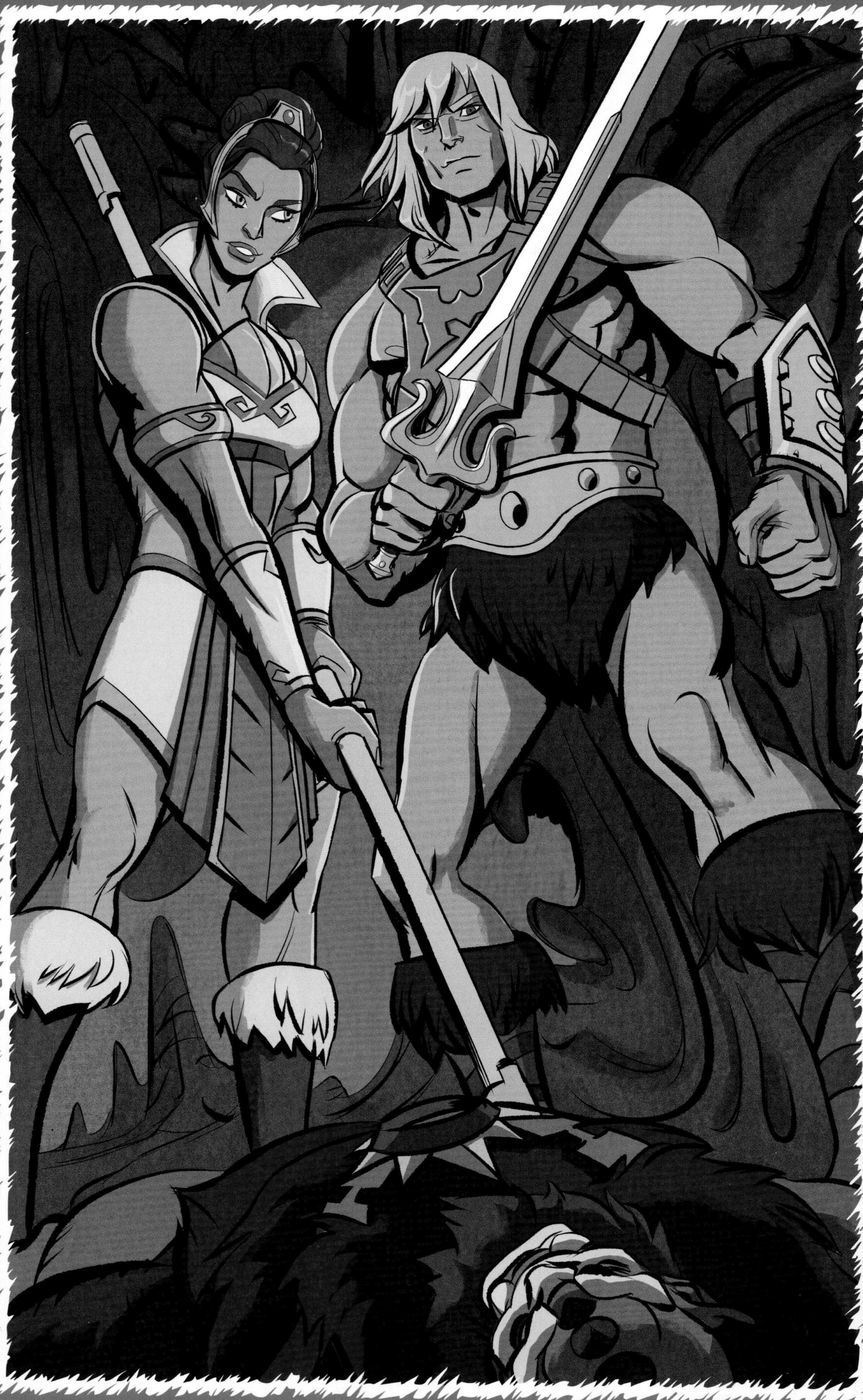

MASTERS OF THE UNIVERSE
REVELATION ™

SECRETS OF GRAYSKULL

◇

Story by
KEVIN SMITH & ROB DAVID

Script by
TIM SHERIDAN

Art by
MINDY LEE

Color Art by
RICO RENZI

Letters by
DERON BENNETT

Collection Cover Artist
STJEPAN SEJIC

Chapter Title Pages by
STJEPAN SEJIC (CHAPTER 1)
DAVE WILKINS (CHAPTER 2–4)

DARK HORSE BO

President & Publisher
MIKE RICHARDSON

Editor
DANIEL CHABON

Assistant Editors
CHUCK HOWITT AND **KONNER KNUDSEN**

Designer
KATHLEEN BARNETT

Digital Art Technician
ADAM PRUETT

SPECIAL THANKS TO **RYAN FERGUSON** AND **ROWENNA OTAZU**

◇

MASTERS OF THE UNIVERSE: REVELATION™

MASTERS OF THE UNIVERSE™ and associated trademarks are owned by and used under license from
Mattel © 2022 Mattel. Dark Horse Books® and the Dark Horse logo are registered trademarks of Dark
Horse Comics LLC. All rights reserved. No portion of this publication may be reproduced or transmitted,
in any form or by any means, without the express written permission of Dark Horse Comics LLC. Names,
characters, places, and incidents featured in this publication either are the product of the author's
imagination or are used fictitiously. Any resemblance to actual persons (living or dead), events,
institutions, or locales, without satiric intent, is coincidental.

Collects issues #1–#4 of the Dark Horse Comics series *Masters of the Universe: Revelation*.

Published by
Dark Horse Books
A division of Dark Horse Comics LLC
10956 SE Main Street
Milwaukie, OR 97222

DarkHorse.com

To find a comics shop in your area, visit comicshoplocator.com

First edition: February 2022
Ebook ISBN 978-1-50672-632-8
Trade Paperback ISBN 978-1-50672-631-1

1 3 5 7 9 10 8 6 4 2

Printed in China

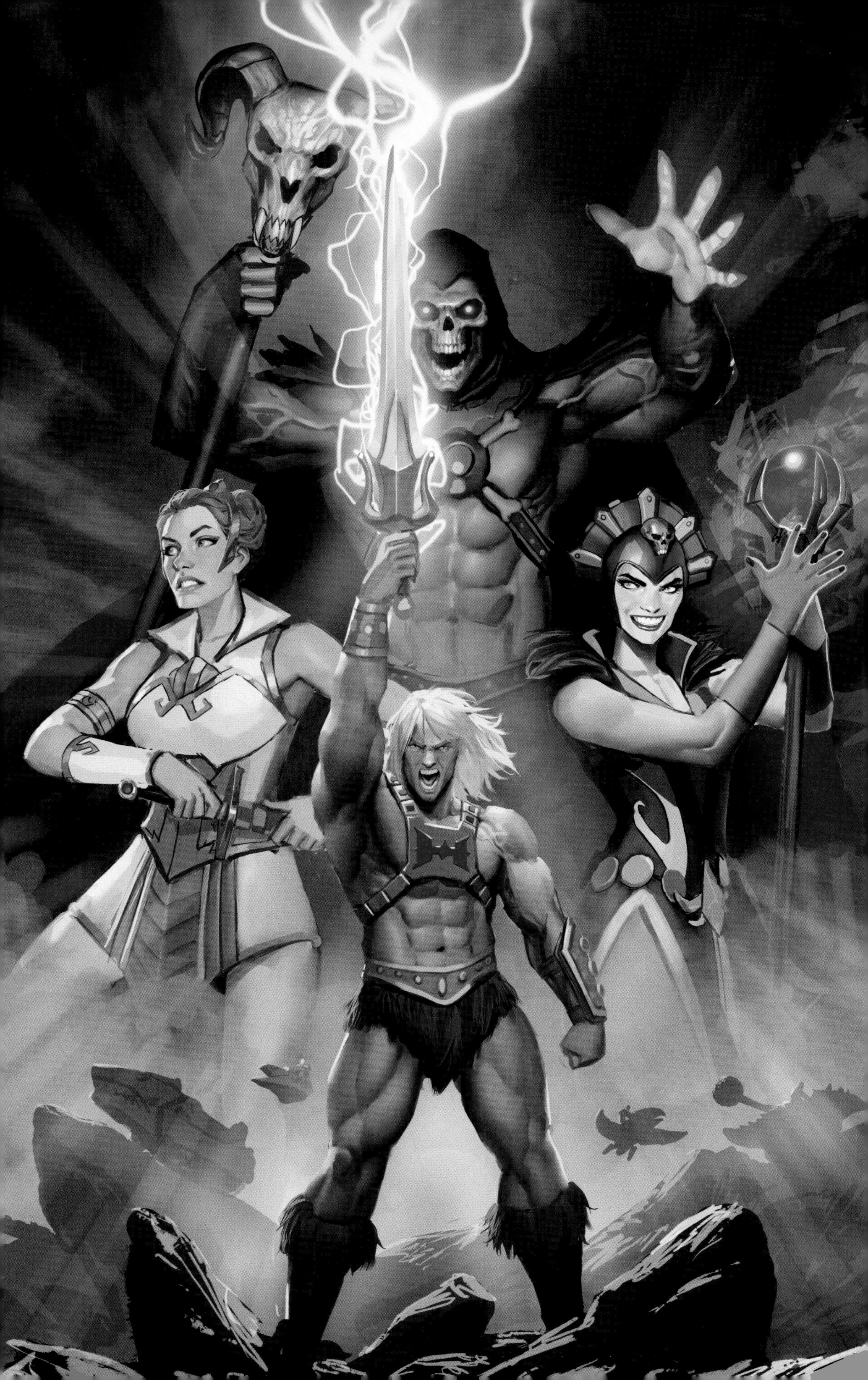

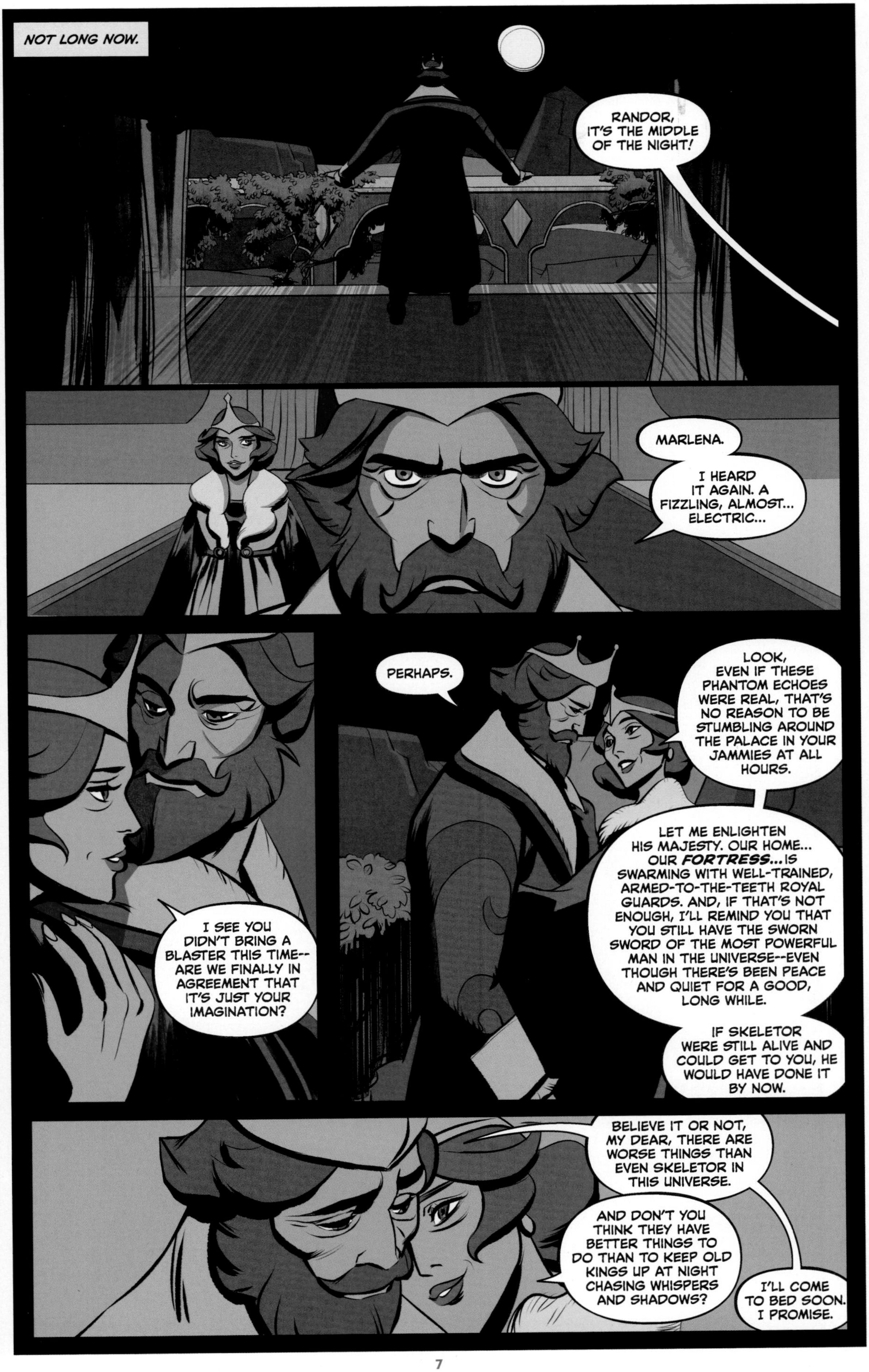
NOT LONG NOW.
RANDOR, IT'S THE MIDDLE OF THE NIGHT!
MARLENA.
I HEARD IT AGAIN. A FIZZLING, ALMOST... ELECTRIC...
I SEE YOU DIDN'T BRING A BLASTER THIS TIME-- ARE WE FINALLY IN AGREEMENT THAT IT'S JUST YOUR IMAGINATION?
PERHAPS.
LOOK, EVEN IF THESE PHANTOM ECHOES WERE REAL, THAT'S NO REASON TO BE STUMBLING AROUND THE PALACE IN YOUR JAMMIES AT ALL HOURS.
LET ME ENLIGHTEN HIS MAJESTY. OUR HOME... OUR *FORTRESS...* IS SWARMING WITH WELL-TRAINED, ARMED-TO-THE-TEETH ROYAL GUARDS. AND, IF THAT'S NOT ENOUGH, I'LL REMIND YOU THAT YOU STILL HAVE THE SWORN SWORD OF THE MOST POWERFUL MAN IN THE UNIVERSE--EVEN THOUGH THERE'S BEEN PEACE AND QUIET FOR A GOOD, LONG WHILE.
IF SKELETOR WERE STILL ALIVE AND COULD GET TO YOU, HE WOULD HAVE DONE IT BY NOW.
BELIEVE IT OR NOT, MY DEAR, THERE ARE WORSE THINGS THAN EVEN SKELETOR IN THIS UNIVERSE.
AND DON'T YOU THINK THEY HAVE BETTER THINGS TO DO THAN TO KEEP OLD KINGS UP AT NIGHT CHASING WHISPERS AND SHADOWS?
I'LL COME TO BED SOON. I PROMISE.

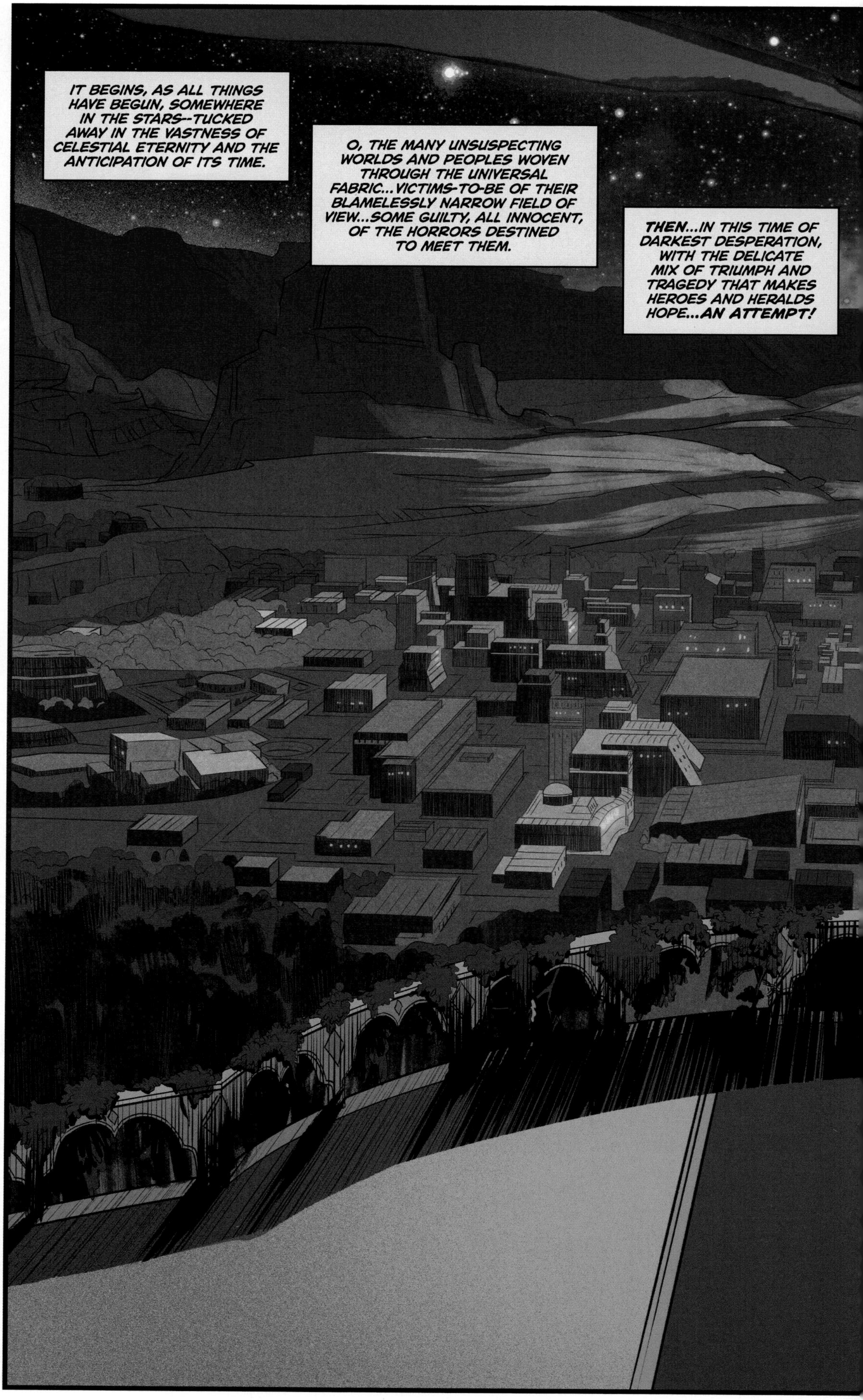
IT BEGINS, AS ALL THINGS HAVE BEGUN, SOMEWHERE IN THE STARS--TUCKED AWAY IN THE VASTNESS OF CELESTIAL ETERNITY AND THE ANTICIPATION OF ITS TIME.
O, THE MANY UNSUSPECTING WORLDS AND PEOPLES WOVEN THROUGH THE UNIVERSAL FABRIC...VICTIMS-TO-BE OF THEIR BLAMELESSLY NARROW FIELD OF VIEW...SOME GUILTY, ALL INNOCENT, OF THE HORRORS DESTINED TO MEET THEM.
THEN...IN THIS TIME OF DARKEST DESPERATION, WITH THE DELICATE MIX OF TRIUMPH AND TRAGEDY THAT MAKES HEROES AND HERALDS HOPE...AN ATTEMPT!

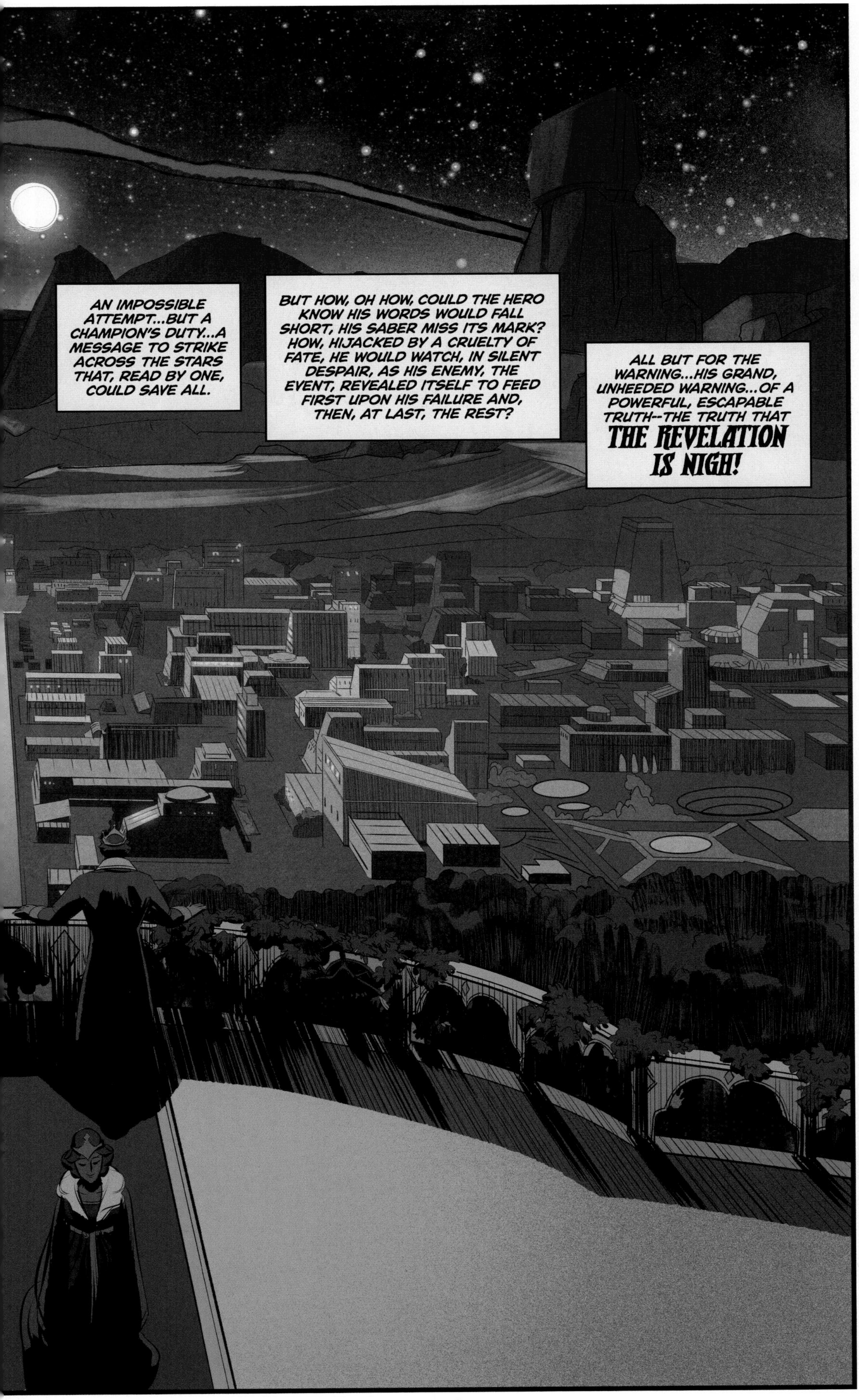

AN IMPOSSIBLE ATTEMPT...BUT A CHAMPION'S DUTY...A MESSAGE TO STRIKE ACROSS THE STARS THAT, READ BY ONE, COULD SAVE ALL.
BUT HOW, OH HOW, COULD THE HERO KNOW HIS WORDS WOULD FALL SHORT, HIS SABER MISS ITS MARK? HOW, HIJACKED BY A CRUELTY OF FATE, HE WOULD WATCH, IN SILENT DESPAIR, AS HIS ENEMY, THE EVENT, REVEALED ITSELF TO FEED FIRST UPON HIS FAILURE AND, THEN, AT LAST, THE REST?
ALL BUT FOR THE WARNING...HIS GRAND, UNHEEDED WARNING...OF A POWERFUL, ESCAPABLE TRUTH--THE TRUTH THAT THE REVELATION IS NIGH!

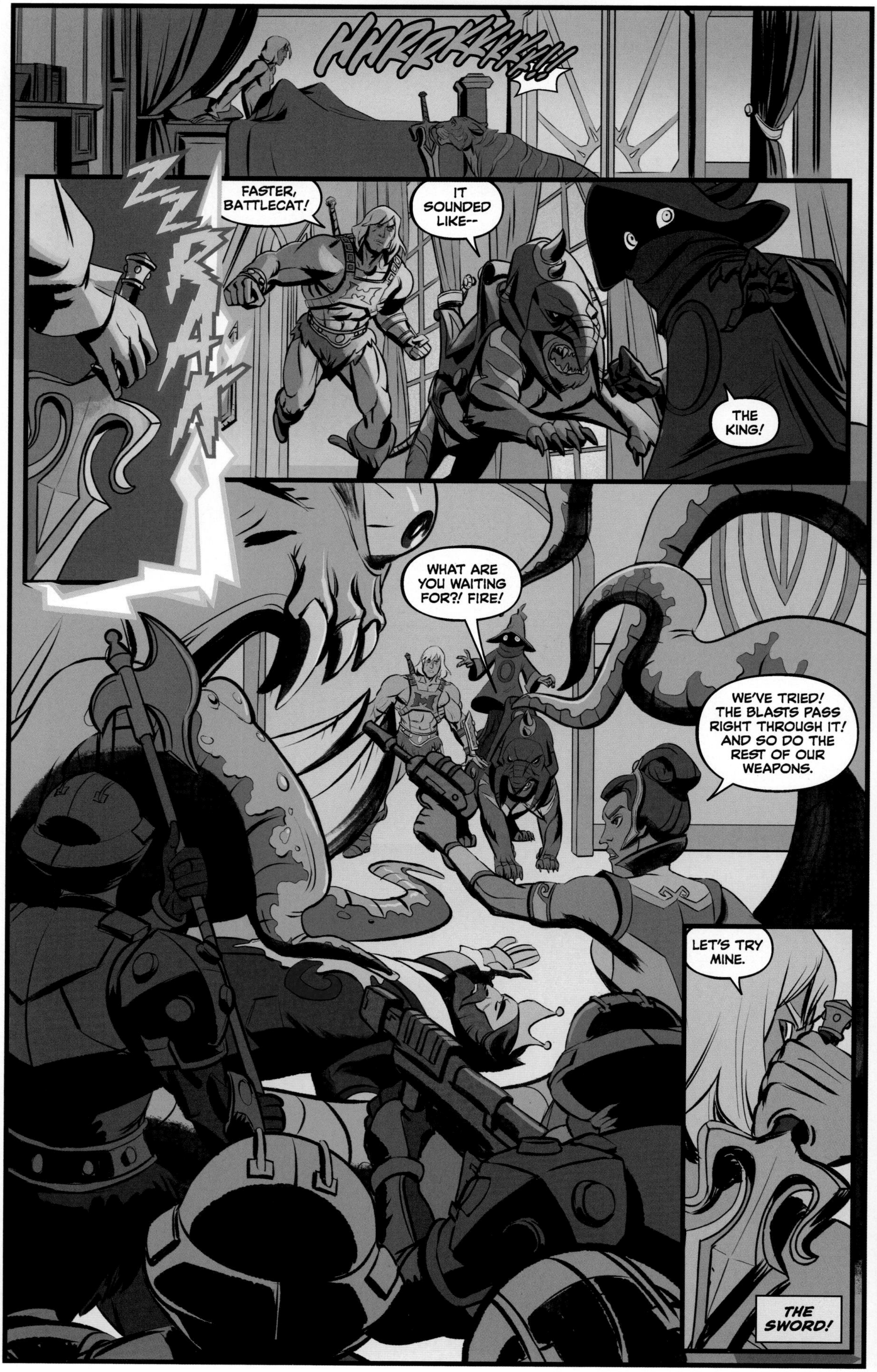

HHRRKKKK!!!
ZZRAKK
FASTER, BATTLECAT!
IT SOUNDED LIKE--
THE KING!
WHAT ARE YOU WAITING FOR?! FIRE!
WE'VE TRIED! THE BLASTS PASS RIGHT THROUGH IT! AND SO DO THE REST OF OUR WEAPONS.
LET'S TRY MINE.
THE SWORD!

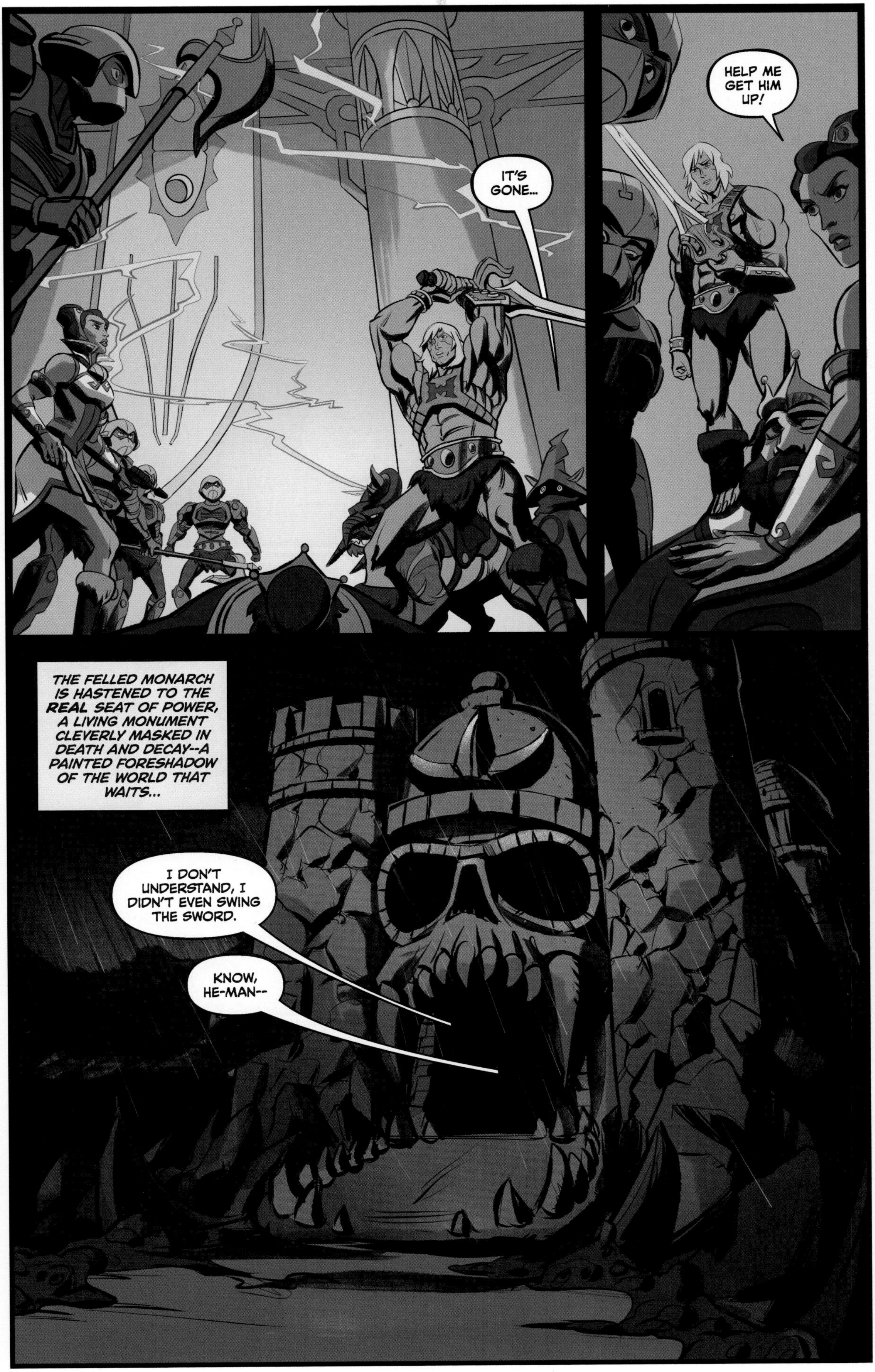
IT'S GONE...
HELP ME GET HIM UP!
THE FELLED MONARCH IS HASTENED TO THE REAL SEAT OF POWER, A LIVING MONUMENT CLEVERLY MASKED IN DEATH AND DECAY--A PAINTED FORESHADOW OF THE WORLD THAT WAITS...
I DON'T UNDERSTAND, I DIDN'T EVEN SWING THE SWORD.
KNOW, HE-MAN--

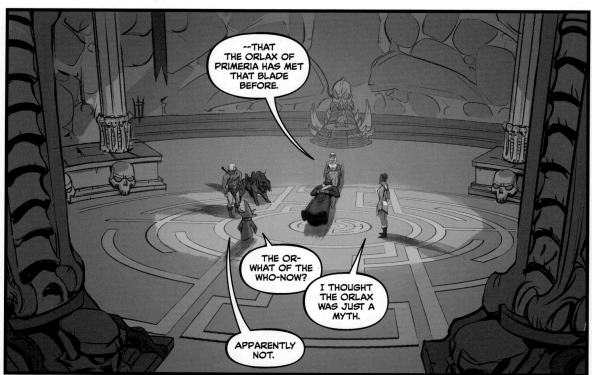

--THAT THE ORLAX OF PRIMERIA HAS MET THAT BLADE BEFORE.

THE OR-WHAT OF THE WHO-NOW?

I THOUGHT THE ORLAX WAS JUST A MYTH.

APPARENTLY NOT.

BUT, SORCERESS, I HAVE NEVER BEFORE HAPPENED UPON THIS CREATURE, LET ALONE RAISED THE SWORD AGAINST IT.

THE LEGEND OF THE ORLAX IS OLDER THAN THE POWER ITSELF. AND YOU ARE NOT THE FIRST TO WIELD ITS SWORD. IF WE COULD KNOW MORE ABOUT THAT LEGEND...

ALL WE NEED TO KNOW RIGHT NOW IS THAT IT TELLS OF THE BEAST'S *MORTAL VENOM.* WHAT OF THE KING?

IF THERE IS POISON IN HIS VEINS, IT MOVES, LIKE THE ORLAX ITSELF, WITH A MAGIC HIDDEN FROM MY SIGHT. WOULD THAT THE BEAST WERE HERE, SO I MIGHT COMMUNE WITH IT, LEARN ITS SECRETS AND USE THEM TO FORMULATE A REMEDY.

MAN-AT-ARMS HAS MOBILIZED THE ENTIRE ROYAL GUARD. THEY'LL FIND IT.

LET US PRAY THEY DO IT IN TIME.

ADAM SHOULD BE HERE.

TEELA, I--

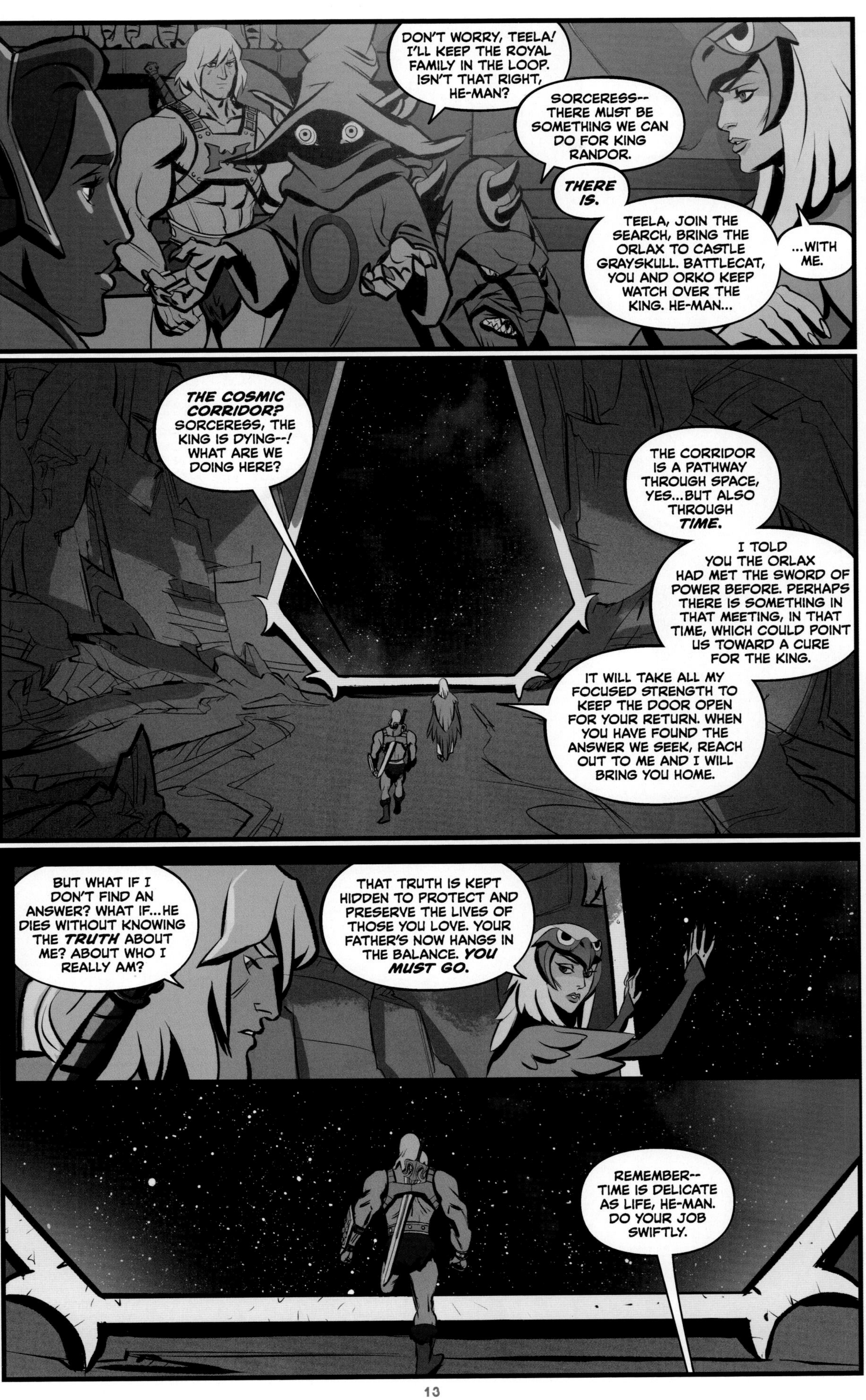
DON'T WORRY, TEELA! I'LL KEEP THE ROYAL FAMILY IN THE LOOP. ISN'T THAT RIGHT, HE-MAN?
SORCERESS-- THERE MUST BE SOMETHING WE CAN DO FOR KING RANDOR.
THERE IS.
TEELA, JOIN THE SEARCH, BRING THE ORLAX TO CASTLE GRAYSKULL. BATTLECAT, YOU AND ORKO KEEP WATCH OVER THE KING. HE-MAN...
...WITH ME.
THE COSMIC CORRIDOR? SORCERESS, THE KING IS DYING--! WHAT ARE WE DOING HERE?
THE CORRIDOR IS A PATHWAY THROUGH SPACE, YES...BUT ALSO THROUGH TIME.
I TOLD YOU THE ORLAX HAD MET THE SWORD OF POWER BEFORE. PERHAPS THERE IS SOMETHING IN THAT MEETING, IN THAT TIME, WHICH COULD POINT US TOWARD A CURE FOR THE KING.
IT WILL TAKE ALL MY FOCUSED STRENGTH TO KEEP THE DOOR OPEN FOR YOUR RETURN. WHEN YOU HAVE FOUND THE ANSWER WE SEEK, REACH OUT TO ME AND I WILL BRING YOU HOME.
BUT WHAT IF I DON'T FIND AN ANSWER? WHAT IF...HE DIES WITHOUT KNOWING THE TRUTH ABOUT ME? ABOUT WHO I REALLY AM?
THAT TRUTH IS KEPT HIDDEN TO PROTECT AND PRESERVE THE LIVES OF THOSE YOU LOVE. YOUR FATHER'S NOW HANGS IN THE BALANCE. YOU MUST GO.
REMEMBER-- TIME IS DELICATE AS LIFE, HE-MAN. DO YOUR JOB SWIFTLY.

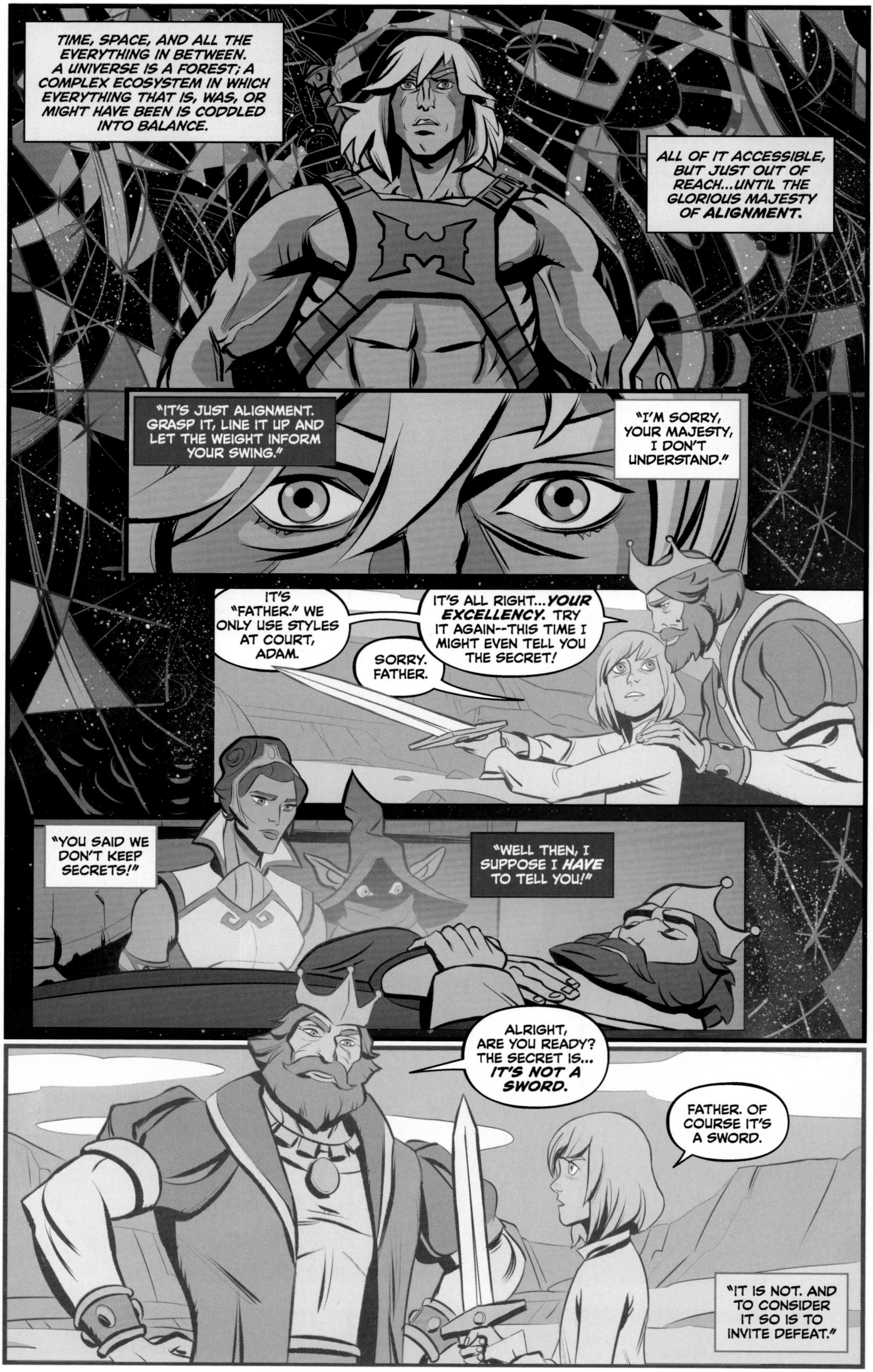
TIME, SPACE, AND ALL THE EVERYTHING IN BETWEEN. A UNIVERSE IS A FOREST; A COMPLEX ECOSYSTEM IN WHICH EVERYTHING THAT IS, WAS, OR MIGHT HAVE BEEN IS CODDLED INTO BALANCE.
ALL OF IT ACCESSIBLE, BUT JUST OUT OF REACH...UNTIL THE GLORIOUS MAJESTY OF ALIGNMENT.
"IT'S JUST ALIGNMENT. GRASP IT, LINE IT UP AND LET THE WEIGHT INFORM YOUR SWING."
"I'M SORRY, YOUR MAJESTY, I DON'T UNDERSTAND."
IT'S "FATHER." WE ONLY USE STYLES AT COURT, ADAM.
SORRY. FATHER.
IT'S ALL RIGHT...YOUR EXCELLENCY. TRY IT AGAIN--THIS TIME I MIGHT EVEN TELL YOU THE SECRET!
"YOU SAID WE DON'T KEEP SECRETS!"
"WELL THEN, I SUPPOSE I HAVE TO TELL YOU!"
ALRIGHT, ARE YOU READY? THE SECRET IS... IT'S NOT A SWORD.
FATHER. OF COURSE IT'S A SWORD.
"IT IS NOT. AND TO CONSIDER IT SO IS TO INVITE DEFEAT."

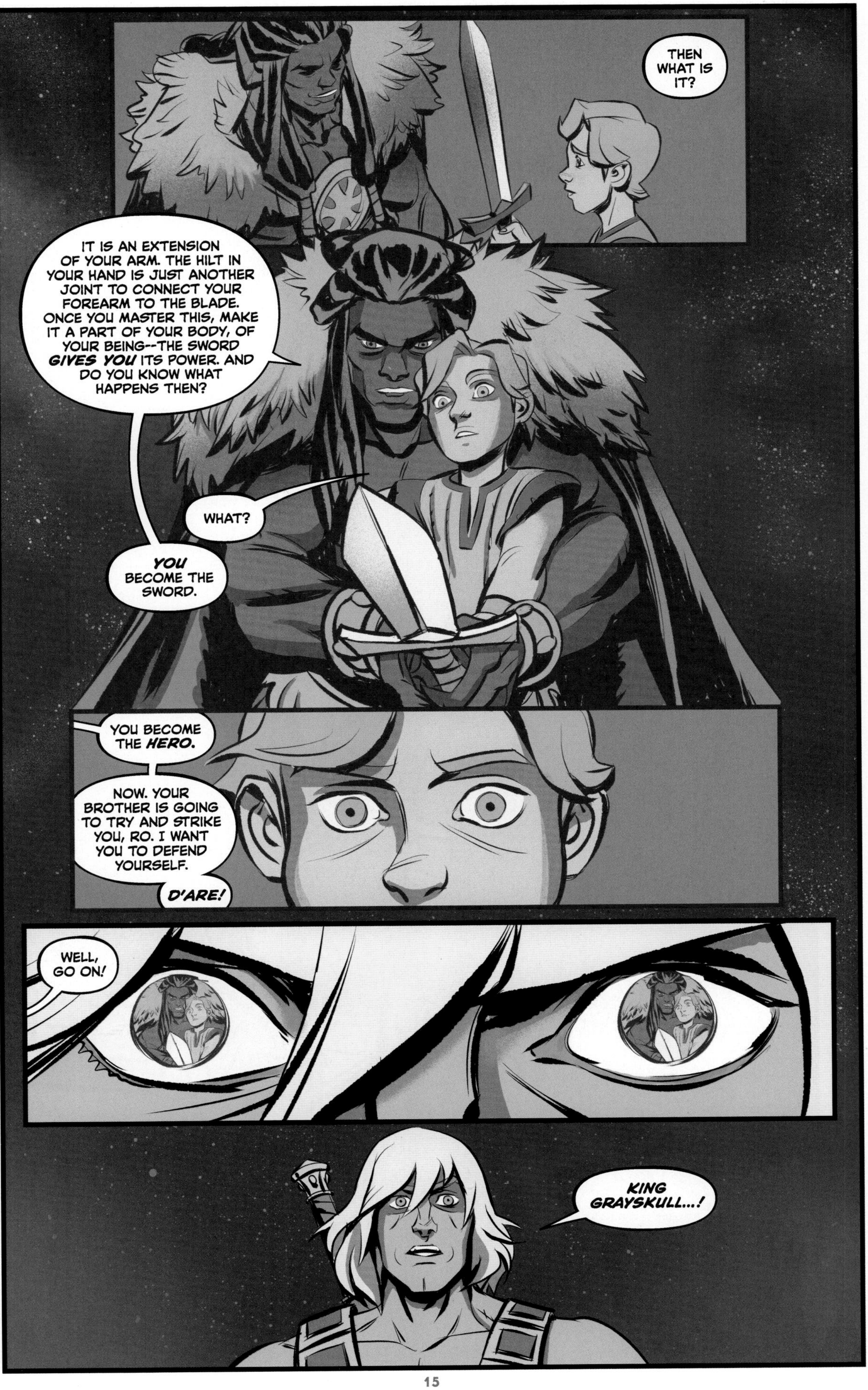
THEN WHAT IS IT?
IT IS AN EXTENSION OF YOUR ARM. THE HILT IN YOUR HAND IS JUST ANOTHER JOINT TO CONNECT YOUR FOREARM TO THE BLADE. ONCE YOU MASTER THIS, MAKE IT A PART OF YOUR BODY, OF YOUR BEING--THE SWORD GIVES YOU ITS POWER. AND DO YOU KNOW WHAT HAPPENS THEN?
WHAT?
YOU BECOME THE SWORD.
YOU BECOME THE HERO.
NOW. YOUR BROTHER IS GOING TO TRY AND STRIKE YOU, RO. I WANT YOU TO DEFEND YOURSELF.
D'ARE!
WELL, GO ON!
KING GRAYSKULL...!

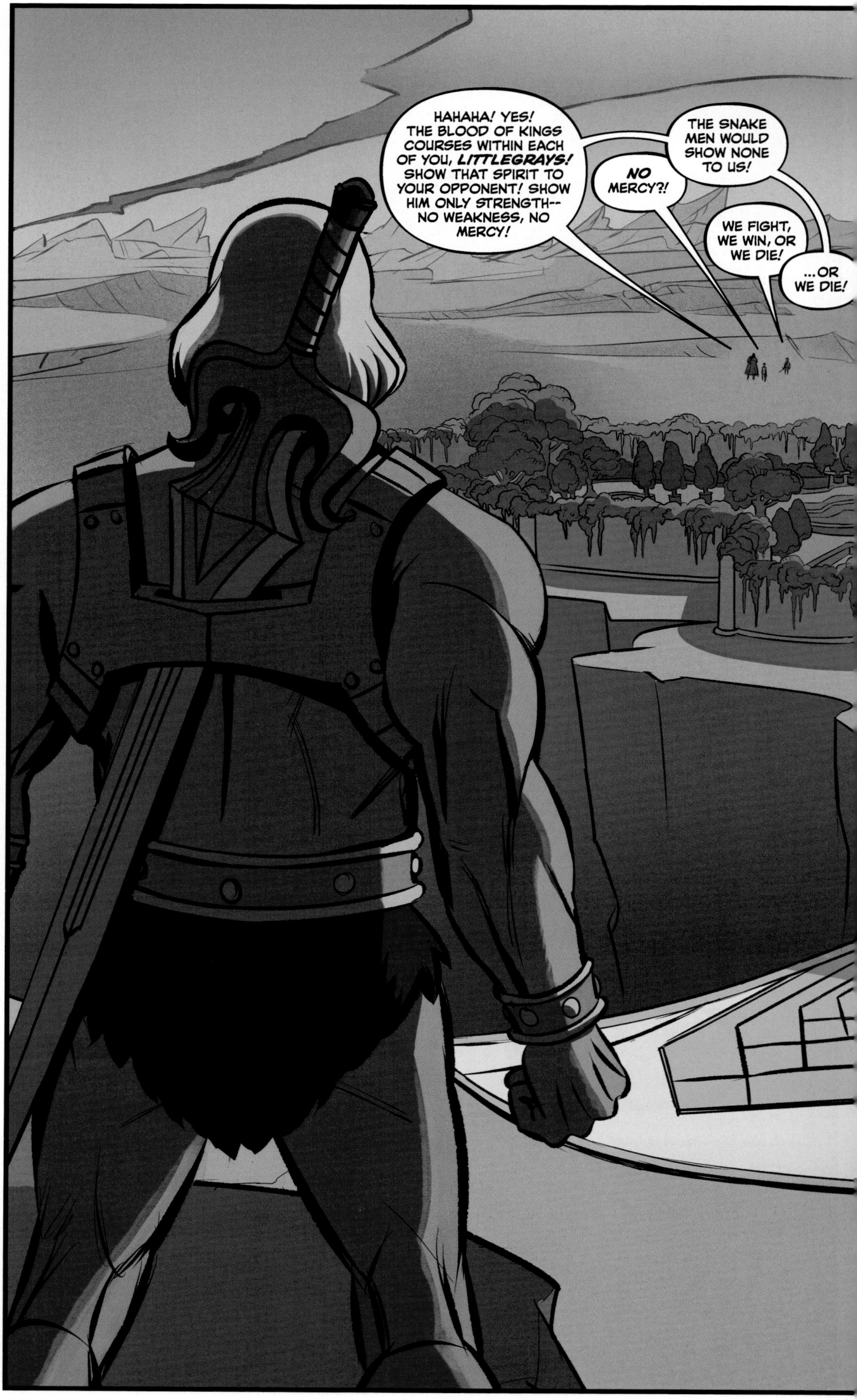
HAHAHA! YES! THE BLOOD OF KINGS COURSES WITHIN EACH OF YOU, ***LITTLEGRAYS!*** SHOW THAT SPIRIT TO YOUR OPPONENT! SHOW HIM ONLY STRENGTH-- NO WEAKNESS, NO MERCY!
NO MERCY?!
THE SNAKE MEN WOULD SHOW NONE TO US!
WE FIGHT, WE WIN, OR WE DIE!
...OR WE DIE!

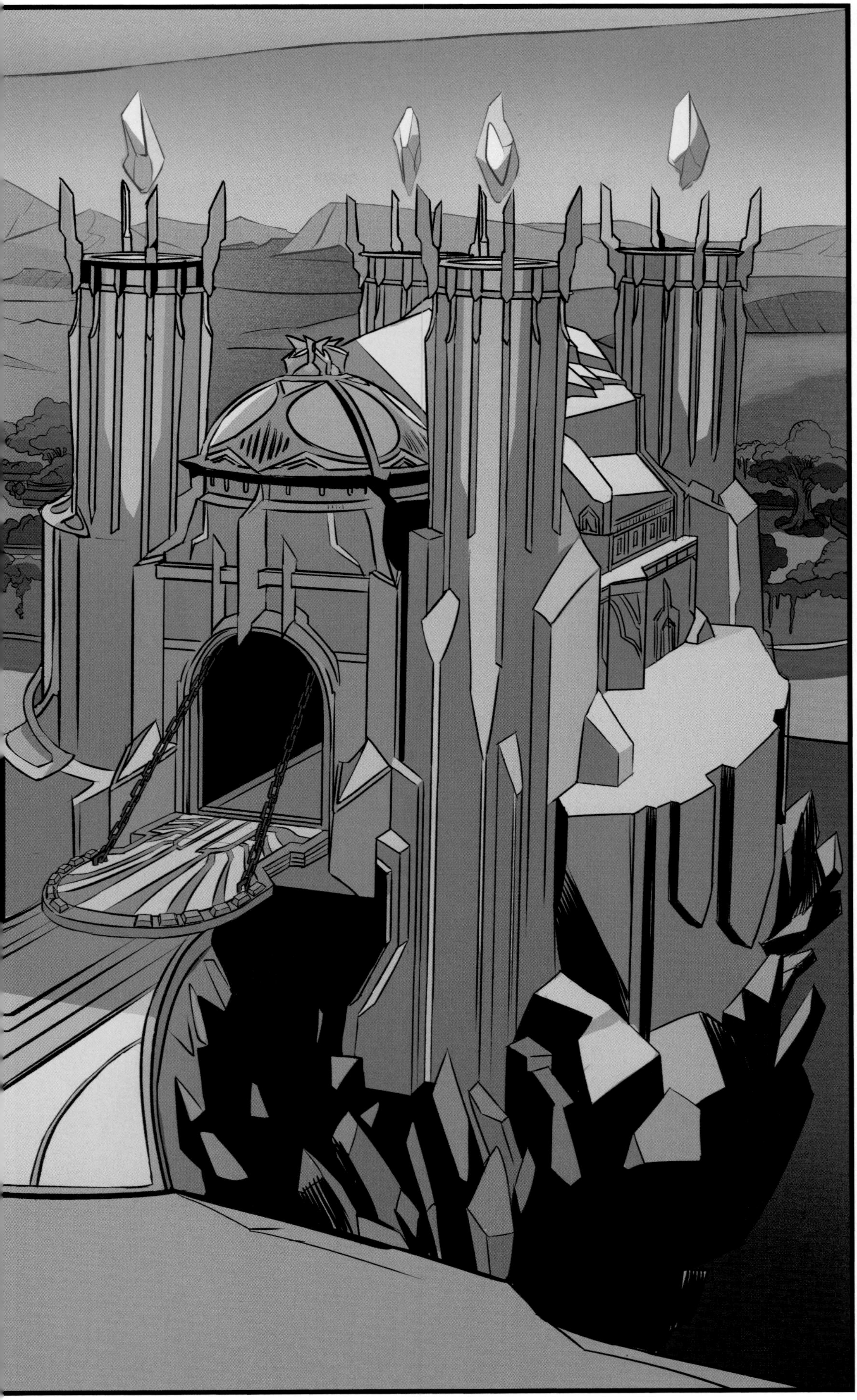

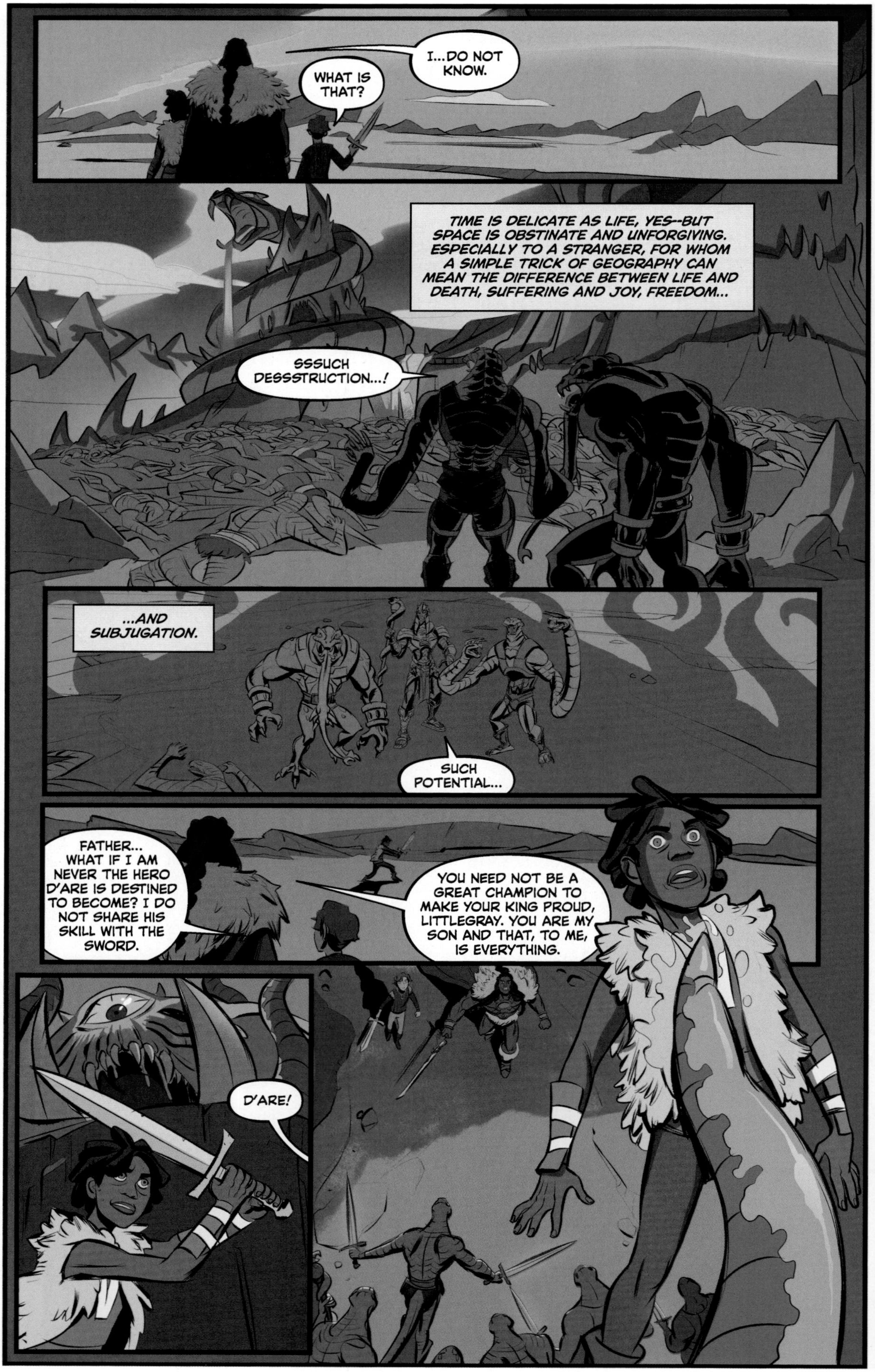
WHAT IS THAT?
I...DO NOT KNOW.
TIME IS DELICATE AS LIFE, YES--BUT SPACE IS OBSTINATE AND UNFORGIVING. ESPECIALLY TO A STRANGER, FOR WHOM A SIMPLE TRICK OF GEOGRAPHY CAN MEAN THE DIFFERENCE BETWEEN LIFE AND DEATH, SUFFERING AND JOY, FREEDOM...
SSSUCH DESSSTRUCTION...!
...AND SUBJUGATION.
SUCH POTENTIAL...
FATHER... WHAT IF I AM NEVER THE HERO D'ARE IS DESTINED TO BECOME? I DO NOT SHARE HIS SKILL WITH THE SWORD.
YOU NEED NOT BE A GREAT CHAMPION TO MAKE YOUR KING PROUD, LITTLEGRAY. YOU ARE MY SON AND THAT, TO ME, IS EVERYTHING.
D'ARE!

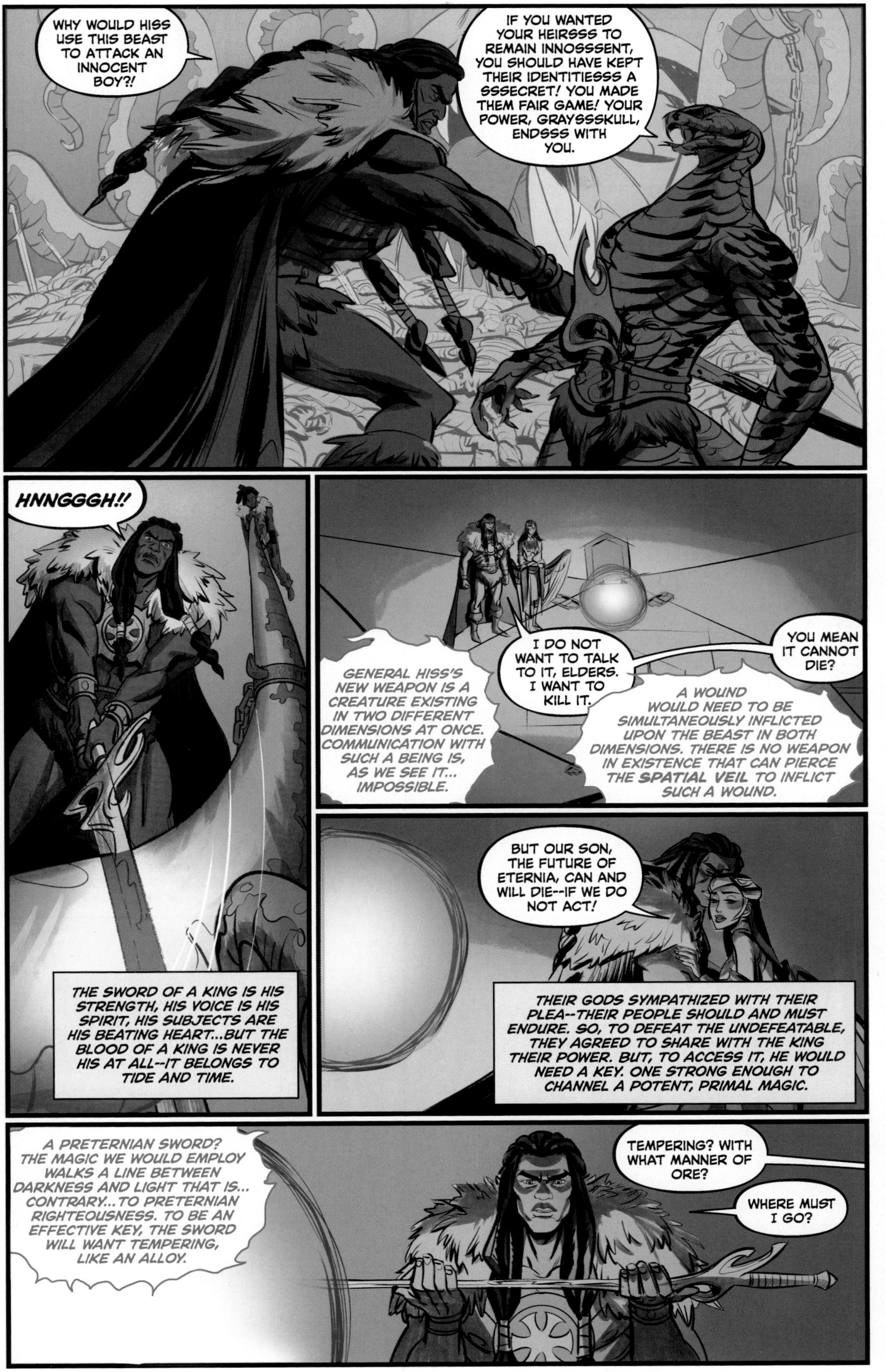
WHY WOULD HISS USE THIS BEAST TO ATTACK AN INNOCENT BOY?!
IF YOU WANTED YOUR HEIRSSS TO REMAIN INNOSSSENT, YOU SHOULD HAVE KEPT THEIR IDENTITIESSS A SSSECRET! YOU MADE THEM FAIR GAME! YOUR POWER, GRAYSSSKULL, ENDSSS WITH YOU.
HNNGGGH!!
THE SWORD OF A KING IS HIS STRENGTH, HIS VOICE IS HIS SPIRIT, HIS SUBJECTS ARE HIS BEATING HEART...BUT THE BLOOD OF A KING IS NEVER HIS AT ALL--IT BELONGS TO TIDE AND TIME.
GENERAL HISS'S NEW WEAPON IS A CREATURE EXISTING IN TWO DIFFERENT DIMENSIONS AT ONCE. COMMUNICATION WITH SUCH A BEING IS, AS WE SEE IT... IMPOSSIBLE.
I DO NOT WANT TO TALK TO IT, ELDERS. I WANT TO KILL IT.
A WOUND WOULD NEED TO BE SIMULTANEOUSLY INFLICTED UPON THE BEAST IN BOTH DIMENSIONS. THERE IS NO WEAPON IN EXISTENCE THAT CAN PIERCE THE SPATIAL VEIL TO INFLICT SUCH A WOUND.
YOU MEAN IT CANNOT DIE?
BUT OUR SON, THE FUTURE OF ETERNIA, CAN AND WILL DIE--IF WE DO NOT ACT!
THEIR GODS SYMPATHIZED WITH THEIR PLEA--THEIR PEOPLE SHOULD AND MUST ENDURE. SO, TO DEFEAT THE UNDEFEATABLE, THEY AGREED TO SHARE WITH THE KING THEIR POWER. BUT, TO ACCESS IT, HE WOULD NEED A KEY. ONE STRONG ENOUGH TO CHANNEL A POTENT, PRIMAL MAGIC.
A PRETERNIAN SWORD? THE MAGIC WE WOULD EMPLOY WALKS A LINE BETWEEN DARKNESS AND LIGHT THAT IS... CONTRARY...TO PRETERNIAN RIGHTEOUSNESS. TO BE AN EFFECTIVE KEY, THE SWORD WILL WANT TEMPERING, LIKE AN ALLOY.
TEMPERING? WITH WHAT MANNER OF ORE?
WHERE MUST I GO?

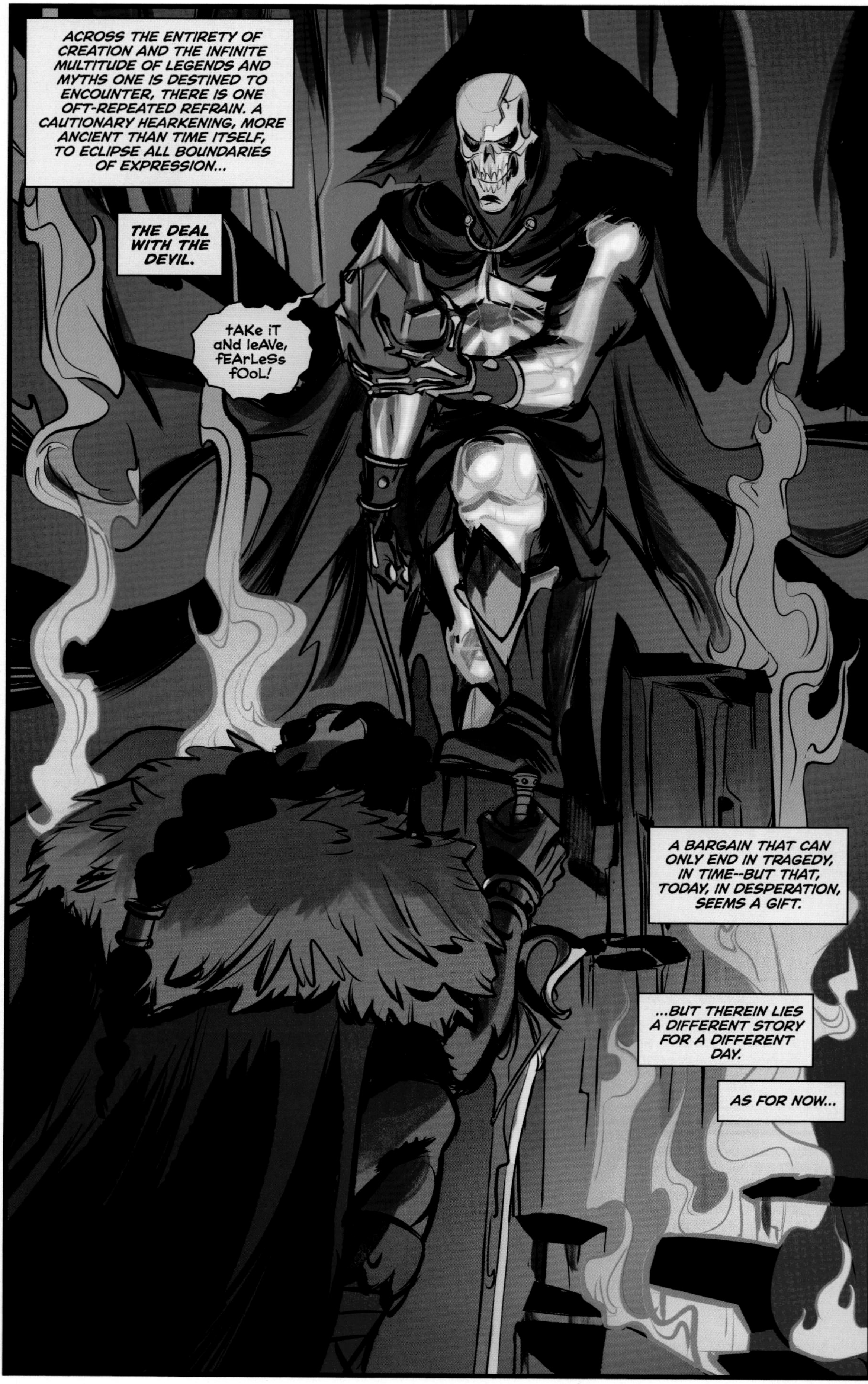
ACROSS THE ENTIRETY OF CREATION AND THE INFINITE MULTITUDE OF LEGENDS AND MYTHS ONE IS DESTINED TO ENCOUNTER, THERE IS ONE OFT-REPEATED REFRAIN. A CAUTIONARY HEARKENING, MORE ANCIENT THAN TIME ITSELF, TO ECLIPSE ALL BOUNDARIES OF EXPRESSION...
THE DEAL WITH THE DEVIL.
tAKe iT aNd leAVe, fEArLeSs fOoL!
A BARGAIN THAT CAN ONLY END IN TRAGEDY, IN TIME--BUT THAT, TODAY, IN DESPERATION, SEEMS A GIFT.
...BUT THEREIN LIES A DIFFERENT STORY FOR A DIFFERENT DAY.
AS FOR NOW...

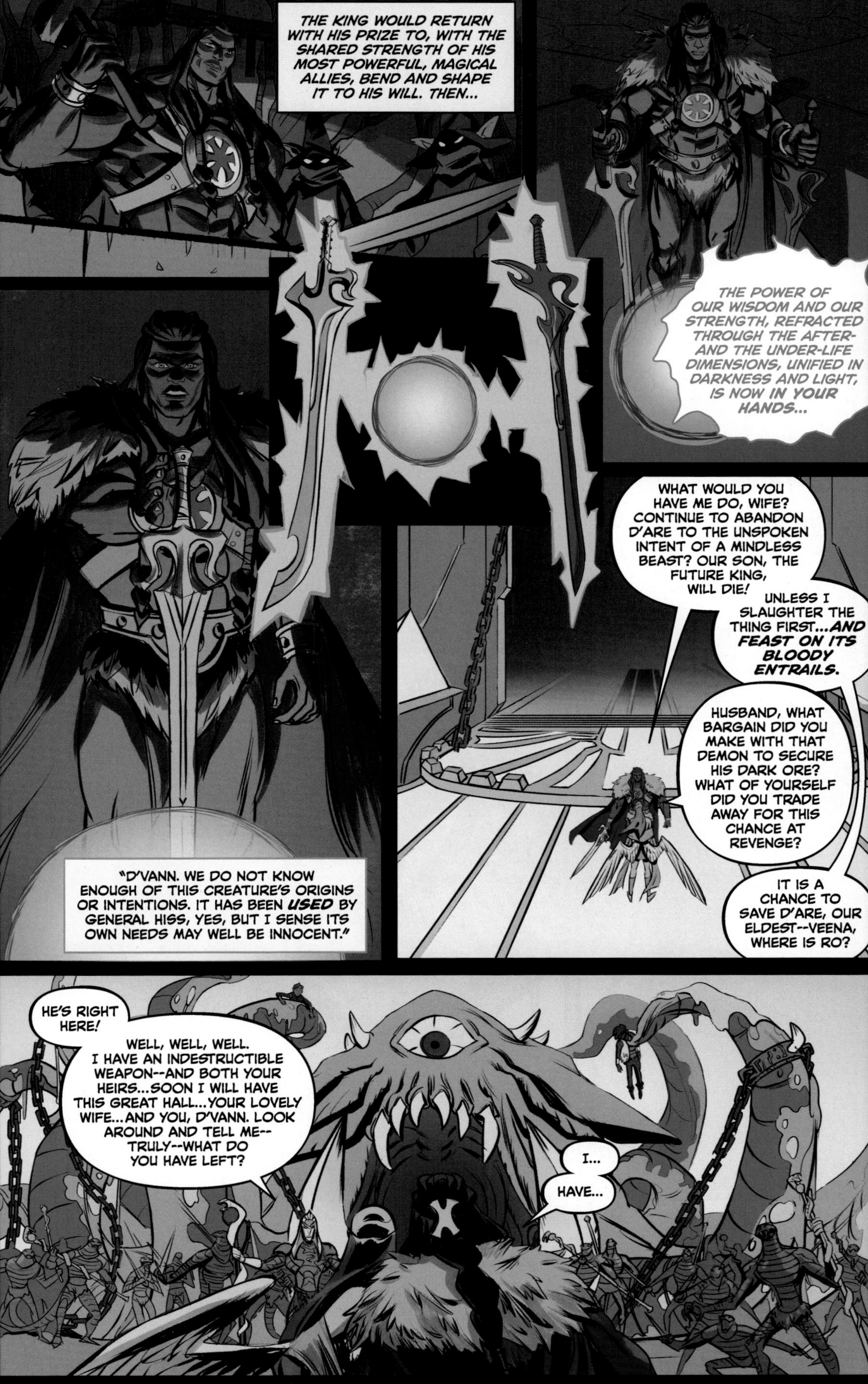
THE KING WOULD RETURN WITH HIS PRIZE TO, WITH THE SHARED STRENGTH OF HIS MOST POWERFUL, MAGICAL ALLIES, BEND AND SHAPE IT TO HIS WILL. THEN...
THE POWER OF OUR WISDOM AND OUR STRENGTH, REFRACTED THROUGH THE AFTER- AND THE UNDER-LIFE DIMENSIONS, UNIFIED IN DARKNESS AND LIGHT, IS NOW IN YOUR HANDS...
"D'VANN. WE DO NOT KNOW ENOUGH OF THIS CREATURE'S ORIGINS OR INTENTIONS. IT HAS BEEN USED BY GENERAL HISS, YES, BUT I SENSE ITS OWN NEEDS MAY WELL BE INNOCENT."
WHAT WOULD YOU HAVE ME DO, WIFE? CONTINUE TO ABANDON D'ARE TO THE UNSPOKEN INTENT OF A MINDLESS BEAST? OUR SON, THE FUTURE KING, WILL DIE!
UNLESS I SLAUGHTER THE THING FIRST...AND FEAST ON ITS BLOODY ENTRAILS.
HUSBAND, WHAT BARGAIN DID YOU MAKE WITH THAT DEMON TO SECURE HIS DARK ORE? WHAT OF YOURSELF DID YOU TRADE AWAY FOR THIS CHANCE AT REVENGE?
IT IS A CHANCE TO SAVE D'ARE, OUR ELDEST--VEENA, WHERE IS RO?
HE'S RIGHT HERE!
WELL, WELL, WELL. I HAVE AN INDESTRUCTIBLE WEAPON--AND BOTH YOUR HEIRS...SOON I WILL HAVE THIS GREAT HALL...YOUR LOVELY WIFE...AND YOU, D'VANN. LOOK AROUND AND TELL ME--TRULY--WHAT DO YOU HAVE LEFT?
I...
HAVE...

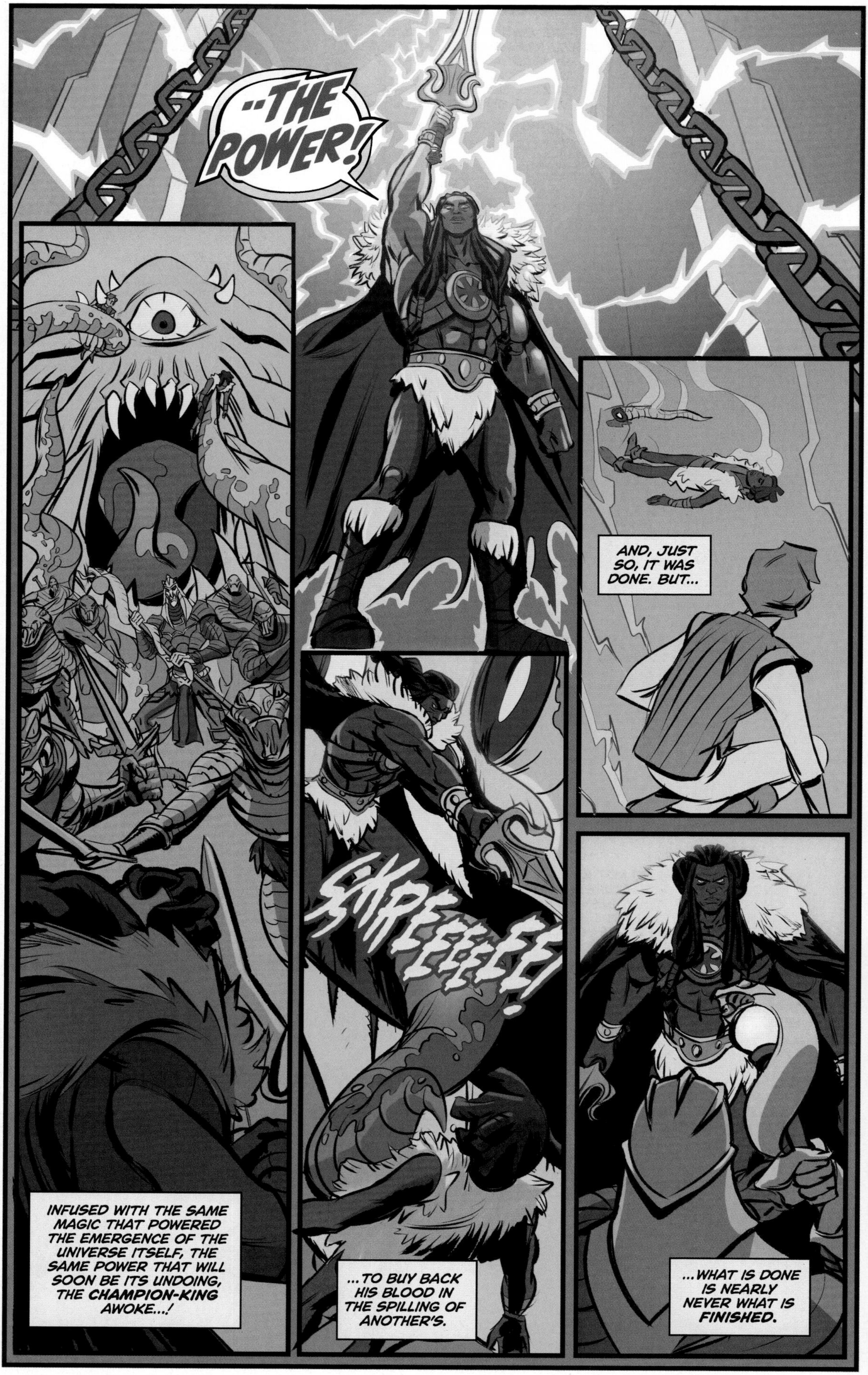

--THE POWER!
INFUSED WITH THE SAME MAGIC THAT POWERED THE EMERGENCE OF THE UNIVERSE ITSELF, THE SAME POWER THAT WILL SOON BE ITS UNDOING, THE CHAMPION-KING AWOKE...!
SKREEEEEEE!
...TO BUY BACK HIS BLOOD IN THE SPILLING OF ANOTHER'S.
AND, JUST SO, IT WAS DONE. BUT...
...WHAT IS DONE IS NEARLY NEVER WHAT IS FINISHED.

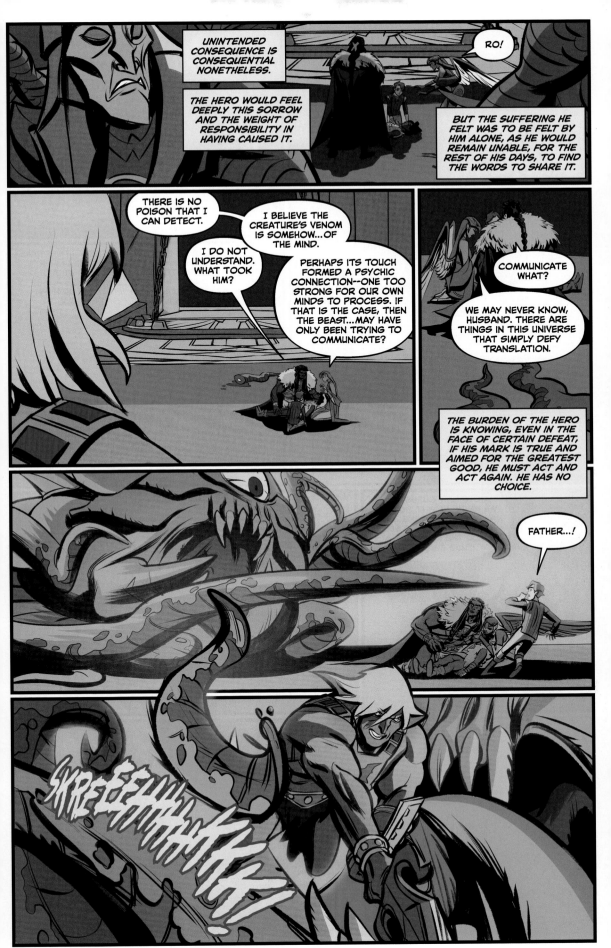

UNINTENDED CONSEQUENCE IS CONSEQUENTIAL NONETHELESS.

THE HERO WOULD FEEL DEEPLY THIS SORROW AND THE WEIGHT OF RESPONSIBILITY IN HAVING CAUSED IT.

RO!

BUT THE SUFFERING HE FELT WAS TO BE FELT BY HIM ALONE, AS HE WOULD REMAIN UNABLE, FOR THE REST OF HIS DAYS, TO FIND THE WORDS TO SHARE IT.

THERE IS NO POISON THAT I CAN DETECT.

I BELIEVE THE CREATURE'S VENOM IS SOMEHOW...OF THE MIND.

I DO NOT UNDERSTAND. WHAT TOOK HIM?

PERHAPS ITS TOUCH FORMED A PSYCHIC CONNECTION--ONE TOO STRONG FOR OUR OWN MINDS TO PROCESS. IF THAT IS THE CASE, THEN THE BEAST...MAY HAVE ONLY BEEN TRYING TO COMMUNICATE?

COMMUNICATE WHAT?

WE MAY NEVER KNOW, HUSBAND. THERE ARE THINGS IN THIS UNIVERSE THAT SIMPLY DEFY TRANSLATION.

THE BURDEN OF THE HERO IS KNOWING, EVEN IN THE FACE OF CERTAIN DEFEAT, IF HIS MARK IS TRUE AND AIMED FOR THE GREATEST GOOD, HE MUST ACT AND ACT AGAIN. HE HAS NO CHOICE.

FATHER...!

SKREEEEEEAAHHHHKK!

23

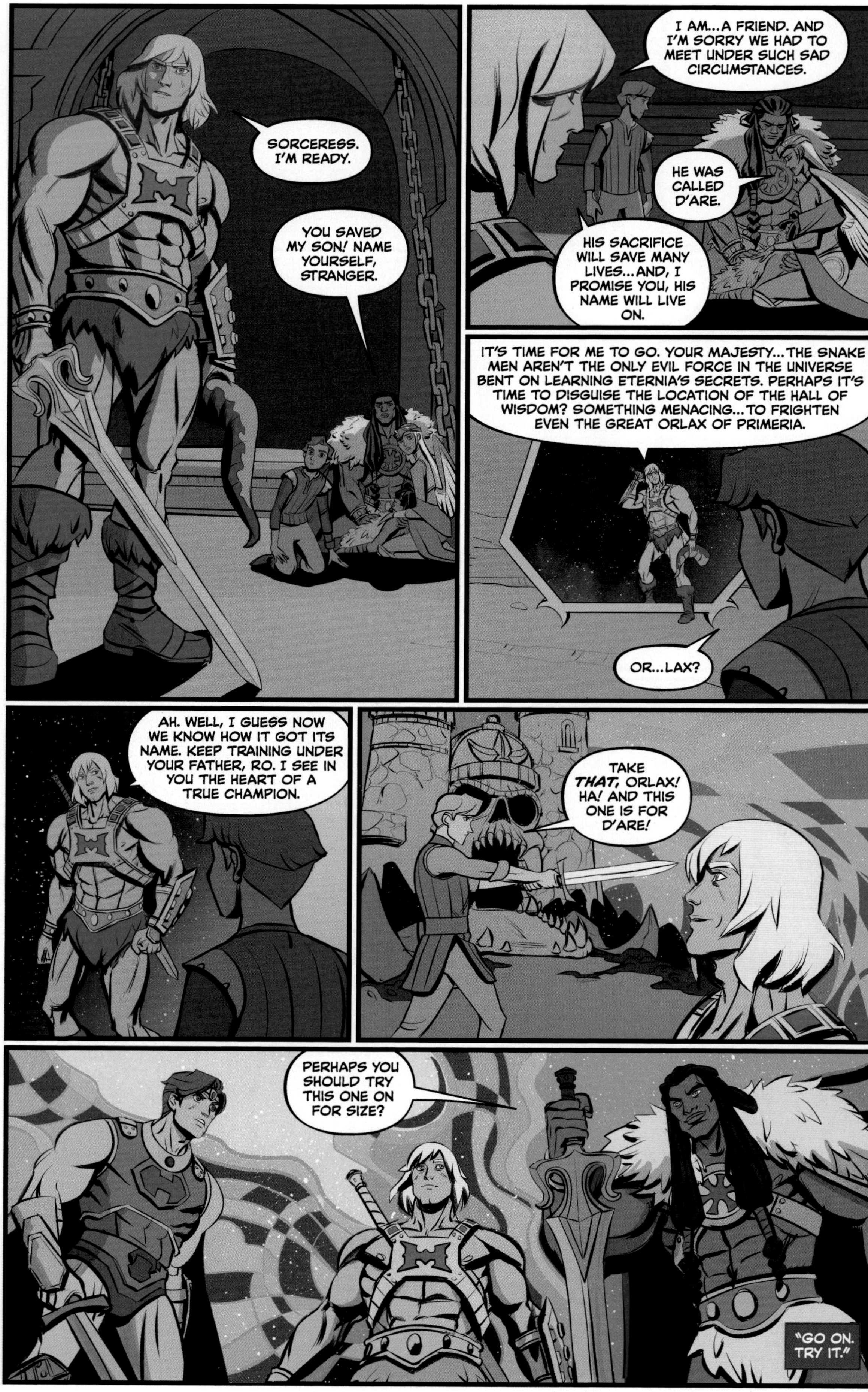
SORCERESS. I'M READY.
YOU SAVED MY SON! NAME YOURSELF, STRANGER.
I AM...A FRIEND. AND I'M SORRY WE HAD TO MEET UNDER SUCH SAD CIRCUMSTANCES.
HE WAS CALLED D'ARE.
HIS SACRIFICE WILL SAVE MANY LIVES...AND, I PROMISE YOU, HIS NAME WILL LIVE ON.
IT'S TIME FOR ME TO GO. YOUR MAJESTY...THE SNAKE MEN AREN'T THE ONLY EVIL FORCE IN THE UNIVERSE BENT ON LEARNING ETERNIA'S SECRETS. PERHAPS IT'S TIME TO DISGUISE THE LOCATION OF THE HALL OF WISDOM? SOMETHING MENACING...TO FRIGHTEN EVEN THE GREAT ORLAX OF PRIMERIA.
OR...LAX?
AH. WELL, I GUESS NOW WE KNOW HOW IT GOT ITS NAME. KEEP TRAINING UNDER YOUR FATHER, RO. I SEE IN YOU THE HEART OF A TRUE CHAMPION.
TAKE *THAT*, ORLAX! HA! AND THIS ONE IS FOR D'ARE!
PERHAPS YOU SHOULD TRY THIS ONE ON FOR SIZE?
"GO ON. TRY IT."

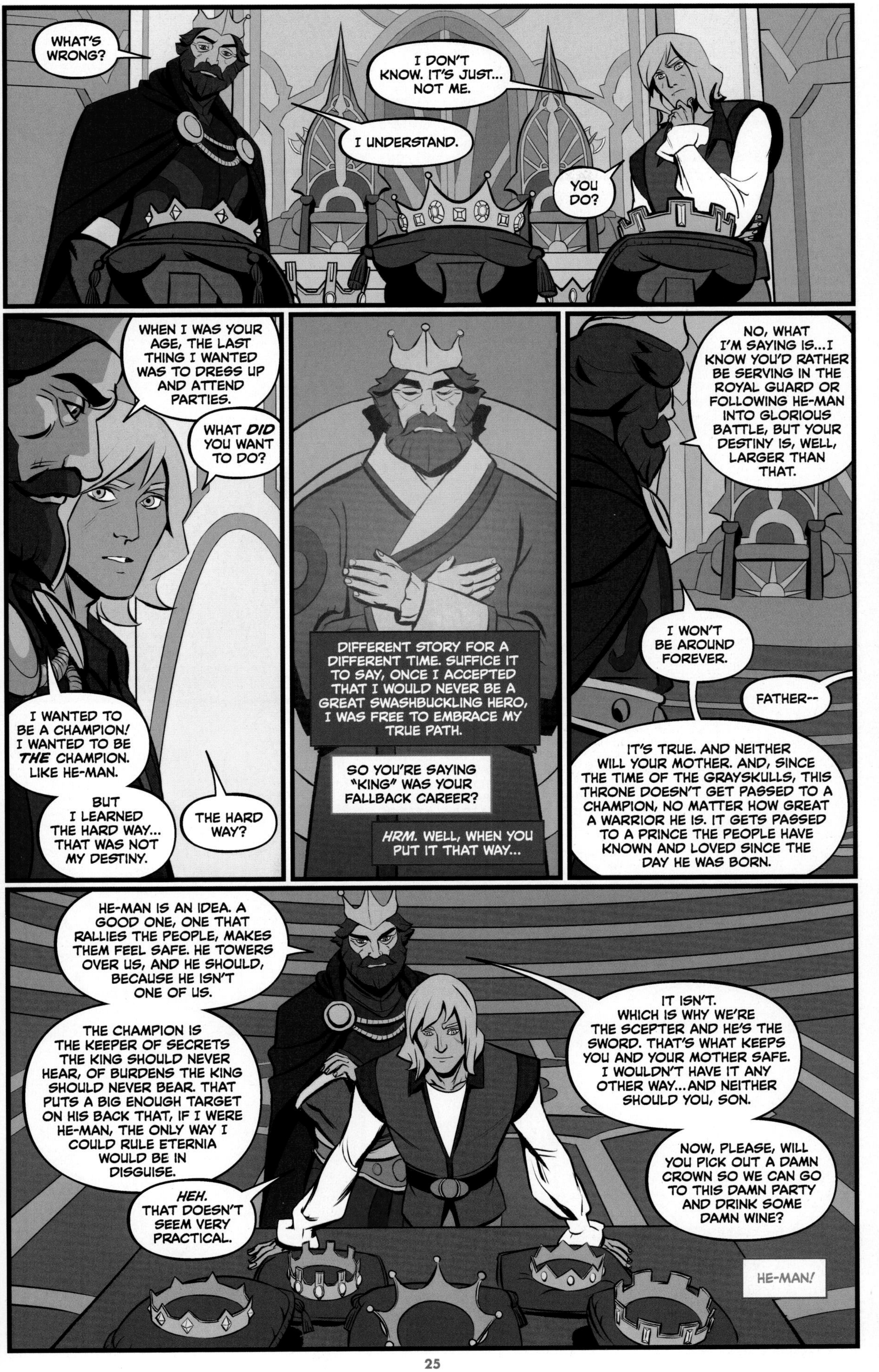
WHAT'S WRONG?
I DON'T KNOW. IT'S JUST... NOT ME.
I UNDERSTAND.
YOU DO?
WHEN I WAS YOUR AGE, THE LAST THING I WANTED WAS TO DRESS UP AND ATTEND PARTIES.
WHAT *DID* YOU WANT TO DO?
I WANTED TO BE A CHAMPION! I WANTED TO BE *THE* CHAMPION. LIKE HE-MAN.
BUT I LEARNED THE HARD WAY... THAT WAS NOT MY DESTINY.
THE HARD WAY?
DIFFERENT STORY FOR A DIFFERENT TIME. SUFFICE IT TO SAY, ONCE I ACCEPTED THAT I WOULD NEVER BE A GREAT SWASHBUCKLING HERO, I WAS FREE TO EMBRACE MY TRUE PATH.
SO YOU'RE SAYING "KING" WAS YOUR FALLBACK CAREER?
HRM. WELL, WHEN YOU PUT IT THAT WAY...
NO, WHAT I'M SAYING IS...I KNOW YOU'D RATHER BE SERVING IN THE ROYAL GUARD OR FOLLOWING HE-MAN INTO GLORIOUS BATTLE, BUT YOUR DESTINY IS, WELL, LARGER THAN THAT.
I WON'T BE AROUND FOREVER.
FATHER--
IT'S TRUE. AND NEITHER WILL YOUR MOTHER. AND, SINCE THE TIME OF THE GRAYSKULLS, THIS THRONE DOESN'T GET PASSED TO A CHAMPION, NO MATTER HOW GREAT A WARRIOR HE IS. IT GETS PASSED TO A PRINCE THE PEOPLE HAVE KNOWN AND LOVED SINCE THE DAY HE WAS BORN.
HE-MAN IS AN IDEA. A GOOD ONE, ONE THAT RALLIES THE PEOPLE, MAKES THEM FEEL SAFE. HE TOWERS OVER US, AND HE SHOULD, BECAUSE HE ISN'T ONE OF US.
THE CHAMPION IS THE KEEPER OF SECRETS THE KING SHOULD NEVER HEAR, OF BURDENS THE KING SHOULD NEVER BEAR. THAT PUTS A BIG ENOUGH TARGET ON HIS BACK THAT, IF I WERE HE-MAN, THE ONLY WAY I COULD RULE ETERNIA WOULD BE IN DISGUISE.
HEH. THAT DOESN'T SEEM VERY PRACTICAL.
IT ISN'T. WHICH IS WHY WE'RE THE SCEPTER AND HE'S THE SWORD. THAT'S WHAT KEEPS YOU AND YOUR MOTHER SAFE. I WOULDN'T HAVE IT ANY OTHER WAY...AND NEITHER SHOULD YOU, SON.
NOW, PLEASE, WILL YOU PICK OUT A DAMN CROWN SO WE CAN GO TO THIS DAMN PARTY AND DRINK SOME DAMN WINE?
HE-MAN!

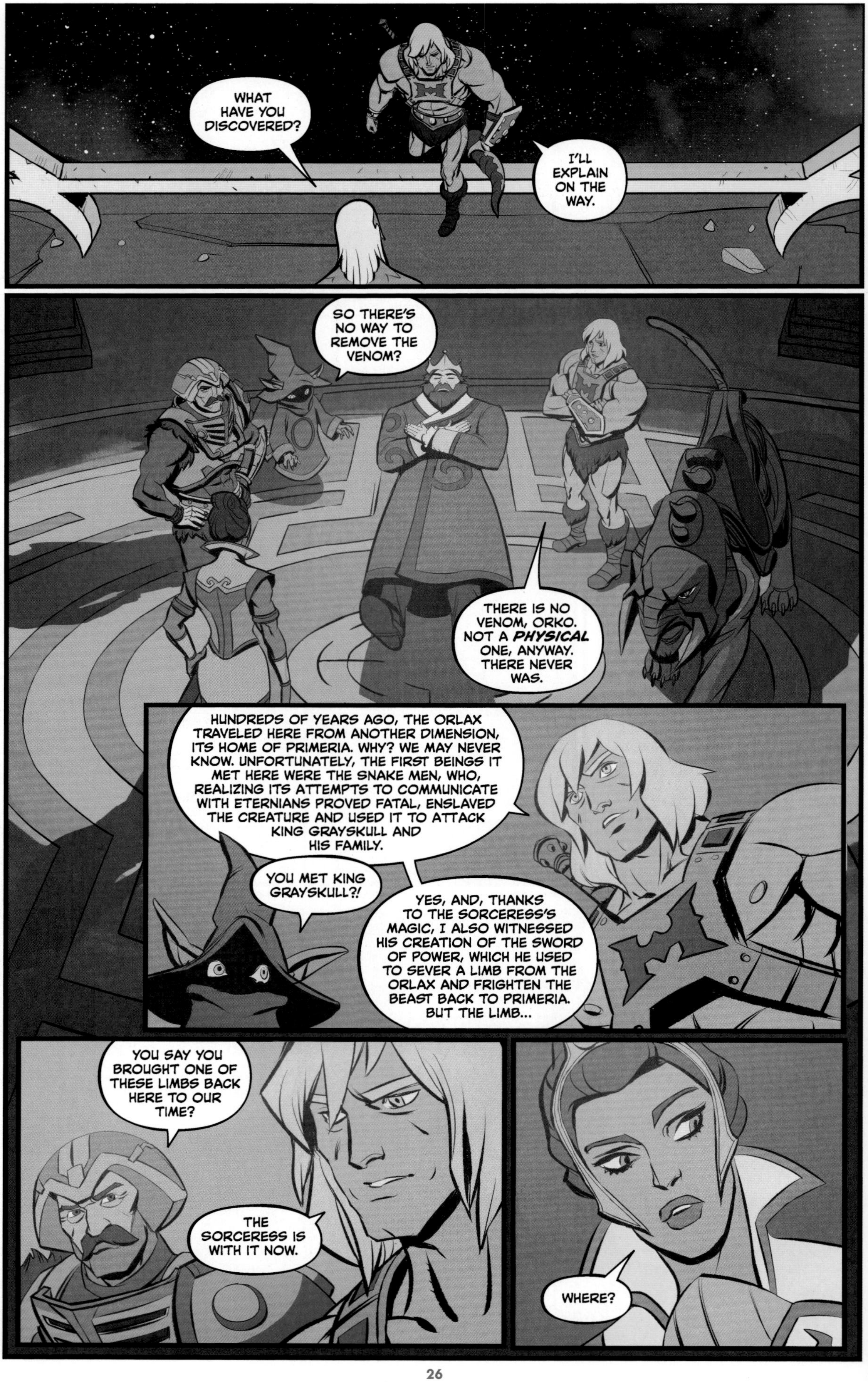
WHAT HAVE YOU DISCOVERED?
I'LL EXPLAIN ON THE WAY.
SO THERE'S NO WAY TO REMOVE THE VENOM?
THERE IS NO VENOM, ORKO. NOT A *PHYSICAL* ONE, ANYWAY. THERE NEVER WAS.
HUNDREDS OF YEARS AGO, THE ORLAX TRAVELED HERE FROM ANOTHER DIMENSION, ITS HOME OF PRIMERIA. WHY? WE MAY NEVER KNOW. UNFORTUNATELY, THE FIRST BEINGS IT MET HERE WERE THE SNAKE MEN, WHO, REALIZING ITS ATTEMPTS TO COMMUNICATE WITH ETERNIANS PROVED FATAL, ENSLAVED THE CREATURE AND USED IT TO ATTACK KING GRAYSKULL AND HIS FAMILY.
YOU MET KING GRAYSKULL?!
YES, AND, THANKS TO THE SORCERESS'S MAGIC, I ALSO WITNESSED HIS CREATION OF THE SWORD OF POWER, WHICH HE USED TO SEVER A LIMB FROM THE ORLAX AND FRIGHTEN THE BEAST BACK TO PRIMERIA. BUT THE LIMB...
YOU SAY YOU BROUGHT ONE OF THESE LIMBS BACK HERE TO OUR TIME?
THE SORCERESS IS WITH IT NOW.
WHERE?

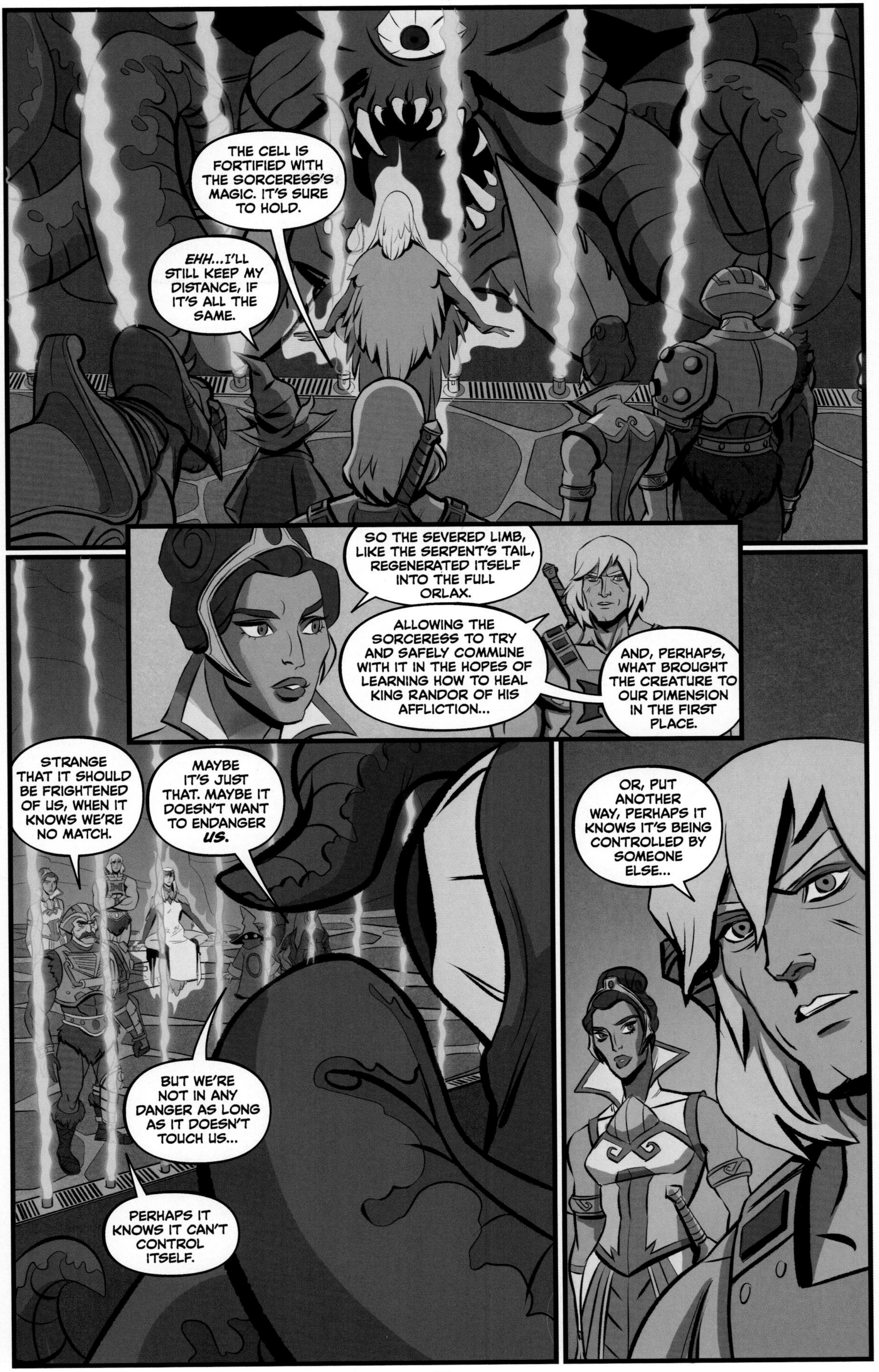
THE CELL IS FORTIFIED WITH THE SORCERESS'S MAGIC. IT'S SURE TO HOLD.
EHH...I'LL STILL KEEP MY DISTANCE, IF IT'S ALL THE SAME.
SO THE SEVERED LIMB, LIKE THE SERPENT'S TAIL, REGENERATED ITSELF INTO THE FULL ORLAX.
ALLOWING THE SORCERESS TO TRY AND SAFELY COMMUNE WITH IT IN THE HOPES OF LEARNING HOW TO HEAL KING RANDOR OF HIS AFFLICTION...
AND, PERHAPS, WHAT BROUGHT THE CREATURE TO OUR DIMENSION IN THE FIRST PLACE.
STRANGE THAT IT SHOULD BE FRIGHTENED OF US, WHEN IT KNOWS WE'RE NO MATCH.
MAYBE IT'S JUST THAT. MAYBE IT DOESN'T WANT TO ENDANGER ***US***.
BUT WE'RE NOT IN ANY DANGER AS LONG AS IT DOESN'T TOUCH US...
PERHAPS IT KNOWS IT CAN'T CONTROL ITSELF.
OR, PUT ANOTHER WAY, PERHAPS IT KNOWS IT'S BEING CONTROLLED BY SOMEONE ELSE...

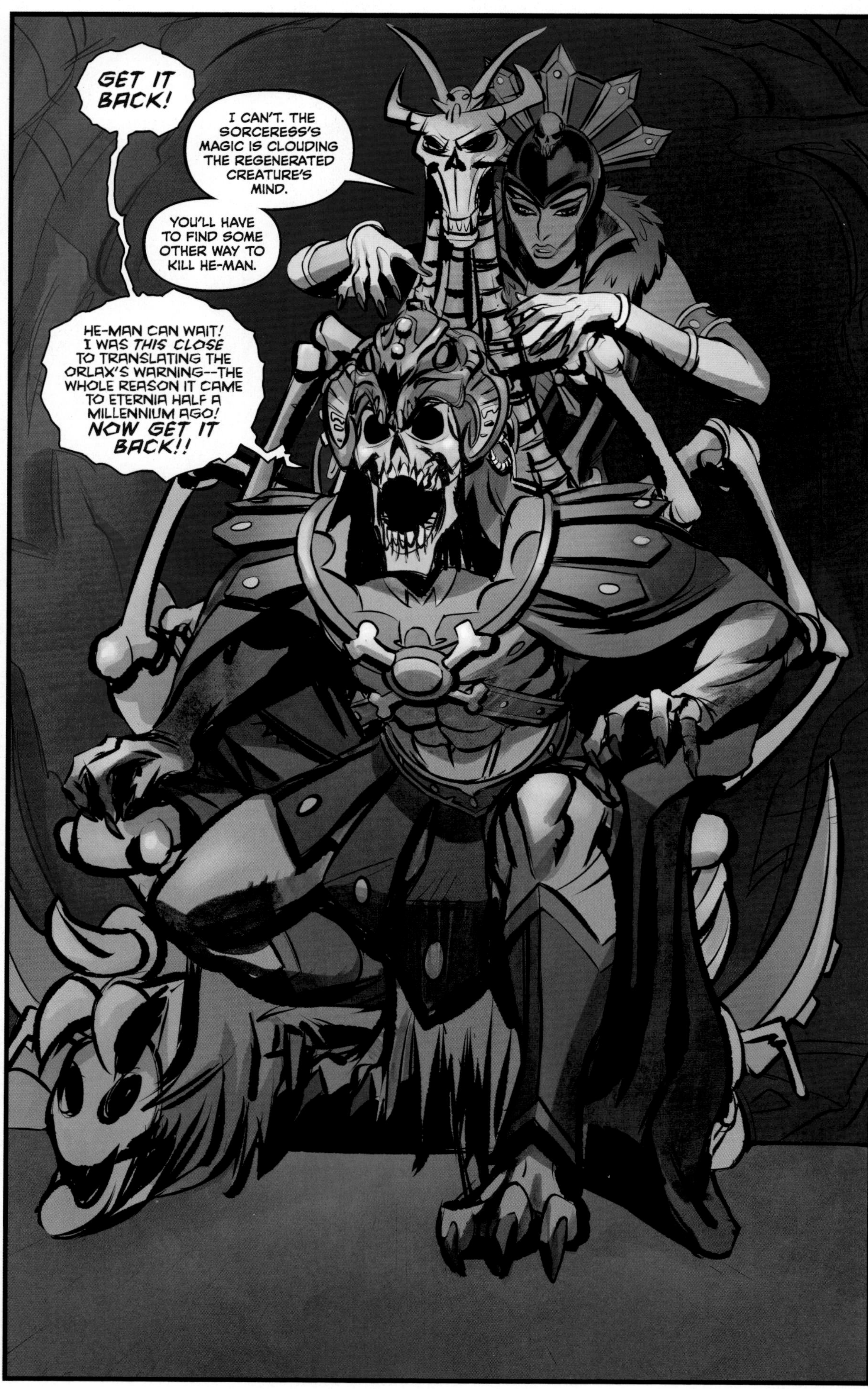
GET IT BACK!
I CAN'T. THE SORCERESS'S MAGIC IS CLOUDING THE REGENERATED CREATURE'S MIND.
YOU'LL HAVE TO FIND SOME OTHER WAY TO KILL HE-MAN.
HE-MAN CAN WAIT! I WAS *THIS CLOSE* TO TRANSLATING THE ORLAX'S WARNING--THE WHOLE REASON IT CAME TO ETERNIA HALF A MILLENNIUM AGO! **NOW GET IT BACK!!**

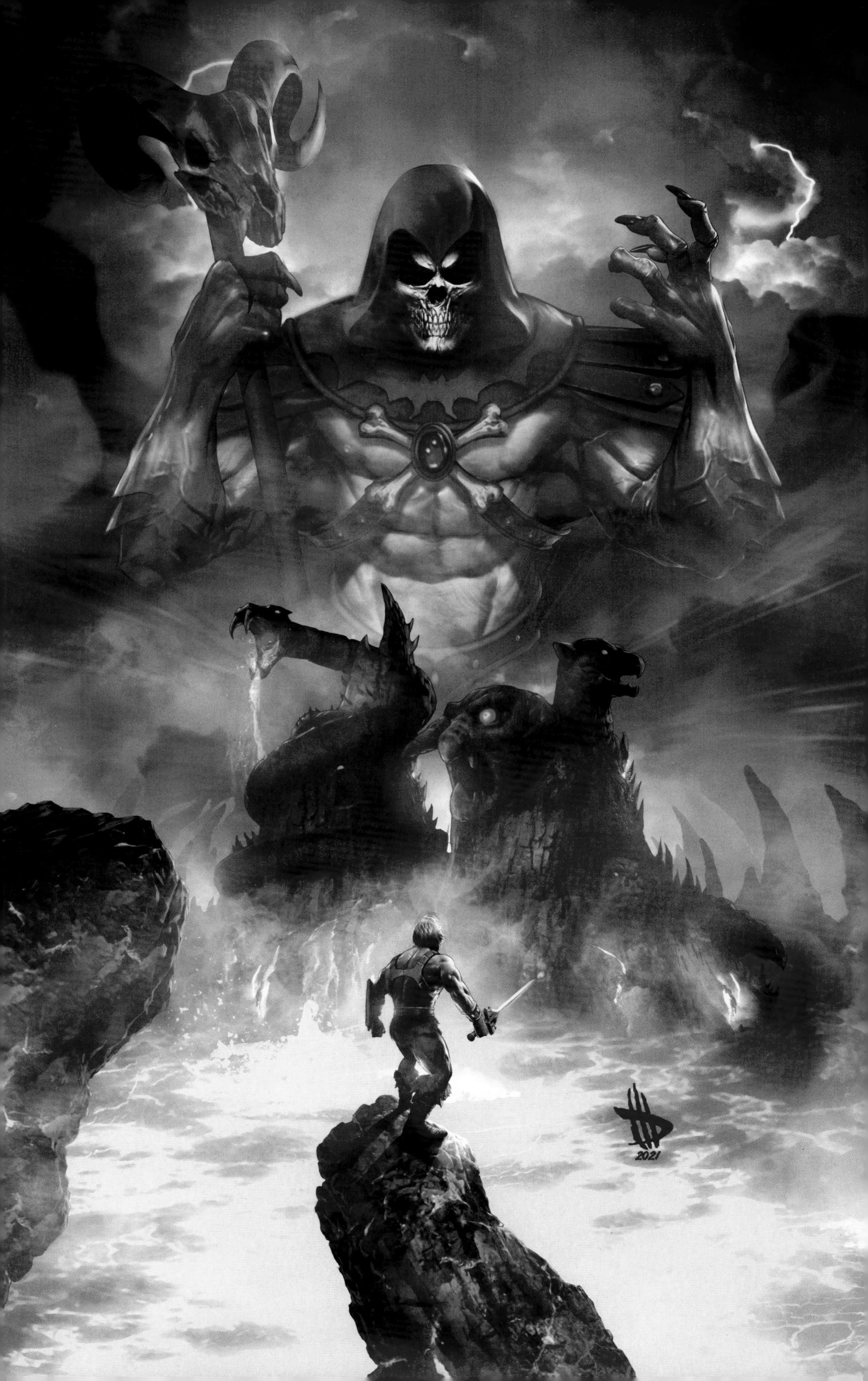
2021

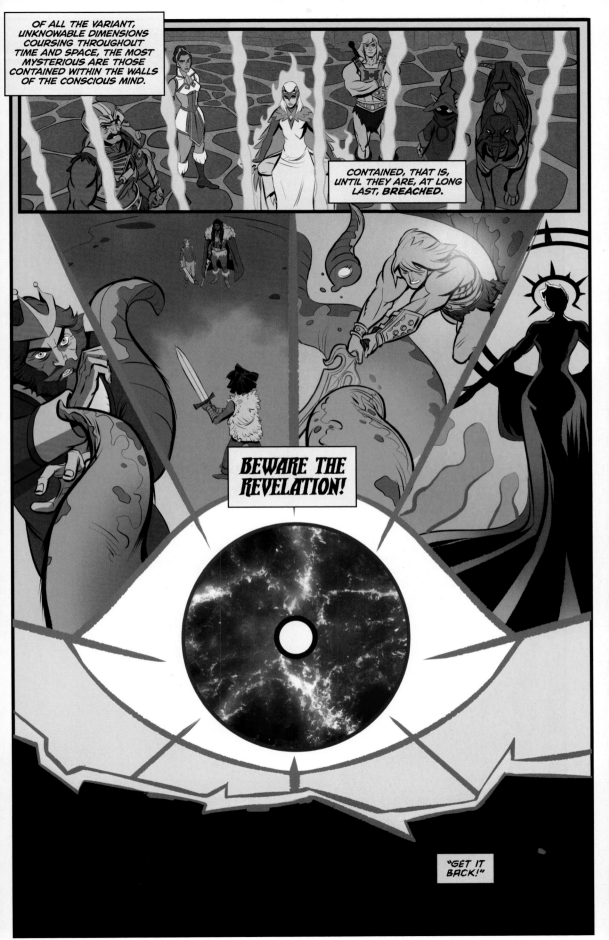

OF ALL THE VARIANT, UNKNOWABLE DIMENSIONS COURSING THROUGHOUT TIME AND SPACE, THE MOST MYSTERIOUS ARE THOSE CONTAINED WITHIN THE WALLS OF THE CONSCIOUS MIND.

CONTAINED, THAT IS, UNTIL THEY ARE, AT LONG LAST, BREACHED.

BEWARE THE REVELATION!

"GET IT BACK!"

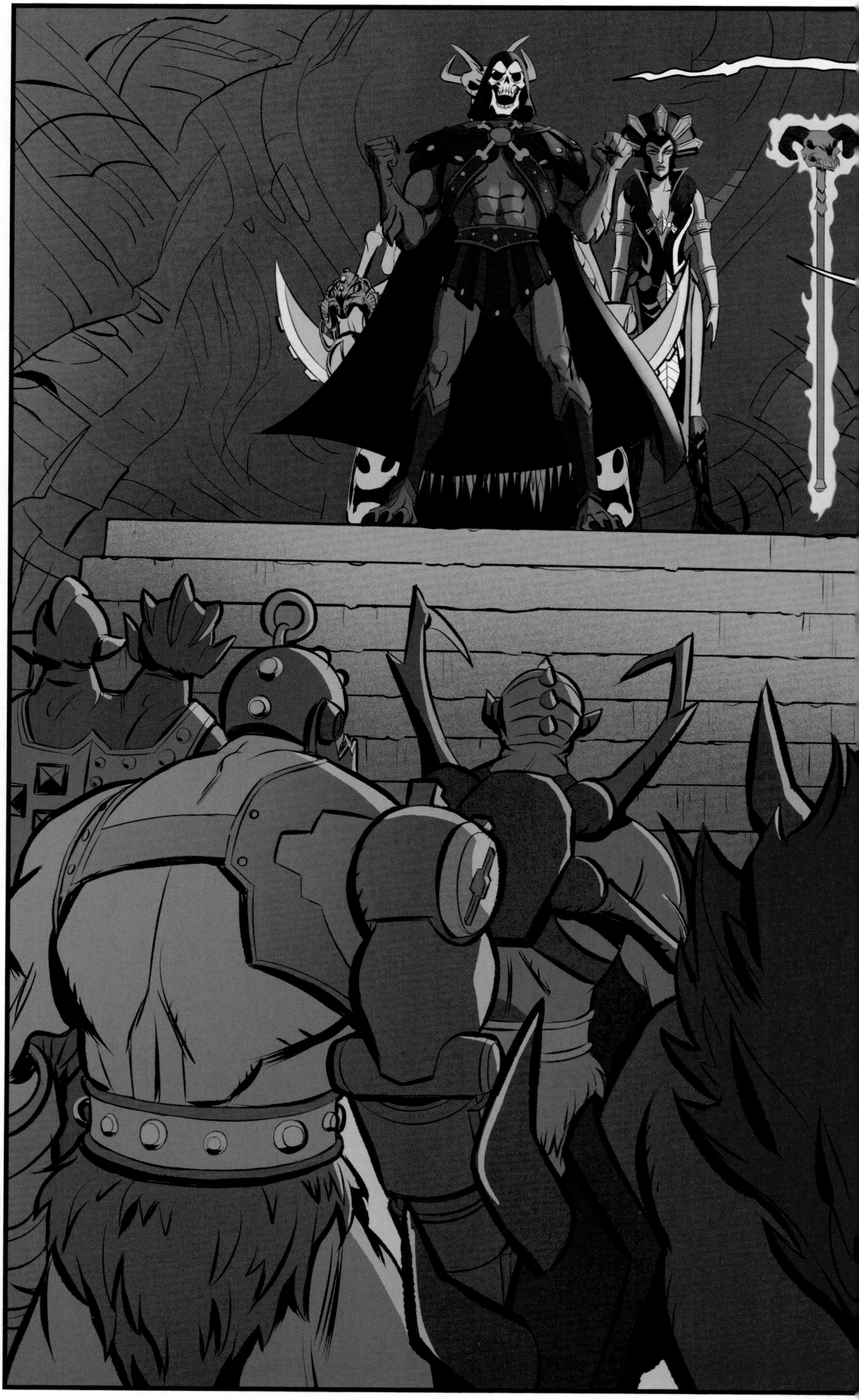

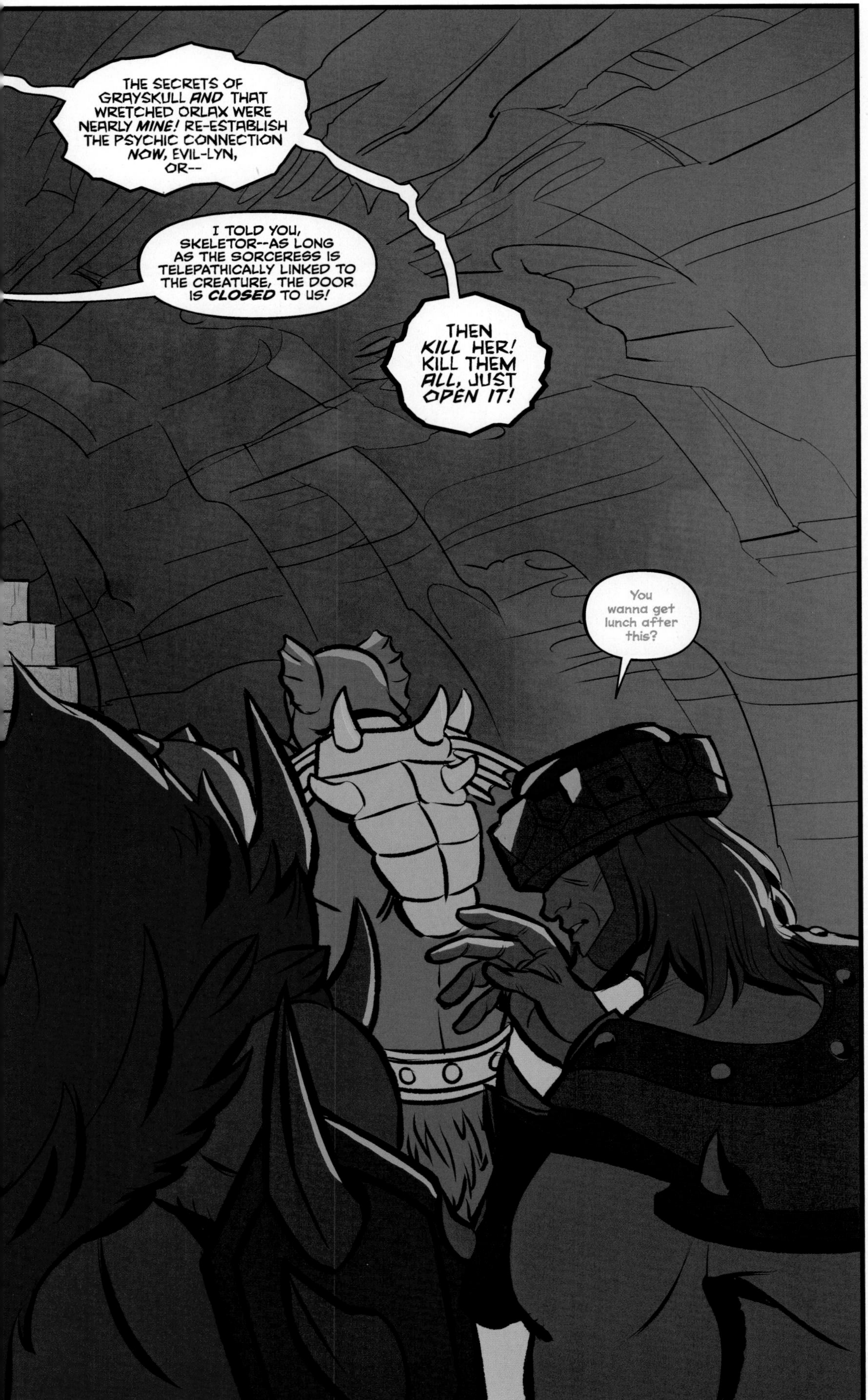
THE SECRETS OF GRAYSKULL *AND* THAT WRETCHED ORLAX WERE NEARLY *MINE!* RE-ESTABLISH THE PSYCHIC CONNECTION *NOW*, EVIL-LYN, OR--
I TOLD YOU, SKELETOR--AS LONG AS THE SORCERESS IS TELEPATHICALLY LINKED TO THE CREATURE, THE DOOR IS *CLOSED* TO US!
THEN *KILL* HER! KILL THEM *ALL*, JUST *OPEN* IT!
You wanna get lunch after this?

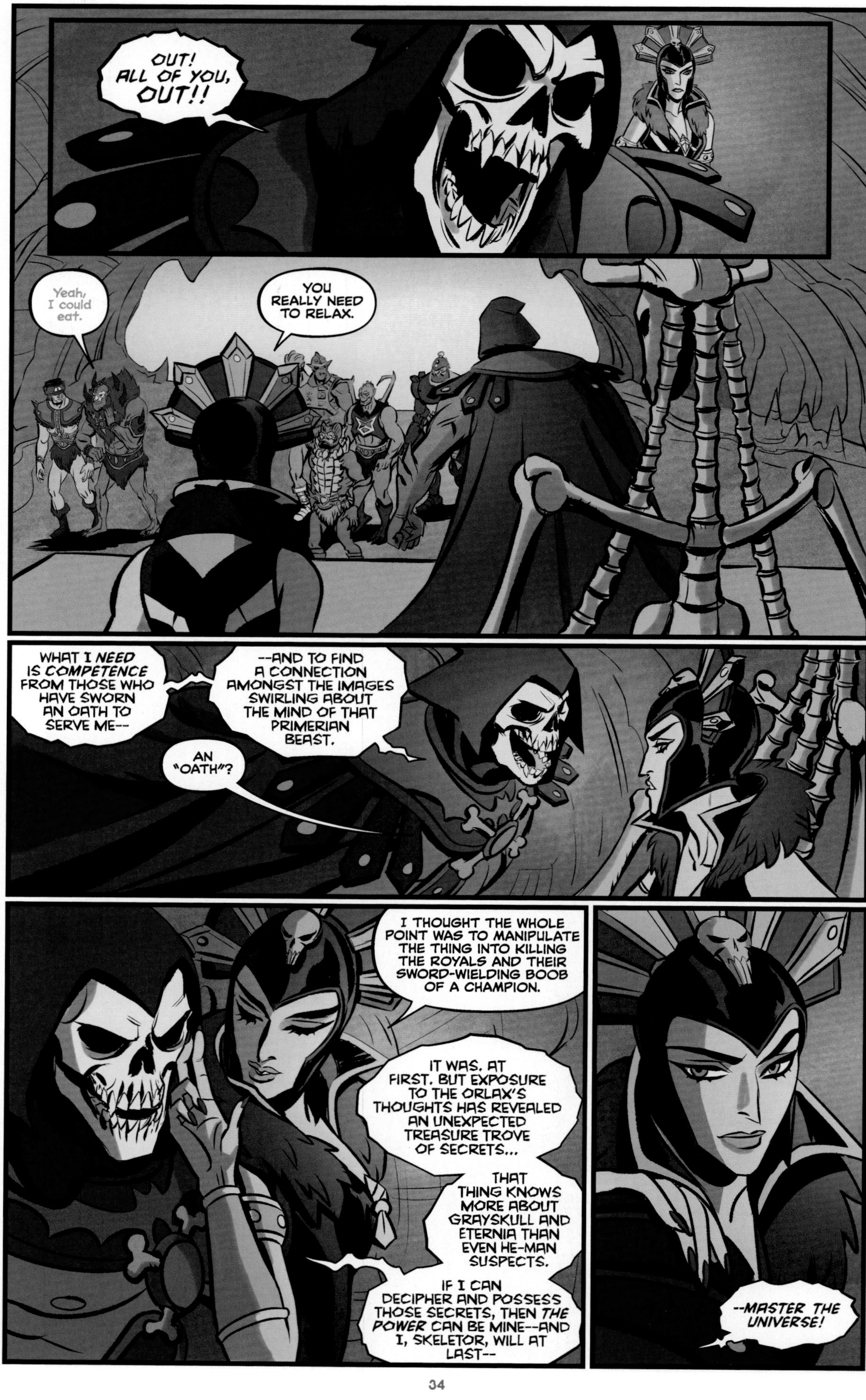
OUT! ALL OF YOU, OUT!!
Yeah, I could eat.
YOU REALLY NEED TO RELAX.
WHAT I NEED IS COMPETENCE FROM THOSE WHO HAVE SWORN AN OATH TO SERVE ME--
--AND TO FIND A CONNECTION AMONGST THE IMAGES SWIRLING ABOUT THE MIND OF THAT PRIMERIAN BEAST.
AN "OATH"?
I THOUGHT THE WHOLE POINT WAS TO MANIPULATE THE THING INTO KILLING THE ROYALS AND THEIR SWORD-WIELDING BOOB OF A CHAMPION.
IT WAS. AT FIRST. BUT EXPOSURE TO THE ORLAX'S THOUGHTS HAS REVEALED AN UNEXPECTED TREASURE TROVE OF SECRETS...
THAT THING KNOWS MORE ABOUT GRAYSKULL AND ETERNIA THAN EVEN HE-MAN SUSPECTS.
IF I CAN DECIPHER AND POSSESS THOSE SECRETS, THEN THE POWER CAN BE MINE--AND I, SKELETOR, WILL AT LAST--
--MASTER THE UNIVERSE!

THE ANSWER IS THERE, DANGLING BEFORE ME, *MOCKING ME!*

D'VANN GRAYSKULL...THE SWORD...THE ANCIENT HALL OF WISDOM...THE PAST!...THEN SOME KIND OF CELESTIAL EVENT... BUT WHAT'S THE *CONNECTION?!*

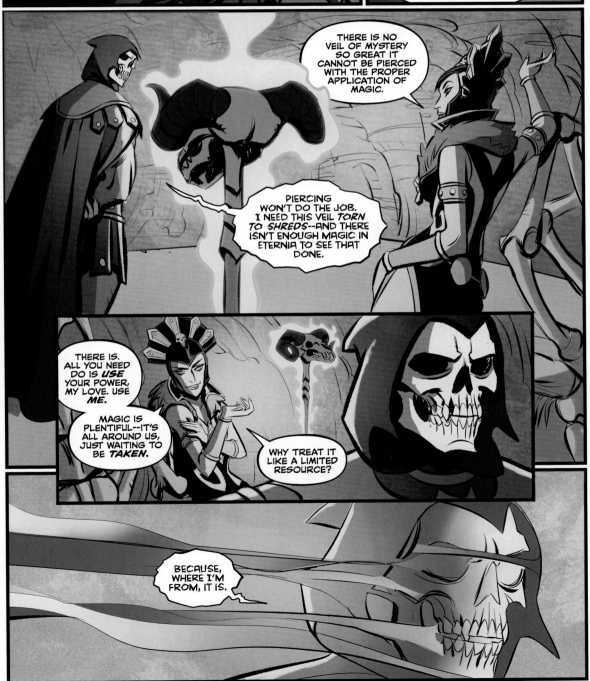

THERE IS NO VEIL OF MYSTERY SO GREAT IT CANNOT BE PIERCED WITH THE PROPER APPLICATION OF MAGIC.

PIERCING WON'T DO THE JOB. I NEED THIS VEIL *TORN TO SHREDS*--AND THERE ISN'T ENOUGH MAGIC IN ETERNIA TO SEE THAT DONE.

THERE IS. ALL YOU NEED DO IS *USE* YOUR POWER, MY LOVE. USE *ME.*

MAGIC IS PLENTIFUL--IT'S ALL AROUND US, JUST WAITING TO BE *TAKEN.*

WHY TREAT IT LIKE A LIMITED RESOURCE?

BECAUSE, WHERE I'M FROM, IT IS.

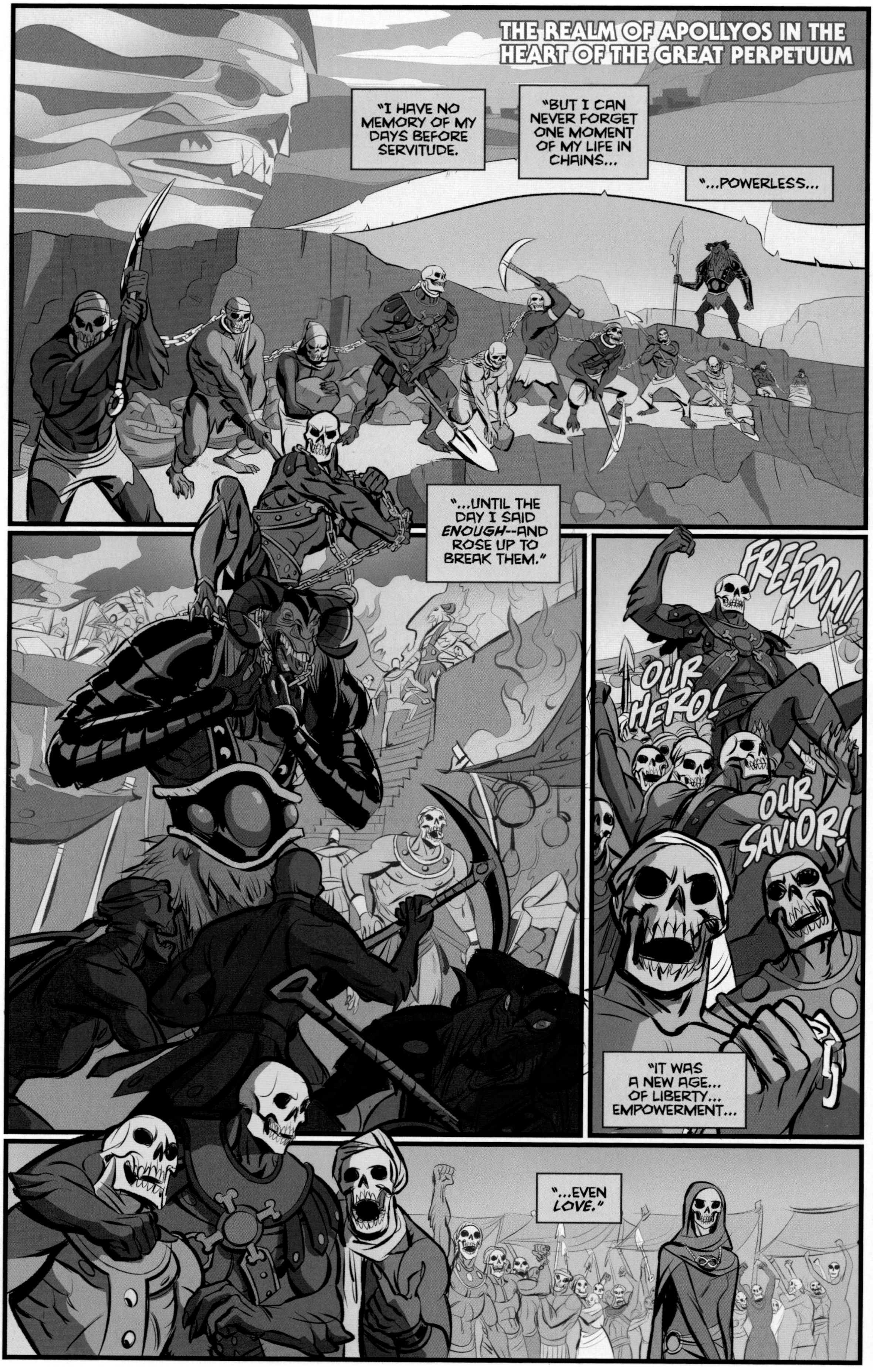
THE REALM OF APOLLYOS IN THE HEART OF THE GREAT PERPETUUM
"I HAVE NO MEMORY OF MY DAYS BEFORE SERVITUDE.
"BUT I CAN NEVER FORGET ONE MOMENT OF MY LIFE IN CHAINS...
"...POWERLESS...
"...UNTIL THE DAY I SAID *ENOUGH*--AND ROSE UP TO BREAK THEM."
FREEDOM!!
OUR HERO!
OUR SAVIOR!
"IT WAS A NEW AGE... OF LIBERTY... EMPOWERMENT...
"...EVEN *LOVE*."

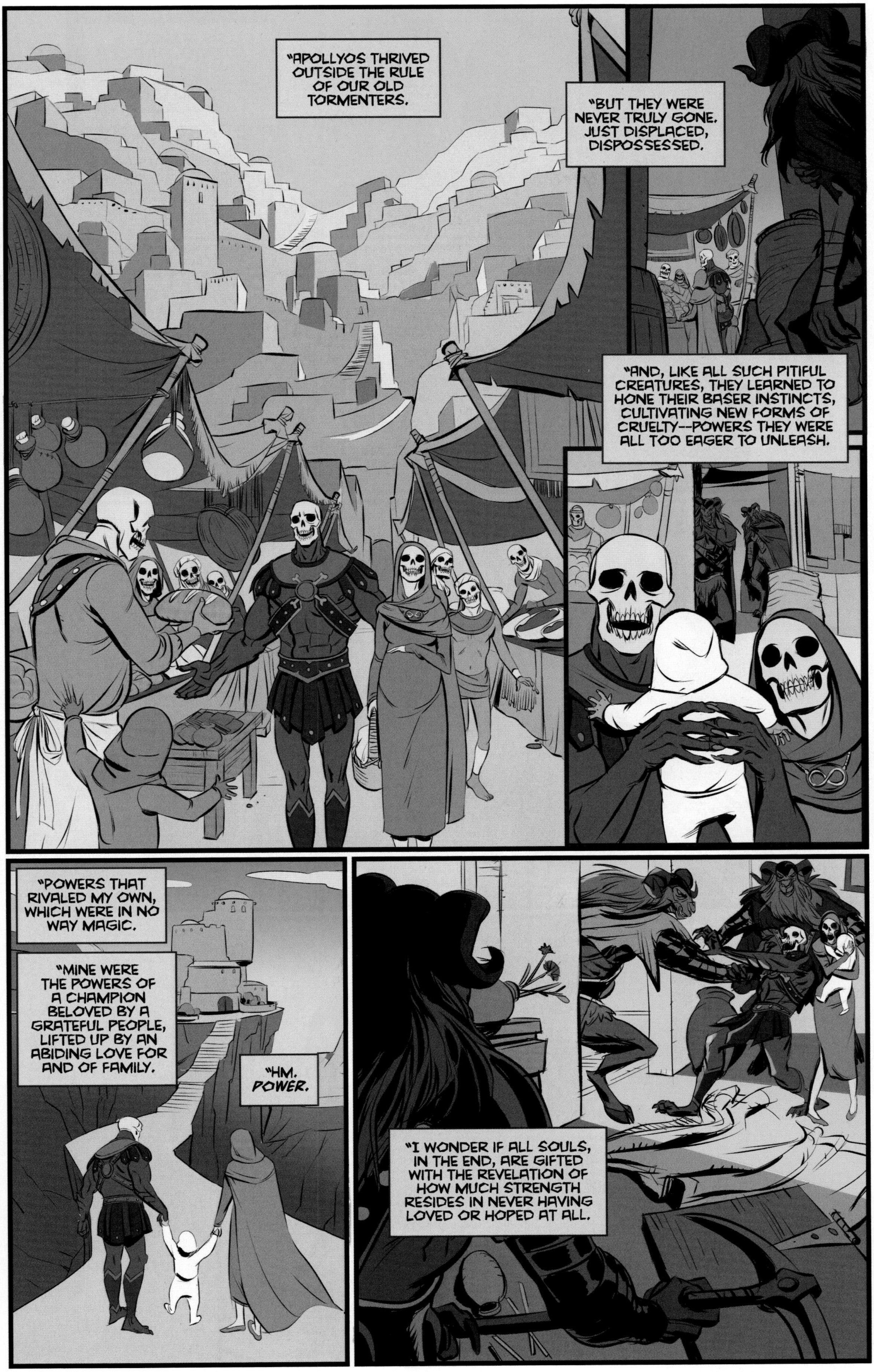
"APOLLYOS THRIVED OUTSIDE THE RULE OF OUR OLD TORMENTERS.
"BUT THEY WERE NEVER TRULY GONE. JUST DISPLACED, DISPOSSESSED.
"AND, LIKE ALL SUCH PITIFUL CREATURES, THEY LEARNED TO HONE THEIR BASER INSTINCTS, CULTIVATING NEW FORMS OF CRUELTY--POWERS THEY WERE ALL TOO EAGER TO UNLEASH.
"POWERS THAT RIVALED MY OWN, WHICH WERE IN NO WAY MAGIC.
"MINE WERE THE POWERS OF A CHAMPION BELOVED BY A GRATEFUL PEOPLE, LIFTED UP BY AN ABIDING LOVE FOR AND OF FAMILY.
"HM. *POWER.*
"I WONDER IF ALL SOULS, IN THE END, ARE GIFTED WITH THE REVELATION OF HOW MUCH STRENGTH RESIDES IN NEVER HAVING LOVED OR HOPED AT ALL.

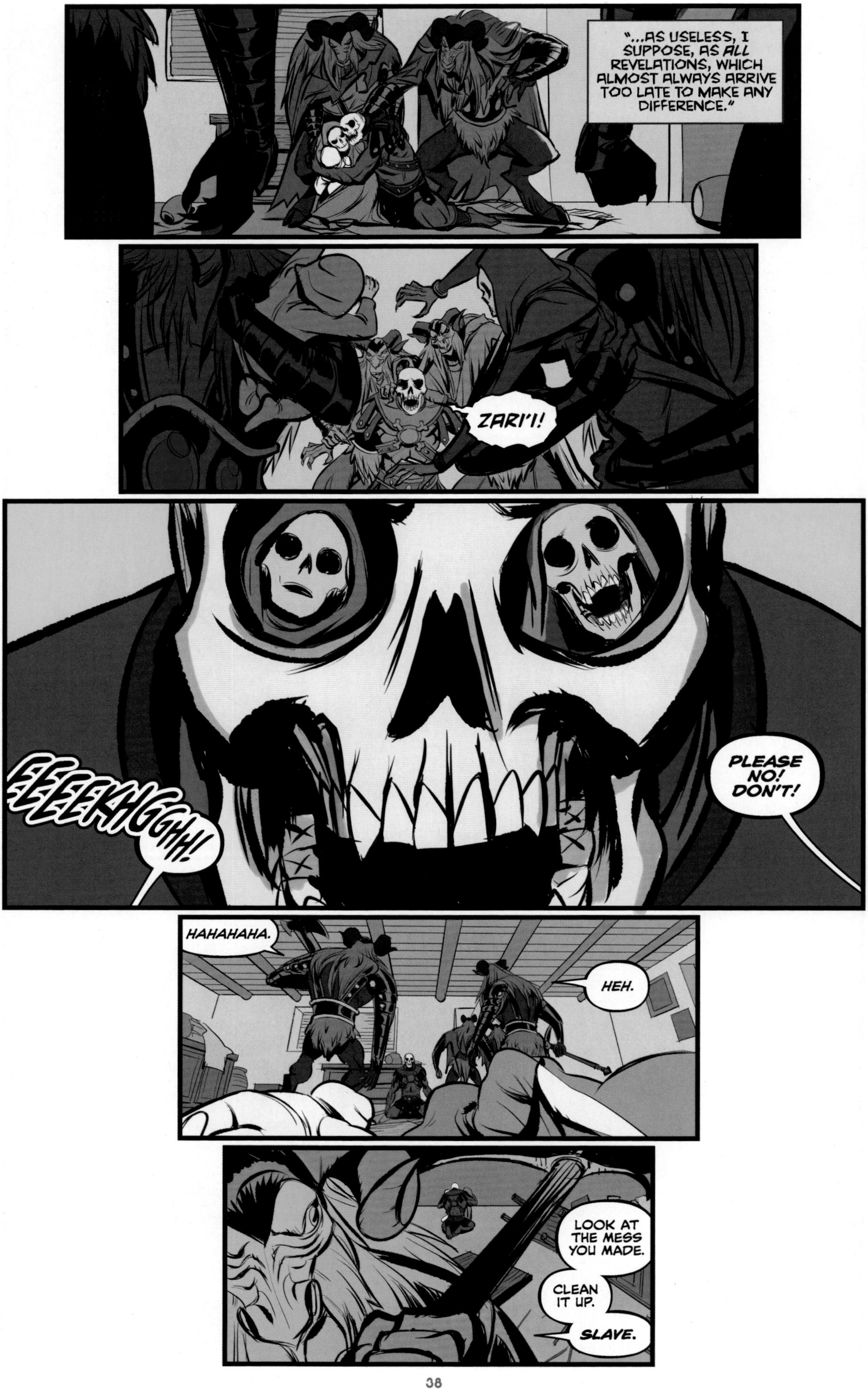
"...AS USELESS, I SUPPOSE, AS ALL REVELATIONS, WHICH ALMOST ALWAYS ARRIVE TOO LATE TO MAKE ANY DIFFERENCE."
ZARI'I!
EEEEEKHGGHH!
PLEASE NO! DON'T!
HAHAHAHA.
HEH.
LOOK AT THE MESS YOU MADE.
CLEAN IT UP.
SLAVE.

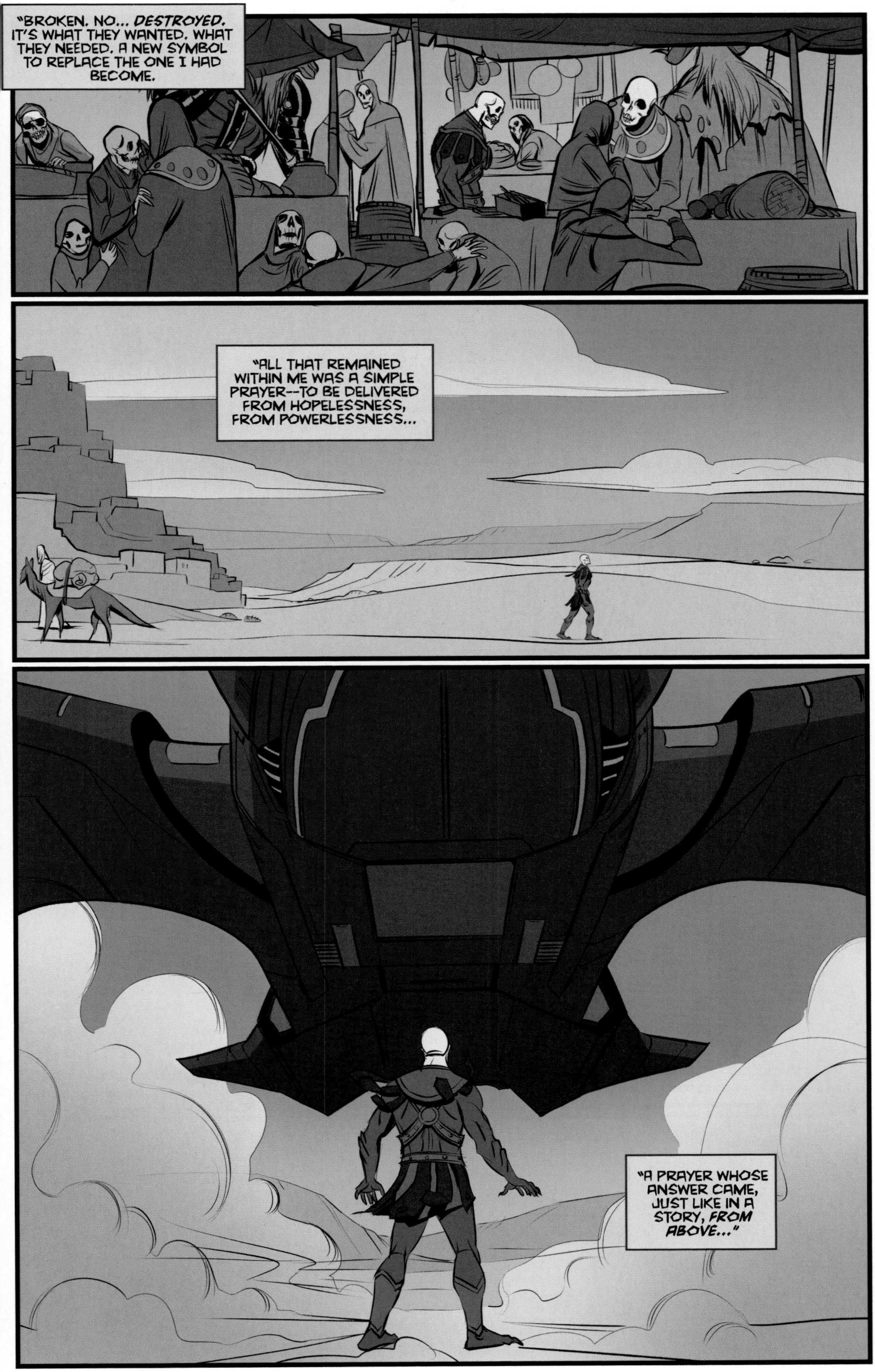
"BROKEN. NO... *DESTROYED.* IT'S WHAT THEY WANTED. WHAT THEY NEEDED. A NEW SYMBOL TO REPLACE THE ONE I HAD BECOME.
"ALL THAT REMAINED WITHIN ME WAS A SIMPLE PRAYER--TO BE DELIVERED FROM HOPELESSNESS, FROM POWERLESSNESS...
"A PRAYER WHOSE ANSWER CAME, JUST LIKE IN A STORY, *FROM ABOVE...*"

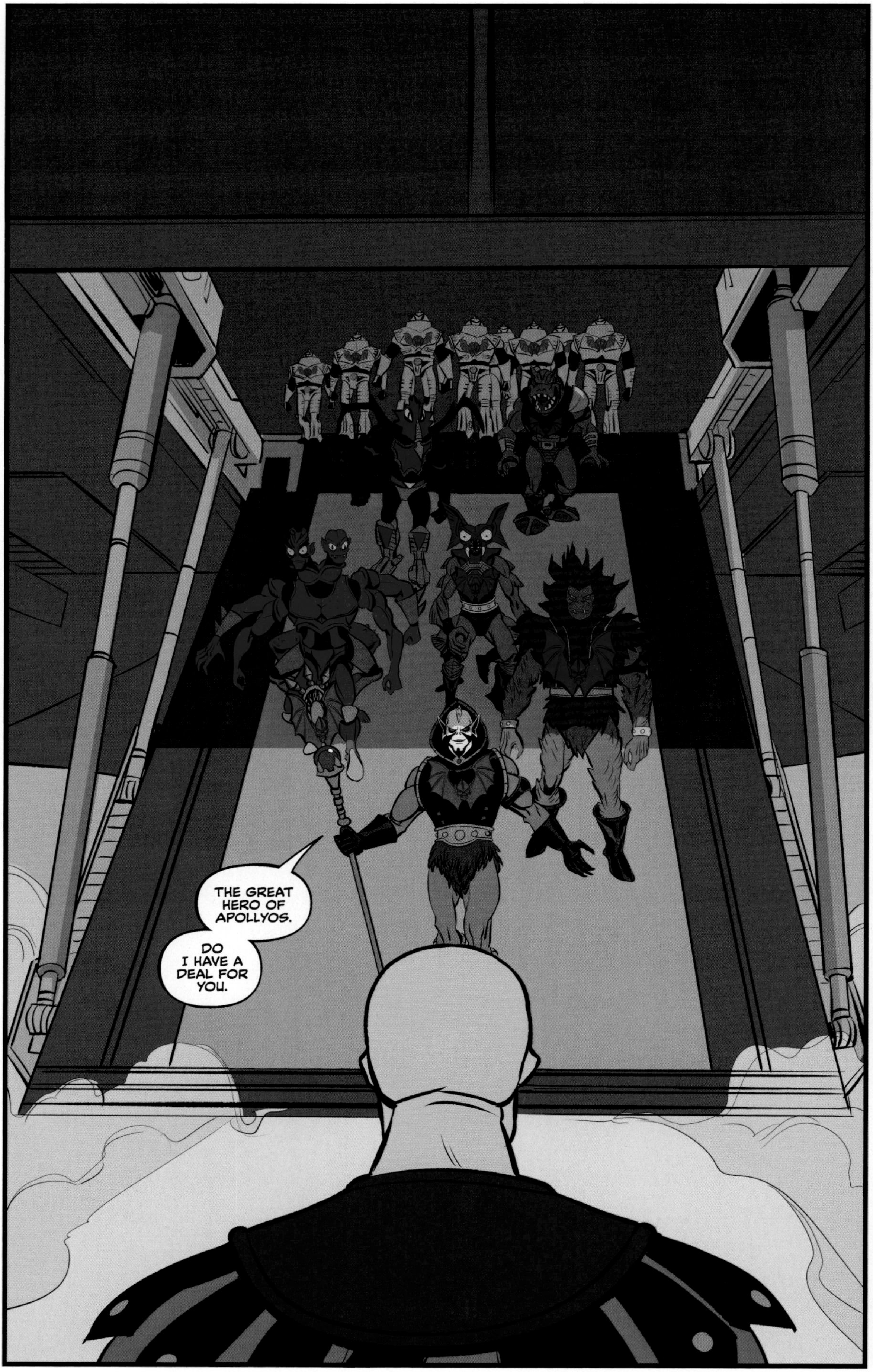
THE GREAT HERO OF APOLLYOS.
DO I HAVE A DEAL FOR YOU.

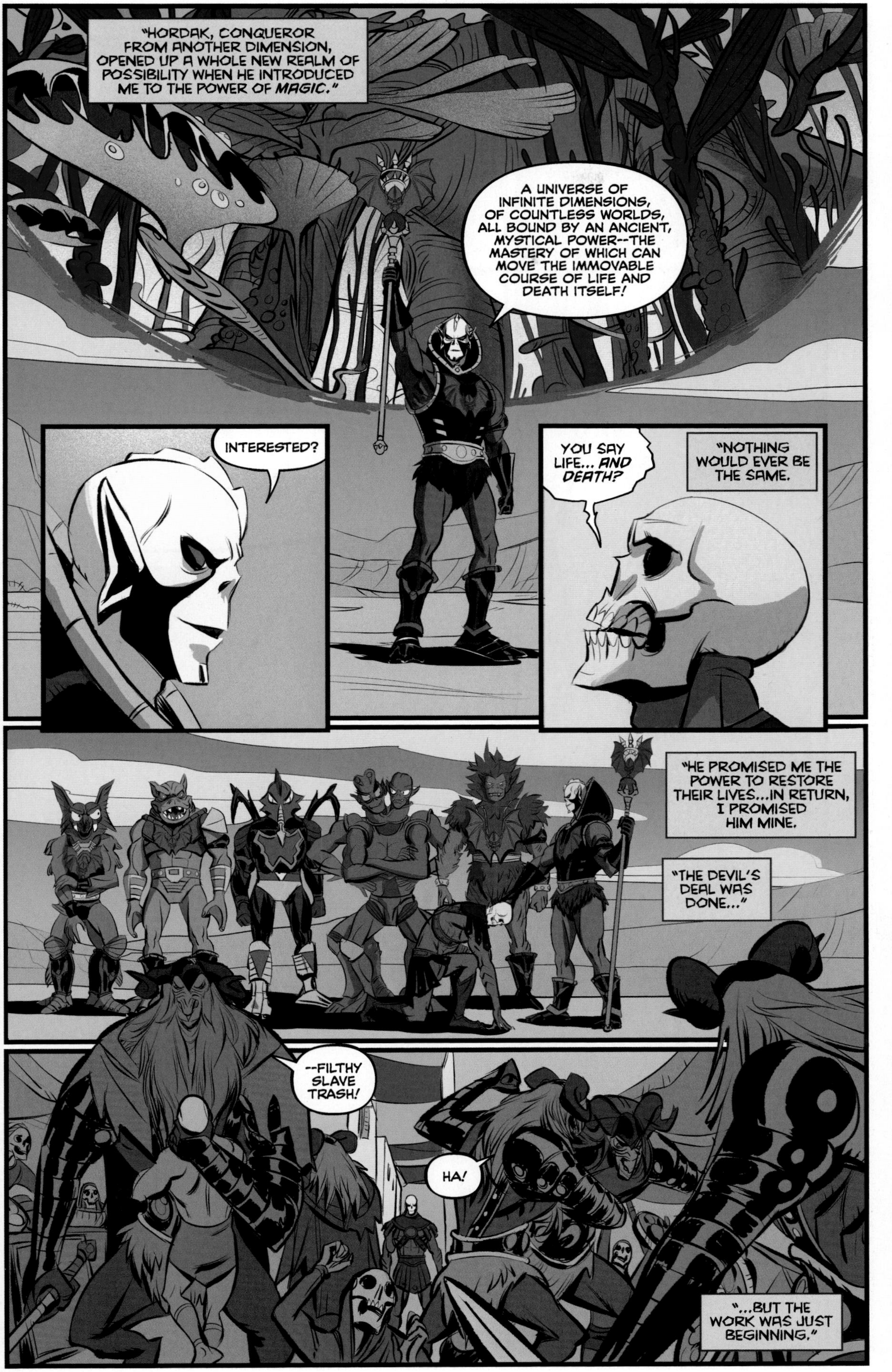
"HORDAK, CONQUEROR FROM ANOTHER DIMENSION, OPENED UP A WHOLE NEW REALM OF POSSIBILITY WHEN HE INTRODUCED ME TO THE POWER OF *MAGIC*."
A UNIVERSE OF INFINITE DIMENSIONS, OF COUNTLESS WORLDS, ALL BOUND BY AN ANCIENT, MYSTICAL POWER--THE MASTERY OF WHICH CAN MOVE THE IMMOVABLE COURSE OF LIFE AND DEATH ITSELF!
INTERESTED?
YOU SAY LIFE... *AND DEATH?*
"NOTHING WOULD EVER BE THE SAME.
"HE PROMISED ME THE POWER TO RESTORE THEIR LIVES...IN RETURN, I PROMISED HIM MINE.
"THE DEVIL'S DEAL WAS DONE..."
--FILTHY SLAVE TRASH!
HA!
"...BUT THE WORK WAS JUST BEGINNING."

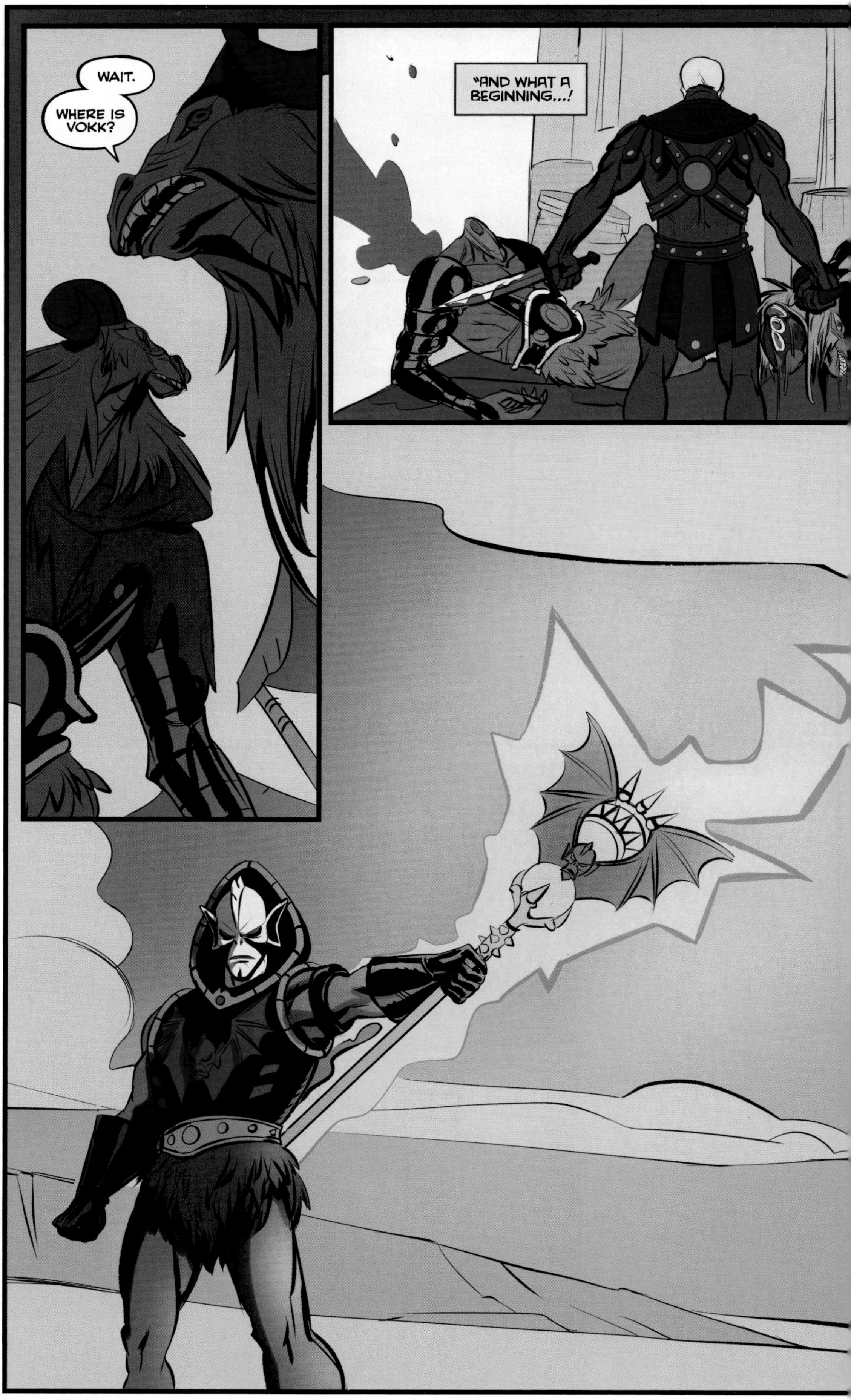
WAIT.
WHERE IS VOKK?
"AND WHAT A BEGINNING...!

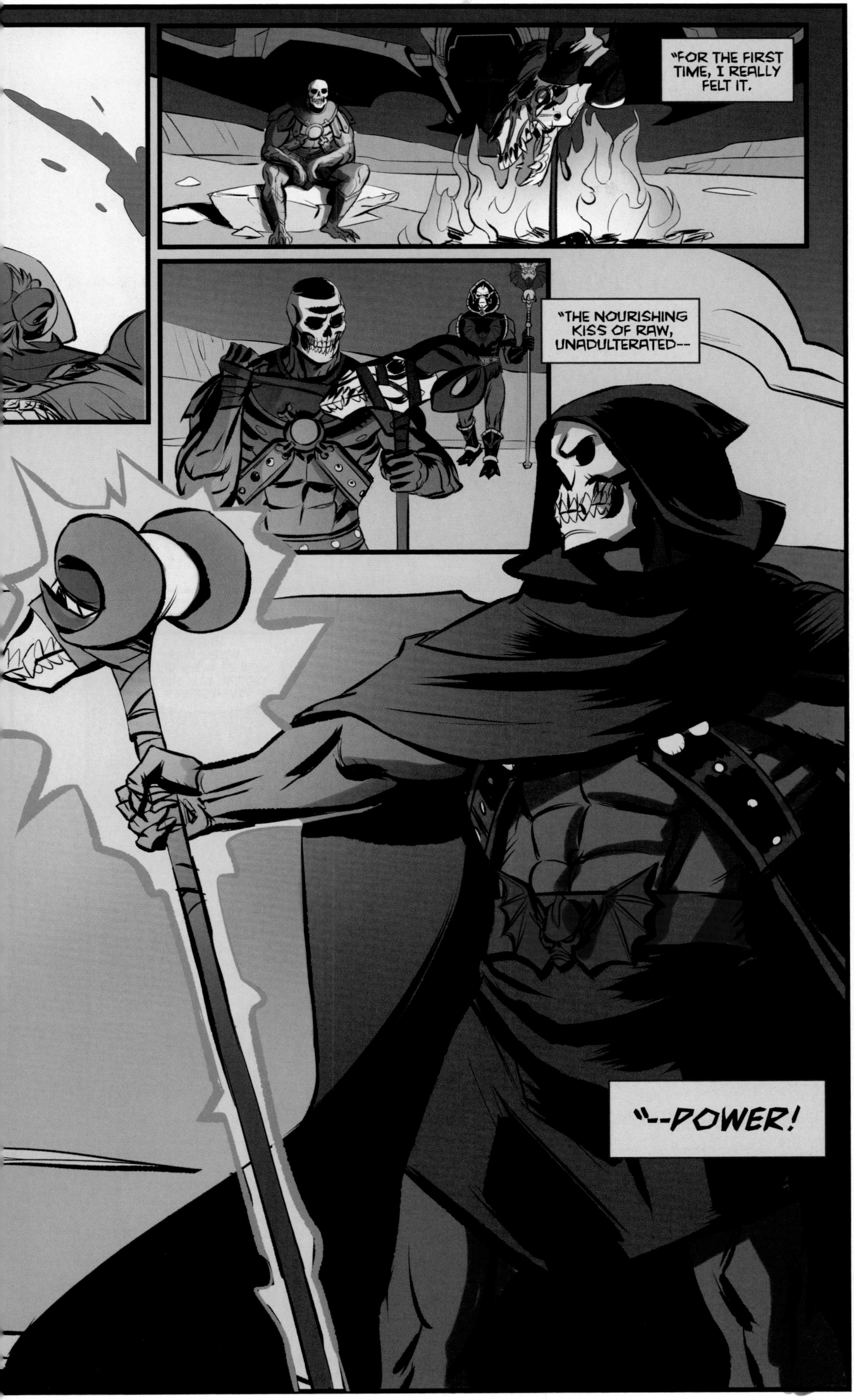
"FOR THE FIRST TIME, I REALLY FELT IT.
"THE NOURISHING KISS OF RAW, UNADULTERATED--
"--POWER!

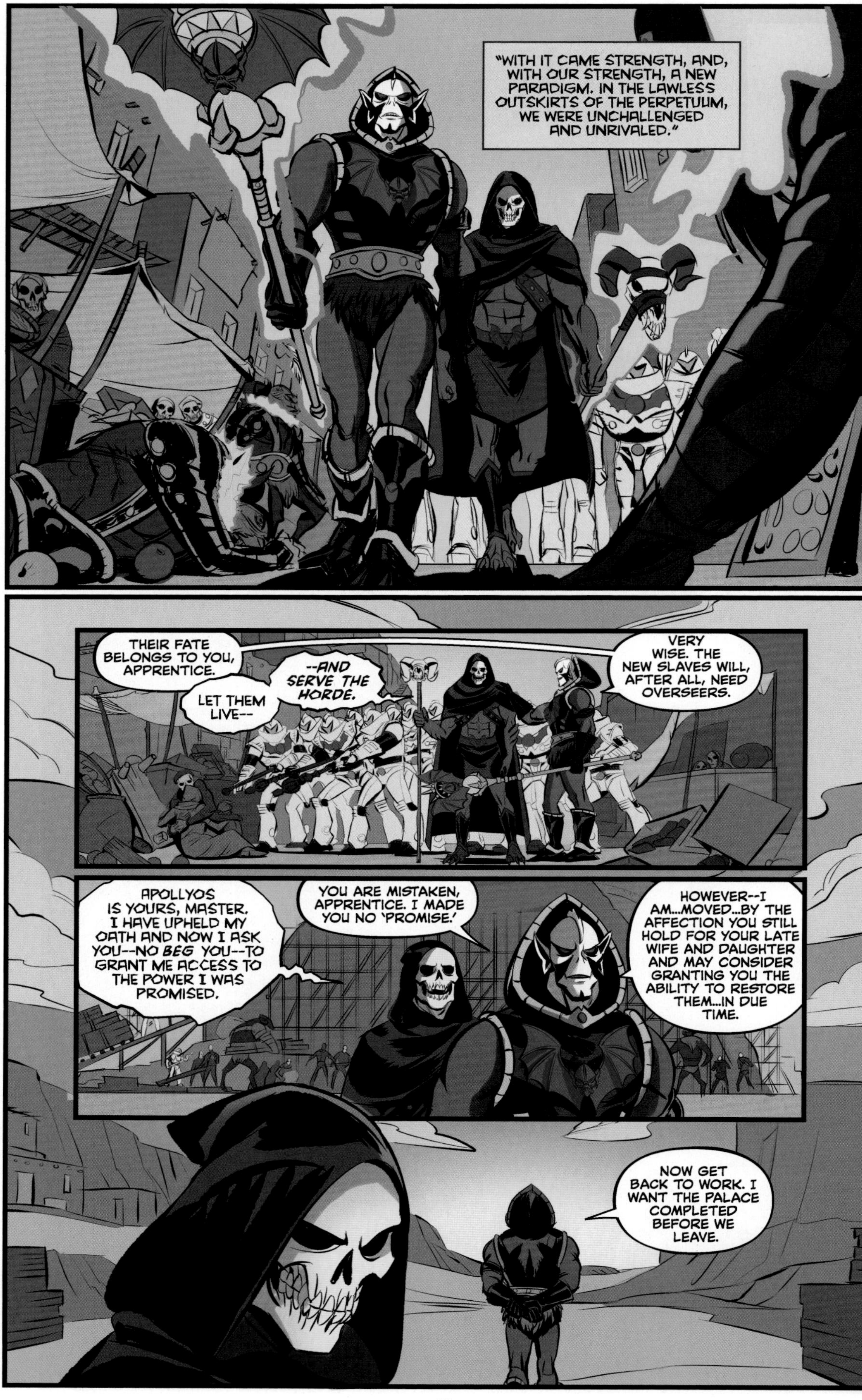
"WITH IT CAME STRENGTH, AND, WITH OUR STRENGTH, A NEW PARADIGM. IN THE LAWLESS OUTSKIRTS OF THE PERPETUUM, WE WERE UNCHALLENGED AND UNRIVALED."
THEIR FATE BELONGS TO YOU, APPRENTICE.
LET THEM LIVE--
--AND SERVE THE HORDE.
VERY WISE. THE NEW SLAVES WILL, AFTER ALL, NEED OVERSEERS.
APOLLYOS IS YOURS, MASTER. I HAVE UPHELD MY OATH AND NOW I ASK YOU--NO BEG YOU--TO GRANT ME ACCESS TO THE POWER I WAS PROMISED.
YOU ARE MISTAKEN, APPRENTICE. I MADE YOU NO 'PROMISE.'
HOWEVER--I AM...MOVED...BY THE AFFECTION YOU STILL HOLD FOR YOUR LATE WIFE AND DAUGHTER AND MAY CONSIDER GRANTING YOU THE ABILITY TO RESTORE THEM...IN DUE TIME.
NOW GET BACK TO WORK. I WANT THE PALACE COMPLETED BEFORE WE LEAVE.

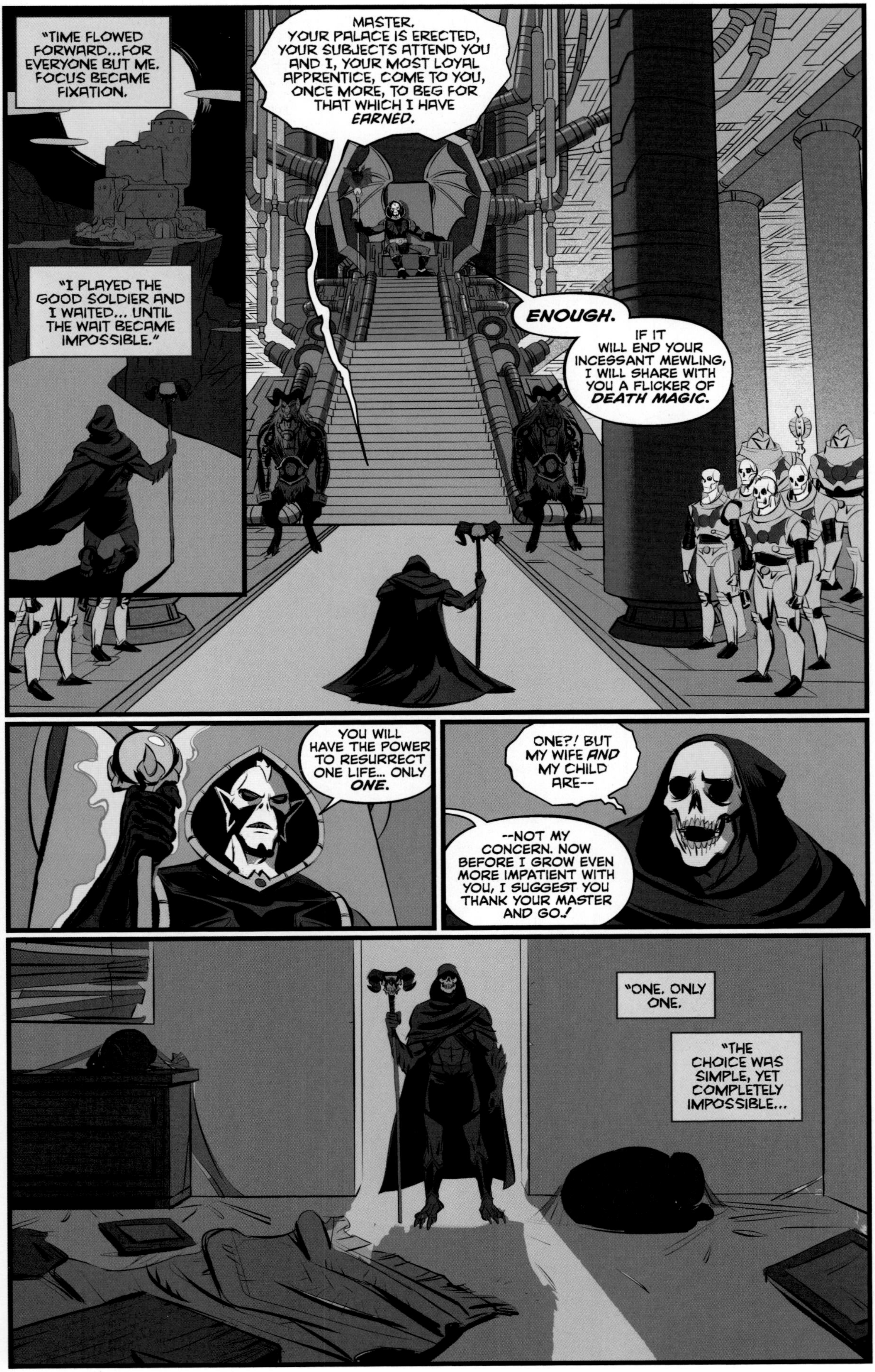
"TIME FLOWED FORWARD...FOR EVERYONE BUT ME. FOCUS BECAME FIXATION.
"I PLAYED THE GOOD SOLDIER AND I WAITED... UNTIL THE WAIT BECAME IMPOSSIBLE."
MASTER. YOUR PALACE IS ERECTED, YOUR SUBJECTS ATTEND YOU AND I, YOUR MOST LOYAL APPRENTICE, COME TO YOU, ONCE MORE, TO BEG FOR THAT WHICH I HAVE EARNED.
ENOUGH.
IF IT WILL END YOUR INCESSANT MEWLING, I WILL SHARE WITH YOU A FLICKER OF DEATH MAGIC.
YOU WILL HAVE THE POWER TO RESURRECT ONE LIFE... ONLY ONE.
ONE?! BUT MY WIFE AND MY CHILD ARE--
--NOT MY CONCERN. NOW BEFORE I GROW EVEN MORE IMPATIENT WITH YOU, I SUGGEST YOU THANK YOUR MASTER AND GO.!
"ONE. ONLY ONE.
"THE CHOICE WAS SIMPLE, YET COMPLETELY IMPOSSIBLE...

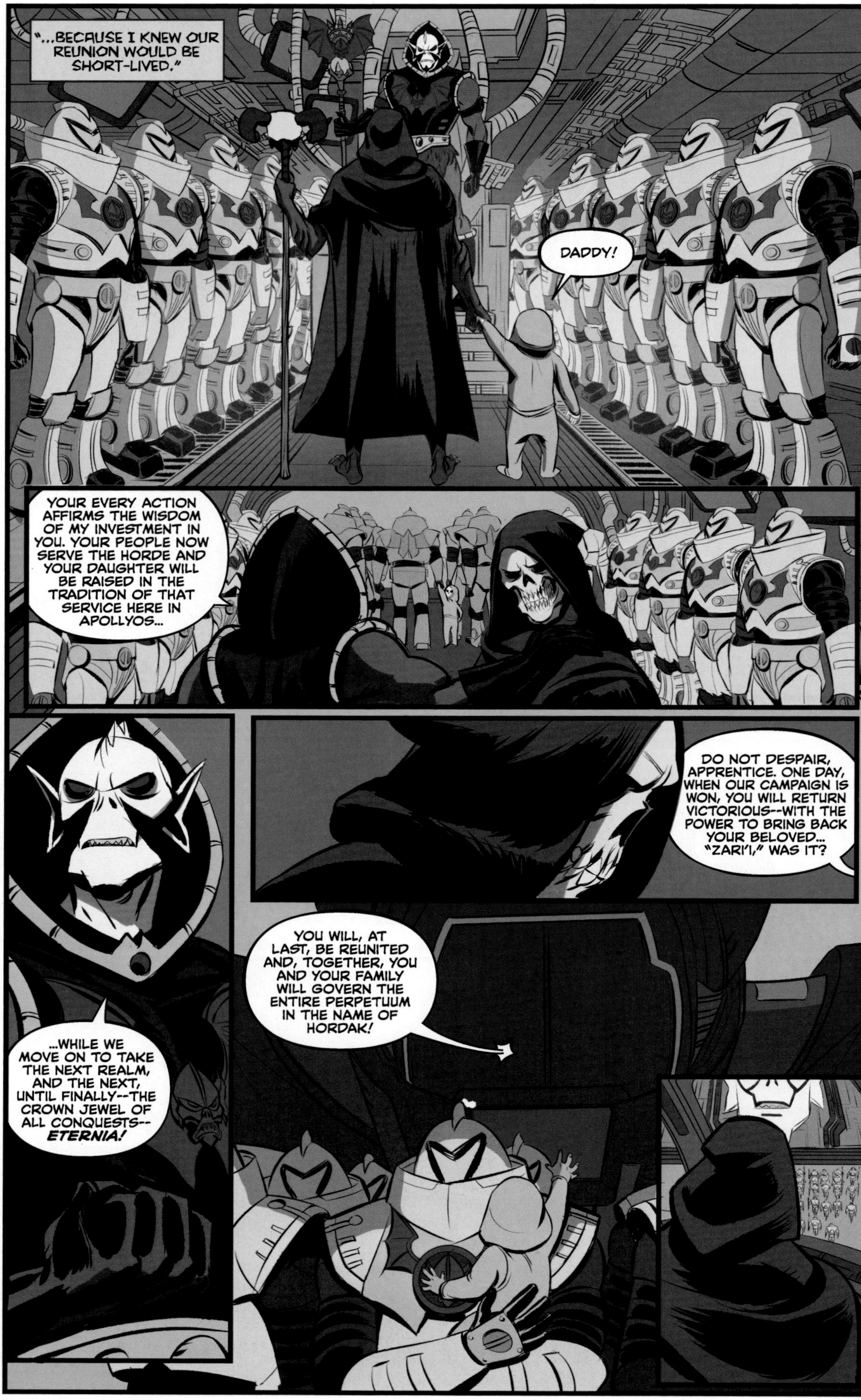
"...BECAUSE I KNEW OUR REUNION WOULD BE SHORT-LIVED."
DADDY!
YOUR EVERY ACTION AFFIRMS THE WISDOM OF MY INVESTMENT IN YOU. YOUR PEOPLE NOW SERVE THE HORDE AND YOUR DAUGHTER WILL BE RAISED IN THE TRADITION OF THAT SERVICE HERE IN APOLLYOS...
DO NOT DESPAIR, APPRENTICE. ONE DAY, WHEN OUR CAMPAIGN IS WON, YOU WILL RETURN VICTORIOUS--WITH THE POWER TO BRING BACK YOUR BELOVED... "ZARI'I," WAS IT?
...WHILE WE MOVE ON TO TAKE THE NEXT REALM, AND THE NEXT, UNTIL FINALLY--THE CROWN JEWEL OF ALL CONQUESTS--*ETERNIA!*
YOU WILL, AT LAST, BE REUNITED AND, TOGETHER, YOU AND YOUR FAMILY WILL GOVERN THE ENTIRE PERPETUUM IN THE NAME OF HORDAK!

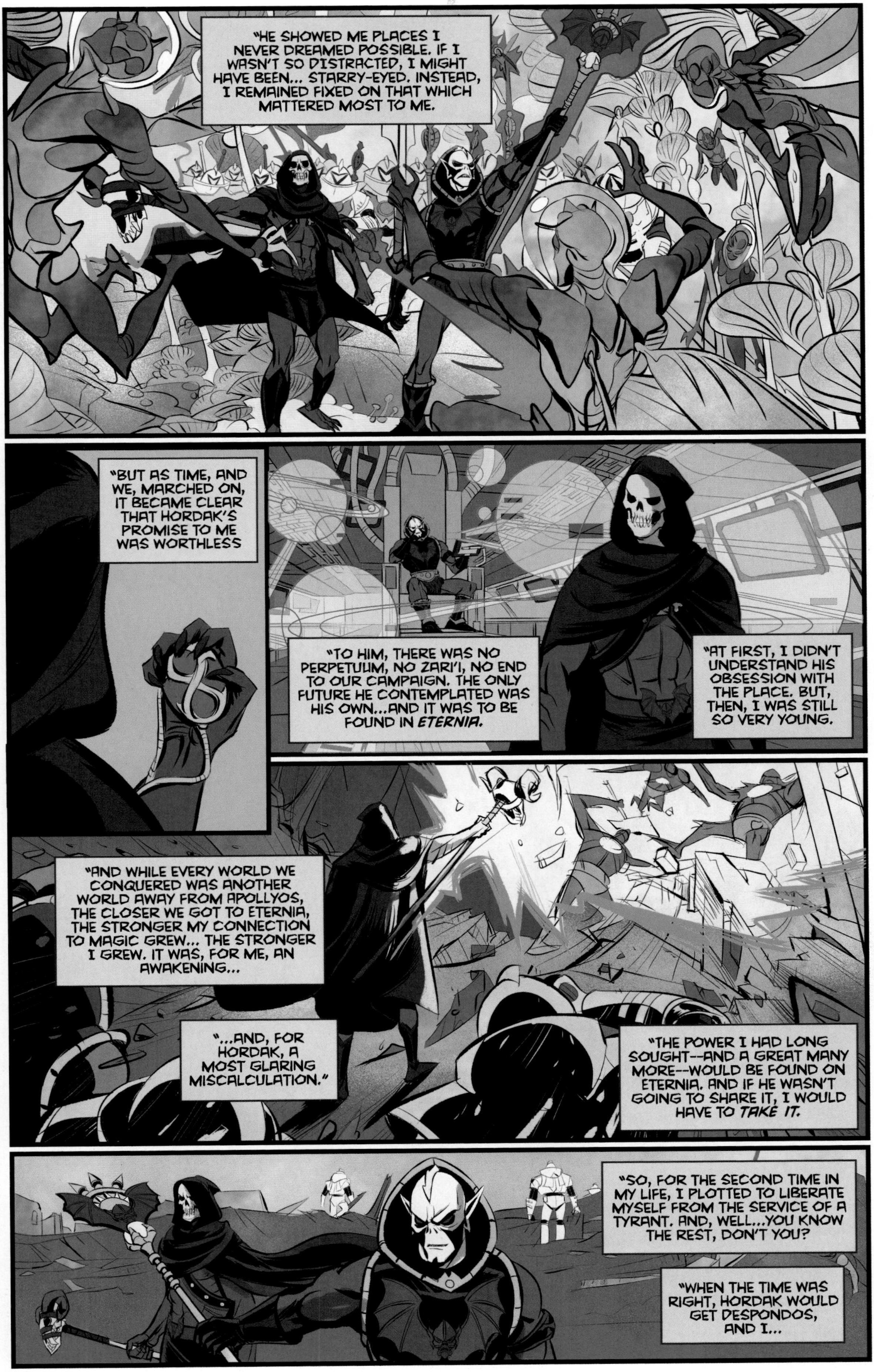
"HE SHOWED ME PLACES I NEVER DREAMED POSSIBLE. IF I WASN'T SO DISTRACTED, I MIGHT HAVE BEEN... STARRY-EYED. INSTEAD, I REMAINED FIXED ON THAT WHICH MATTERED MOST TO ME.
"BUT AS TIME, AND WE, MARCHED ON, IT BECAME CLEAR THAT HORDAK'S PROMISE TO ME WAS WORTHLESS
"TO HIM, THERE WAS NO PERPETUUM, NO ZARI'I, NO END TO OUR CAMPAIGN. THE ONLY FUTURE HE CONTEMPLATED WAS HIS OWN...AND IT WAS TO BE FOUND IN *ETERNIA.*
"AT FIRST, I DIDN'T UNDERSTAND HIS OBSESSION WITH THE PLACE. BUT, THEN, I WAS STILL SO VERY YOUNG.
"AND WHILE EVERY WORLD WE CONQUERED WAS ANOTHER WORLD AWAY FROM APOLLYOS, THE CLOSER WE GOT TO ETERNIA, THE STRONGER MY CONNECTION TO MAGIC GREW... THE STRONGER I GREW. IT WAS, FOR ME, AN AWAKENING...
"...AND, FOR HORDAK, A MOST GLARING MISCALCULATION."
"THE POWER I HAD LONG SOUGHT--AND A GREAT MANY MORE--WOULD BE FOUND ON ETERNIA. AND IF HE WASN'T GOING TO SHARE IT, I WOULD HAVE TO *TAKE IT.*
"SO, FOR THE SECOND TIME IN MY LIFE, I PLOTTED TO LIBERATE MYSELF FROM THE SERVICE OF A TYRANT. AND, WELL...YOU KNOW THE REST, DON'T YOU?
"WHEN THE TIME WAS RIGHT, HORDAK WOULD GET DESPONDOS, AND I...

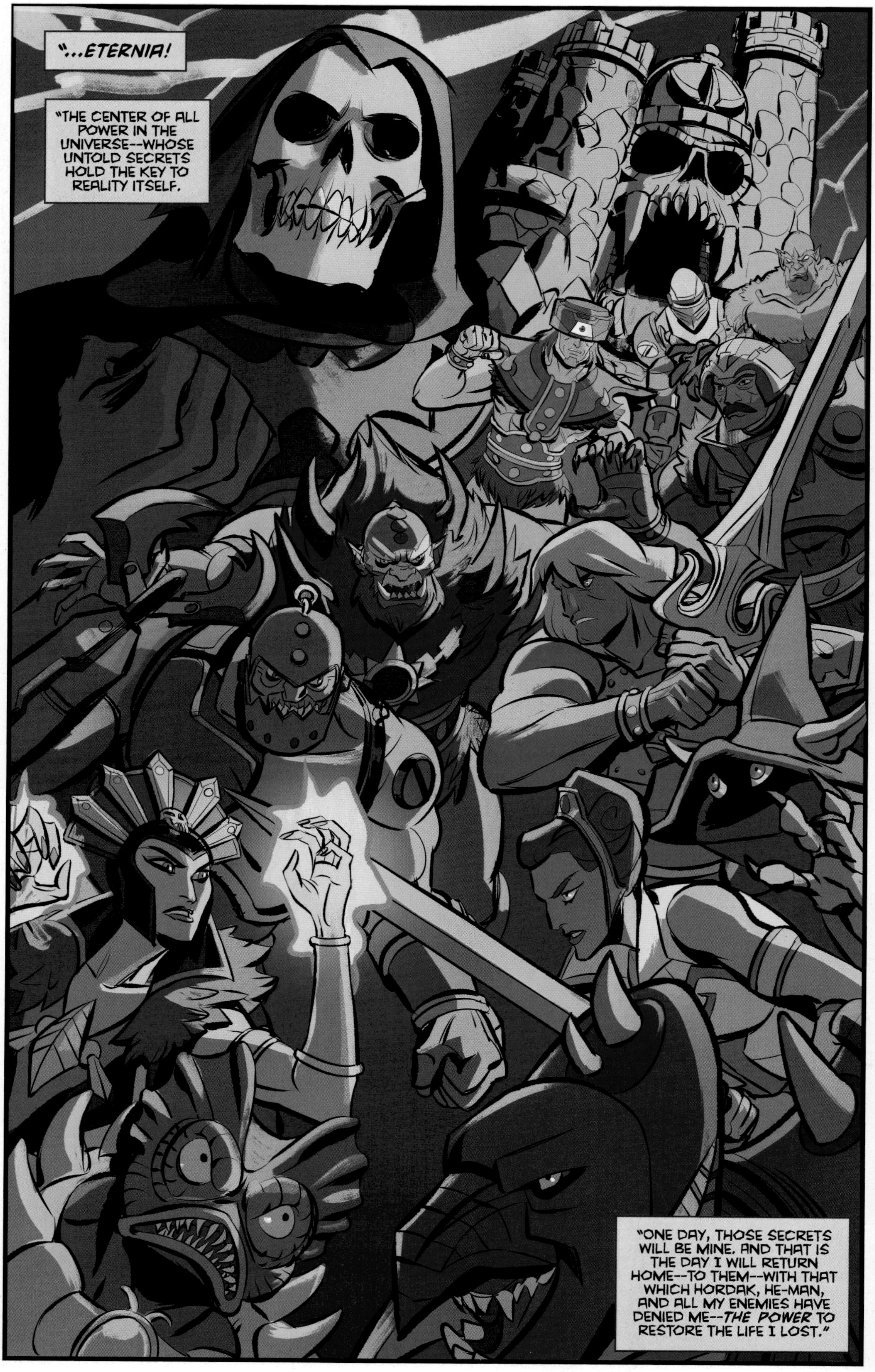
"...ETERNIA!
"THE CENTER OF ALL POWER IN THE UNIVERSE--WHOSE UNTOLD SECRETS HOLD THE KEY TO REALITY ITSELF.
"ONE DAY, THOSE SECRETS WILL BE MINE. AND THAT IS THE DAY I WILL RETURN HOME--TO THEM--WITH THAT WHICH HORDAK, HE-MAN, AND ALL MY ENEMIES HAVE DENIED ME--*THE POWER* TO RESTORE THE LIFE I LOST."

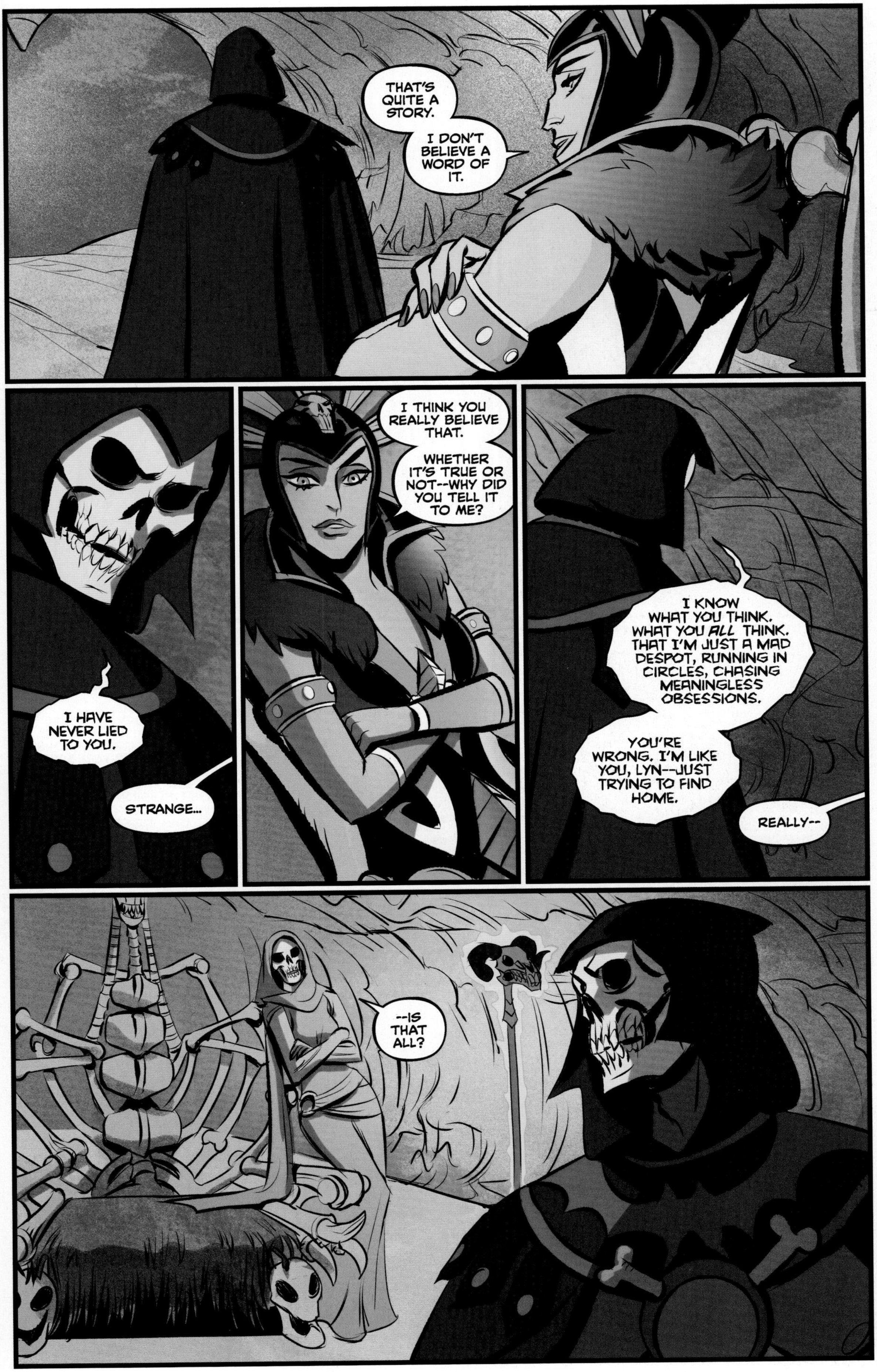
THAT'S QUITE A STORY.
I DON'T BELIEVE A WORD OF IT.
I HAVE NEVER LIED TO YOU.
STRANGE...
I THINK YOU REALLY BELIEVE THAT.
WHETHER IT'S TRUE OR NOT--WHY DID YOU TELL IT TO ME?
I KNOW WHAT YOU THINK. WHAT YOU *ALL* THINK. THAT I'M JUST A MAD DESPOT, RUNNING IN CIRCLES, CHASING MEANINGLESS OBSESSIONS.
YOU'RE WRONG. I'M LIKE YOU, LYN--JUST TRYING TO FIND HOME.
REALLY--
--IS THAT ALL?

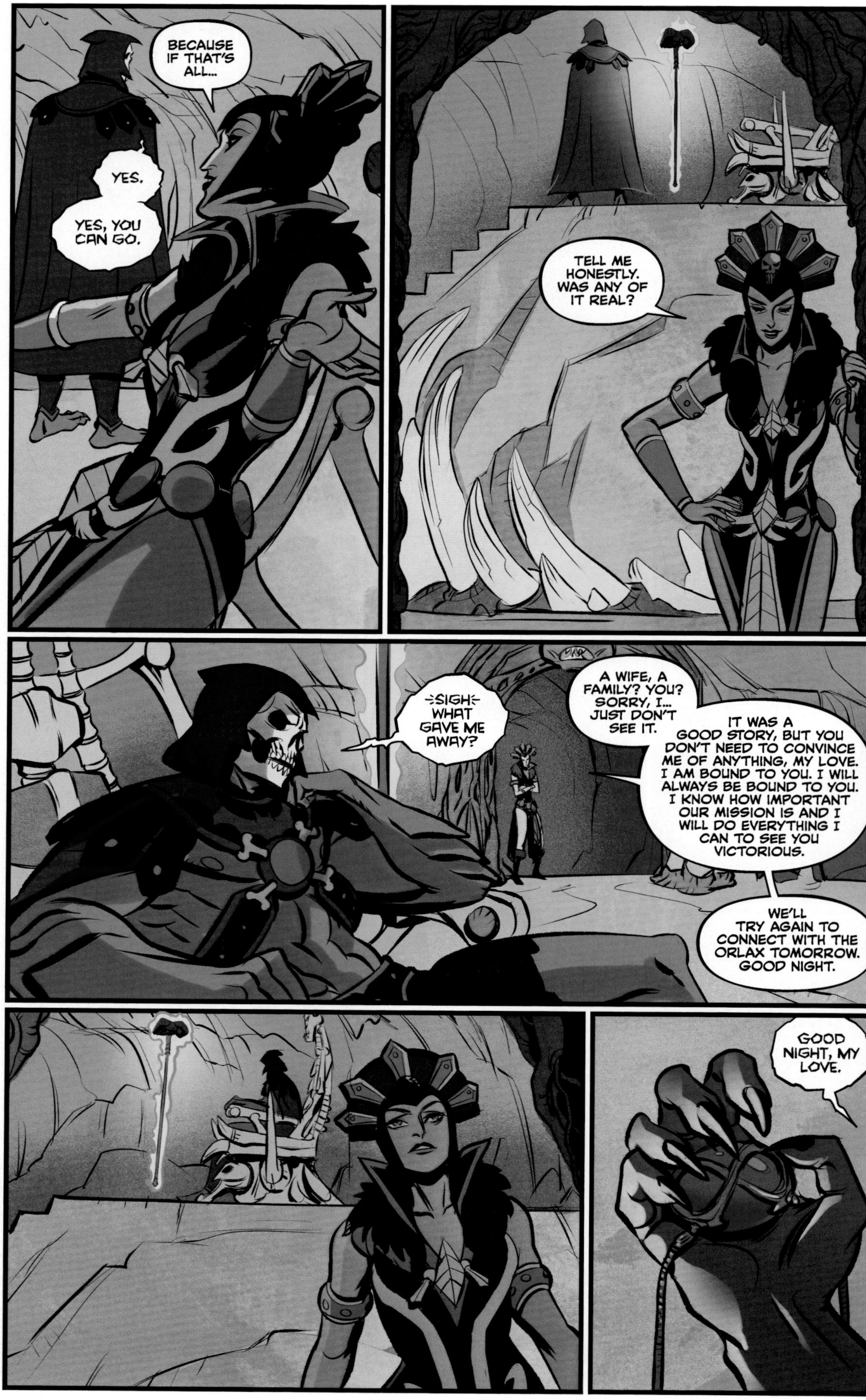
BECAUSE IF THAT'S ALL...
YES.
YES, YOU CAN GO.
TELL ME HONESTLY. WAS ANY OF IT REAL?
-SIGH- WHAT GAVE ME AWAY?
A WIFE, A FAMILY? YOU? SORRY, I... JUST DON'T SEE IT.
IT WAS A GOOD STORY, BUT YOU DON'T NEED TO CONVINCE ME OF ANYTHING, MY LOVE. I AM BOUND TO YOU. I WILL ALWAYS BE BOUND TO YOU. I KNOW HOW IMPORTANT OUR MISSION IS AND I WILL DO EVERYTHING I CAN TO SEE YOU VICTORIOUS.
WE'LL TRY AGAIN TO CONNECT WITH THE ORLAX TOMORROW. GOOD NIGHT.
GOOD NIGHT, MY LOVE.

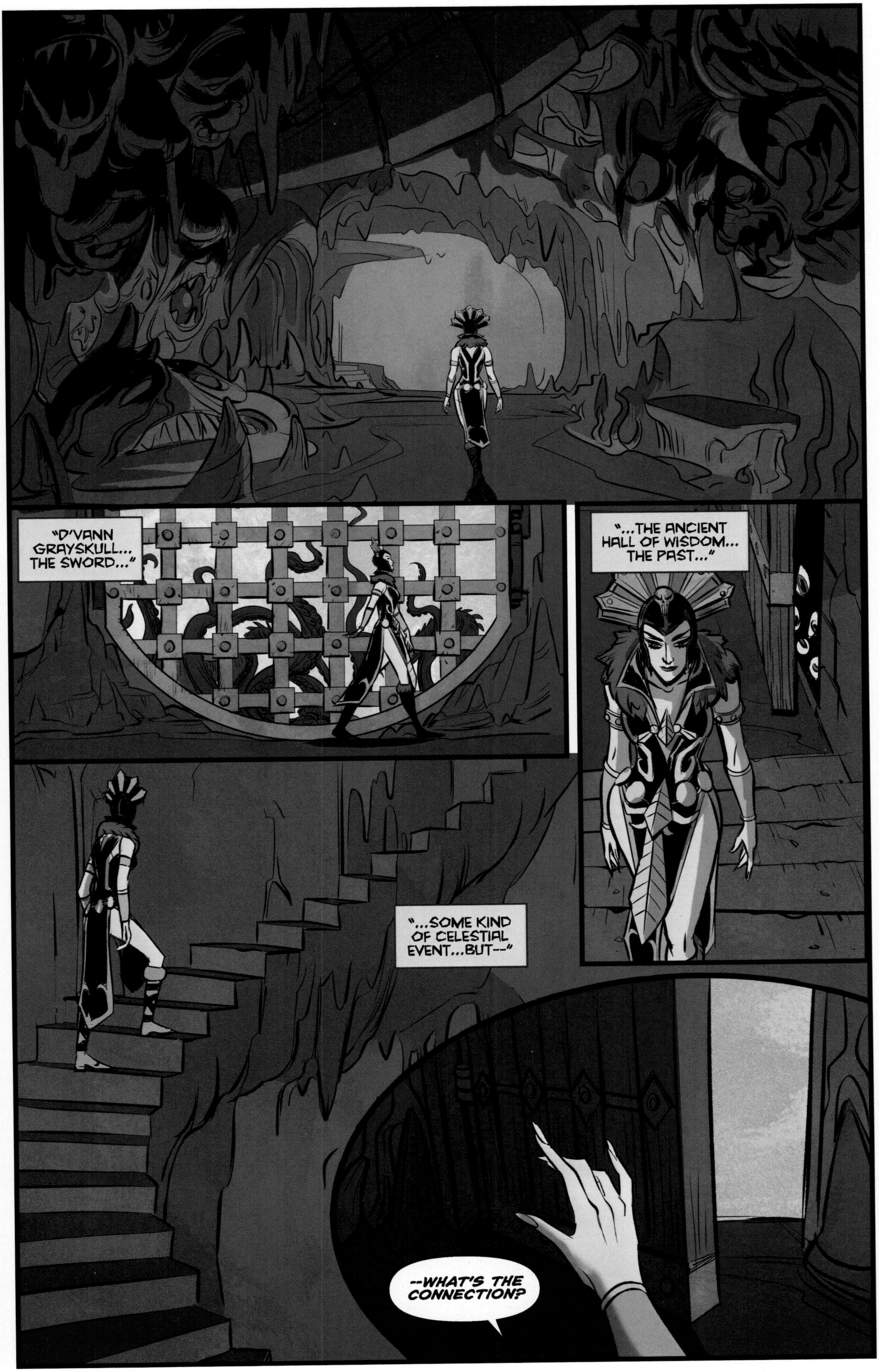
"D'VANN GRAYSKULL... THE SWORD..."
"...THE ANCIENT HALL OF WISDOM... THE PAST..."
"...SOME KIND OF CELESTIAL EVENT...BUT--"
--WHAT'S THE CONNECTION?

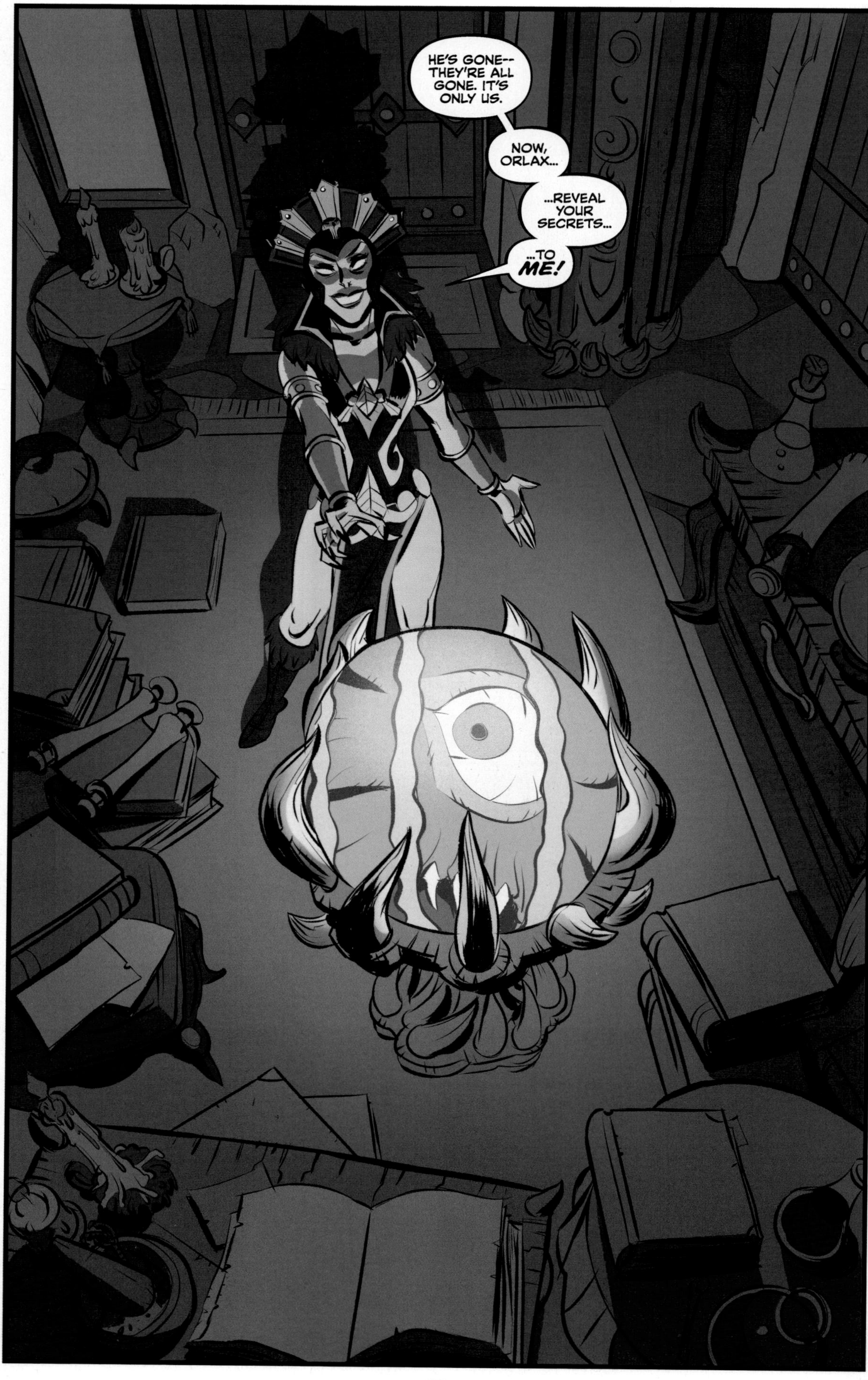
HE'S GONE-- THEY'RE ALL GONE. IT'S ONLY US.
NOW, ORLAX...
...REVEAL YOUR SECRETS...
...TO ME!

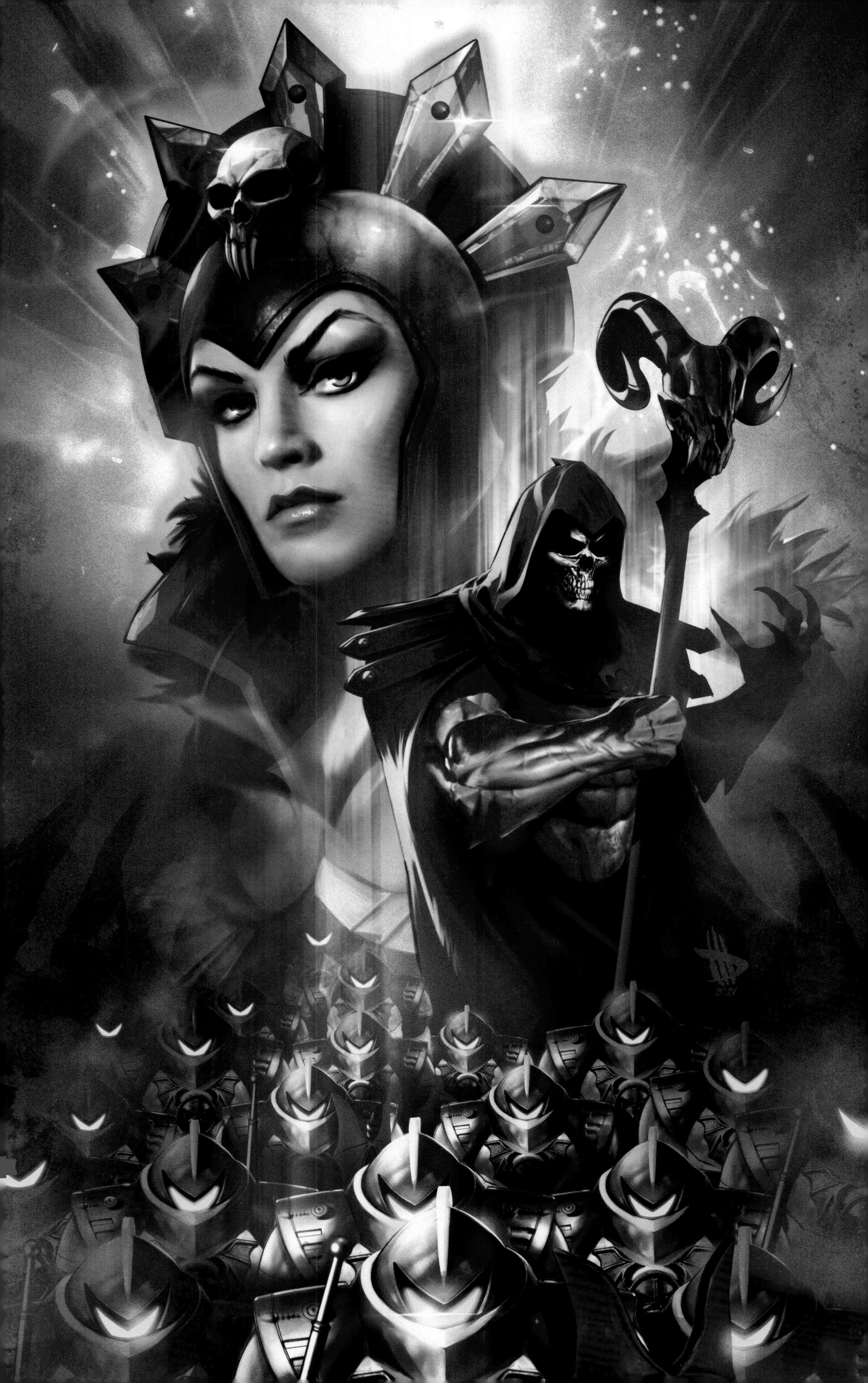

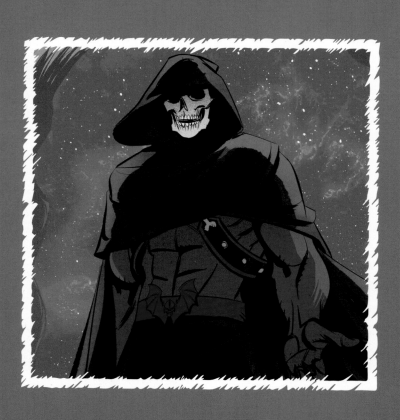

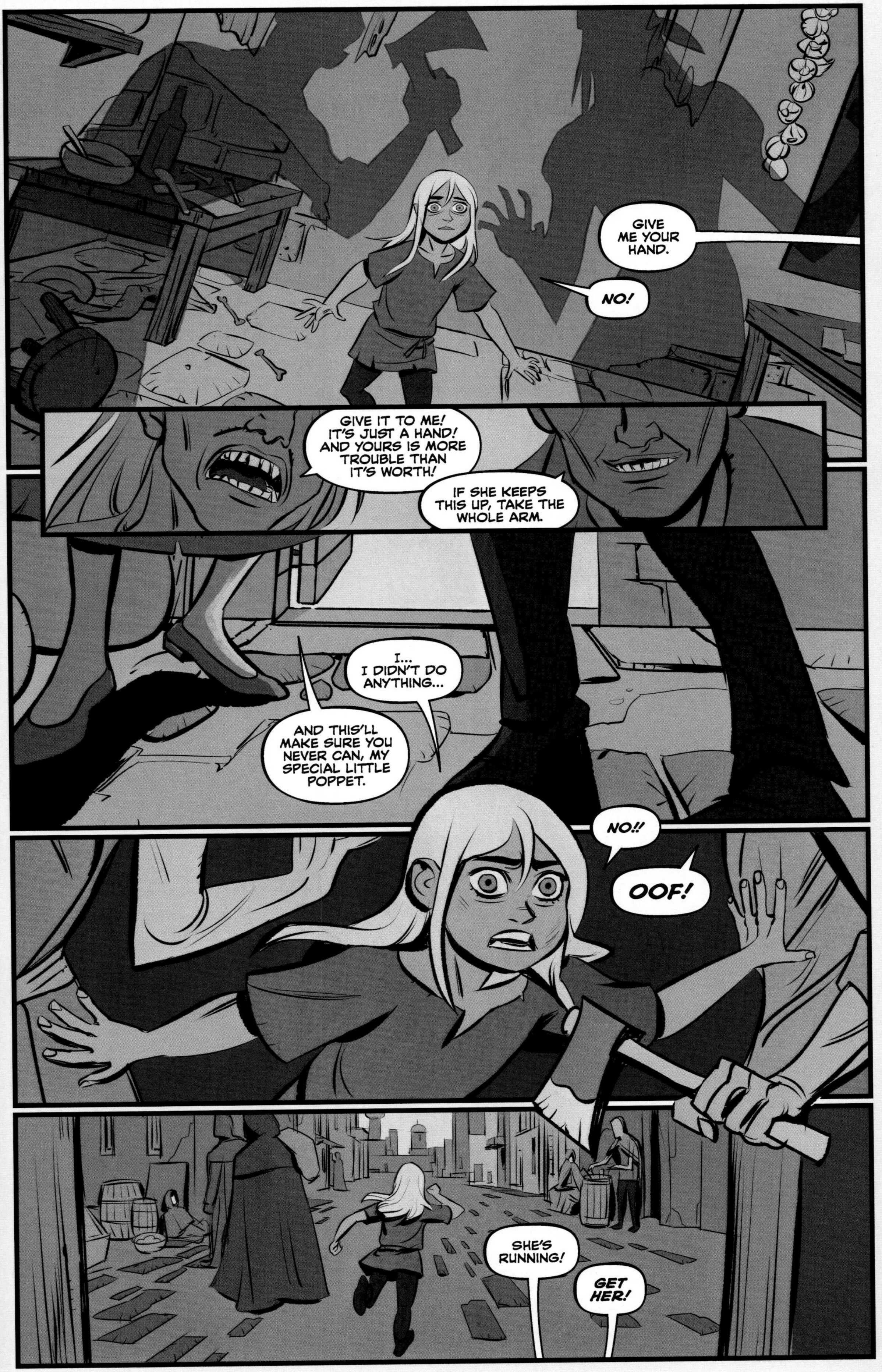
GIVE ME YOUR HAND.
NO!
GIVE IT TO ME! IT'S JUST A HAND! AND YOURS IS MORE TROUBLE THAN IT'S WORTH!
IF SHE KEEPS THIS UP, TAKE THE WHOLE ARM.
I... I DIDN'T DO ANYTHING...
AND THIS'LL MAKE SURE YOU NEVER CAN, MY SPECIAL LITTLE POPPET.
NO!!
OOF!
SHE'S RUNNING!
GET HER!

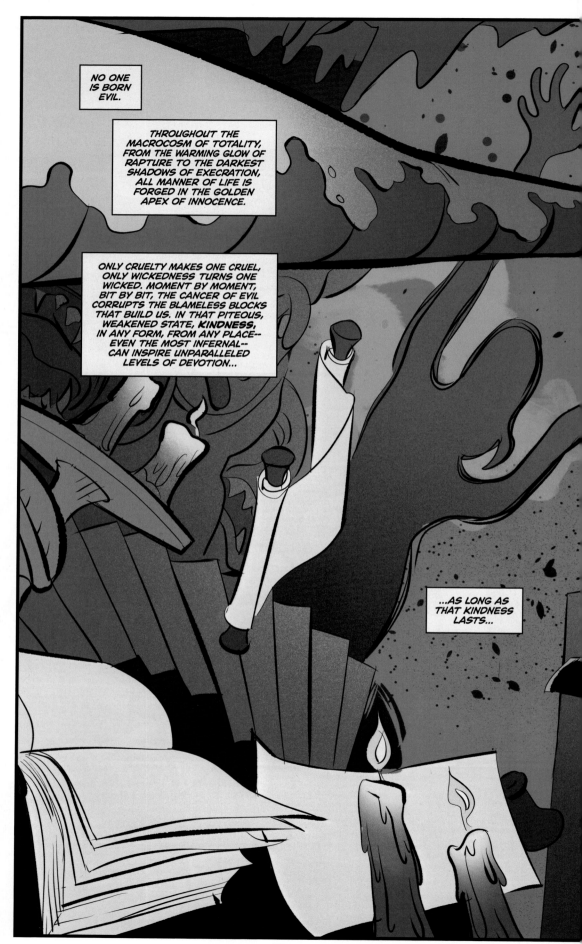

NO ONE IS BORN EVIL.

THROUGHOUT THE MACROCOSM OF TOTALITY, FROM THE WARMING GLOW OF RAPTURE TO THE DARKEST SHADOWS OF EXECRATION, ALL MANNER OF LIFE IS FORGED IN THE GOLDEN APEX OF INNOCENCE.

ONLY CRUELTY MAKES ONE CRUEL, ONLY WICKEDNESS TURNS ONE WICKED. MOMENT BY MOMENT, BIT BY BIT, THE CANCER OF EVIL CORRUPTS THE BLAMELESS BLOCKS THAT BUILD US. IN THAT PITEOUS, WEAKENED STATE, *KINDNESS,* IN ANY FORM, FROM ANY PLACE-- EVEN THE MOST INFERNAL-- CAN INSPIRE UNPARALLELED LEVELS OF DEVOTION...

...AS LONG AS THAT KINDNESS LASTS...

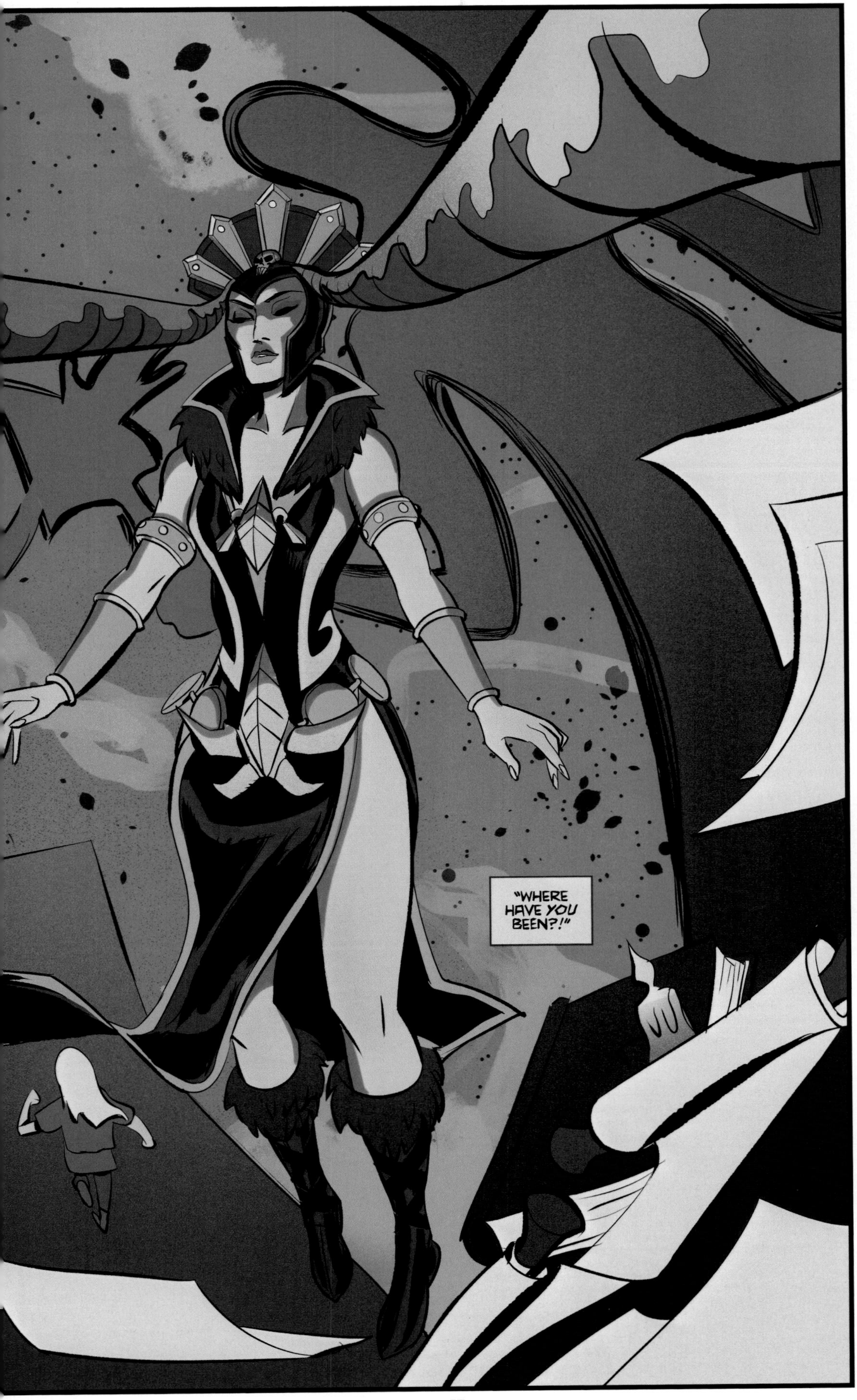
"WHERE HAVE YOU BEEN?!"

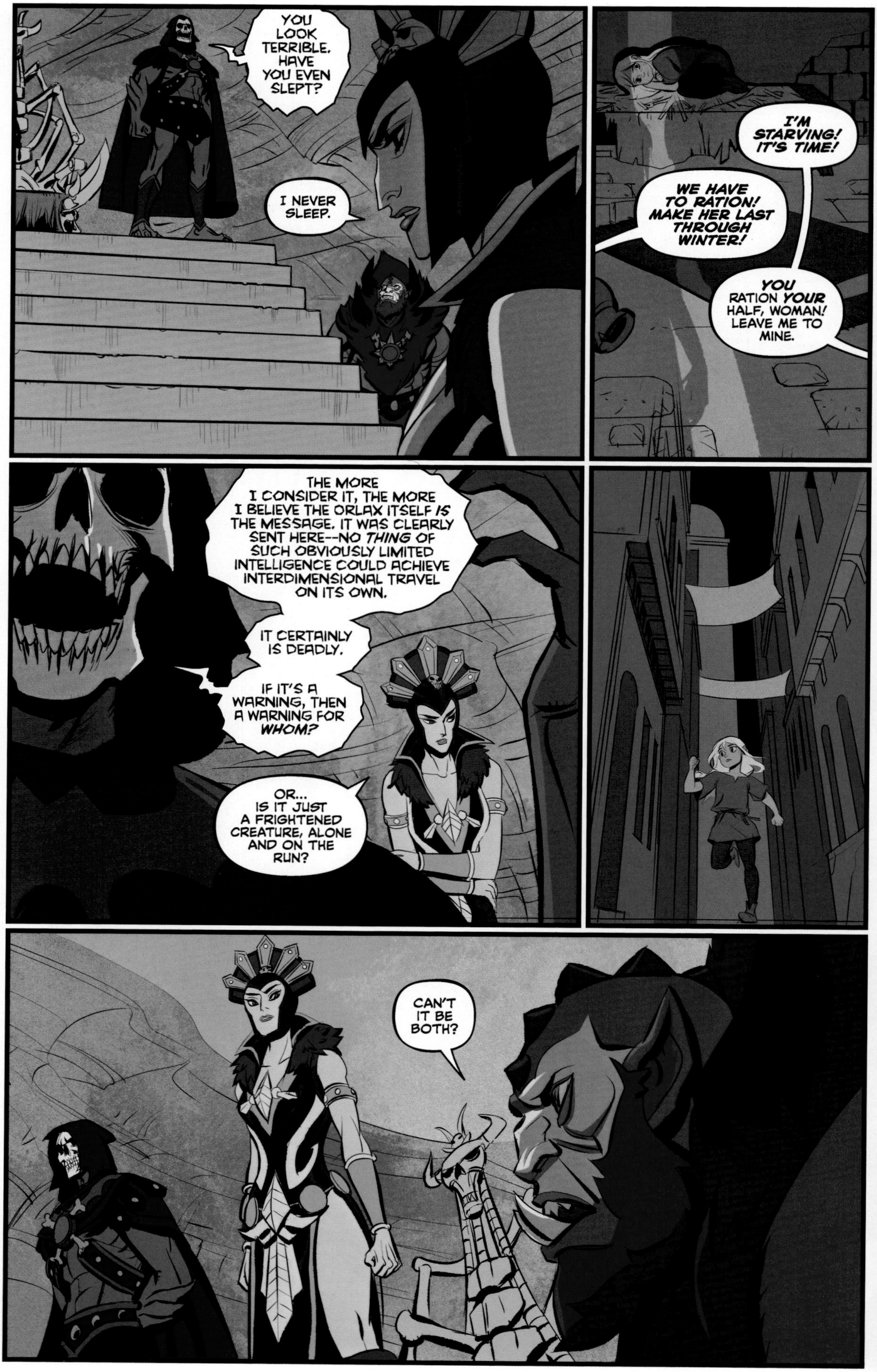
YOU LOOK TERRIBLE. HAVE YOU EVEN SLEPT?
I NEVER SLEEP.
I'M STARVING! IT'S TIME!
WE HAVE TO RATION! MAKE HER LAST THROUGH WINTER!
YOU RATION YOUR HALF, WOMAN! LEAVE ME TO MINE.
THE MORE I CONSIDER IT, THE MORE I BELIEVE THE ORLAX ITSELF IS THE MESSAGE. IT WAS CLEARLY SENT HERE--NO THING OF SUCH OBVIOUSLY LIMITED INTELLIGENCE COULD ACHIEVE INTERDIMENSIONAL TRAVEL ON ITS OWN.
IT CERTAINLY IS DEADLY.
IF IT'S A WARNING, THEN A WARNING FOR WHOM?
OR... IS IT JUST A FRIGHTENED CREATURE, ALONE AND ON THE RUN?
CAN'T IT BE BOTH?

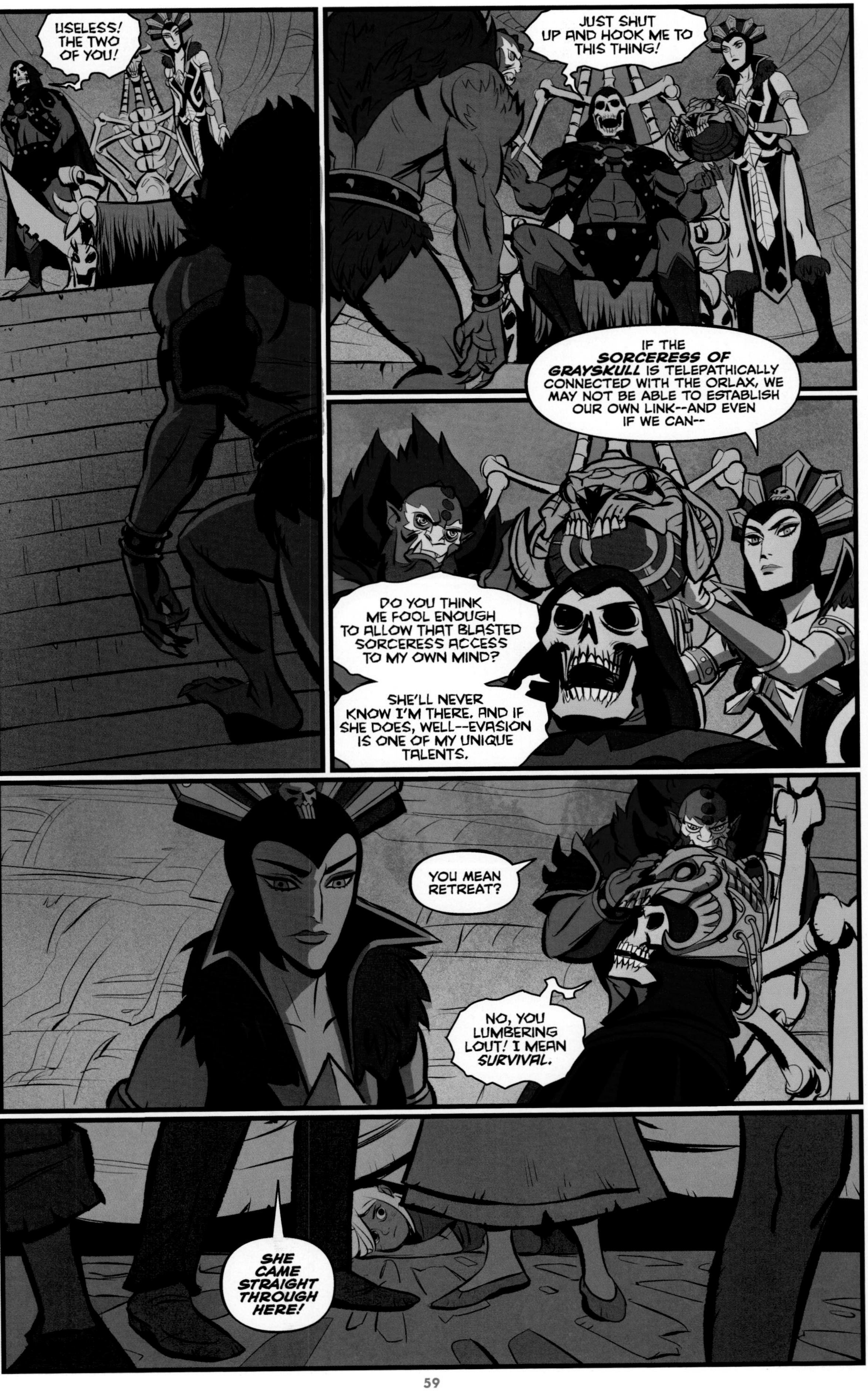
USELESS! THE TWO OF YOU!
JUST SHUT UP AND HOOK ME TO THIS THING!
IF THE SORCERESS OF GRAYSKULL IS TELEPATHICALLY CONNECTED WITH THE ORLAX, WE MAY NOT BE ABLE TO ESTABLISH OUR OWN LINK--AND EVEN IF WE CAN--
DO YOU THINK ME FOOL ENOUGH TO ALLOW THAT BLASTED SORCERESS ACCESS TO MY OWN MIND?
SHE'LL NEVER KNOW I'M THERE. AND IF SHE DOES, WELL--EVASION IS ONE OF MY UNIQUE TALENTS.
YOU MEAN RETREAT?
NO, YOU LUMBERING LOUT! I MEAN SURVIVAL.
SHE CAME STRAIGHT THROUGH HERE!

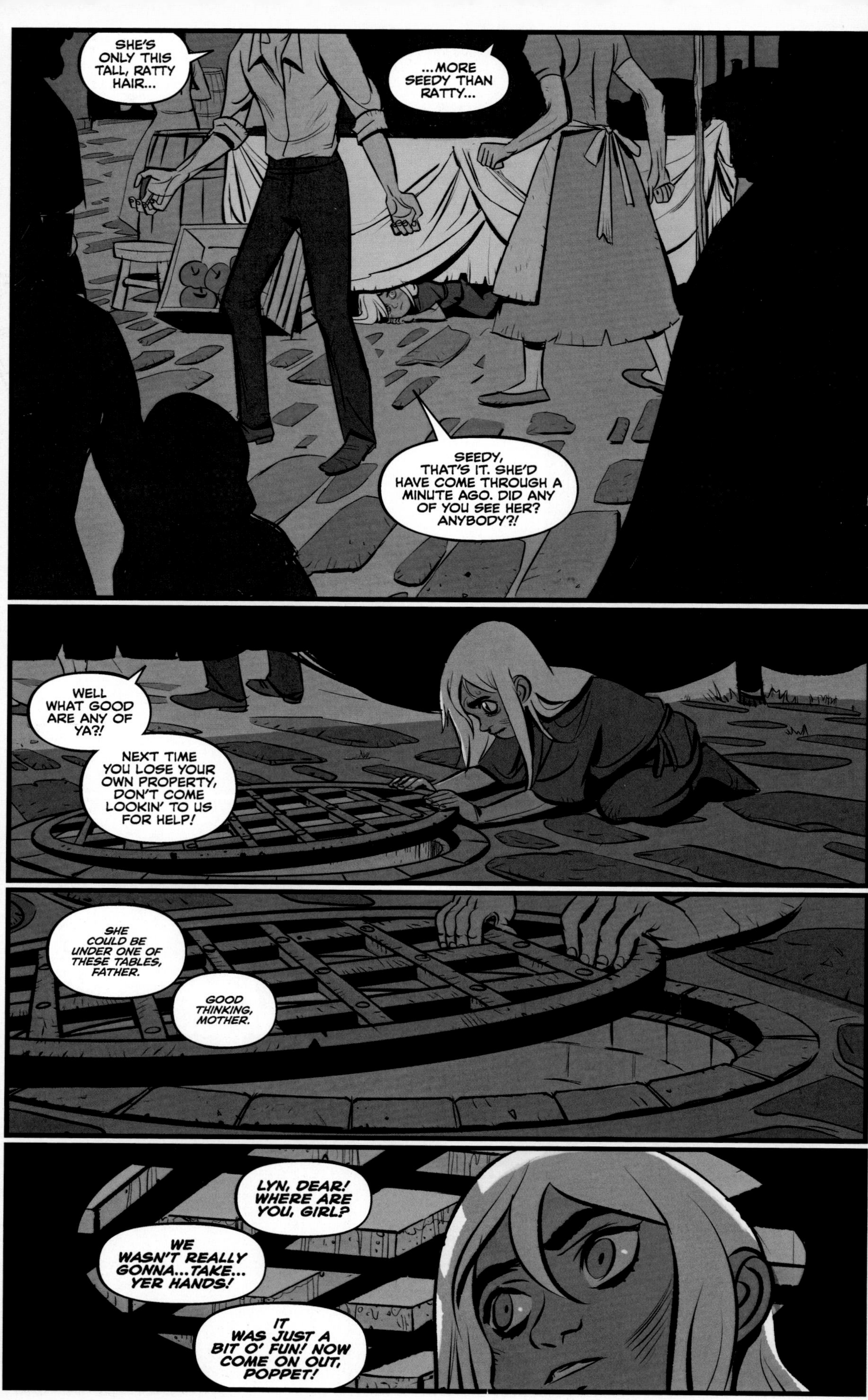
SHE'S ONLY THIS TALL, RATTY HAIR...
...MORE SEEDY THAN RATTY...
SEEDY, THAT'S IT. SHE'D HAVE COME THROUGH A MINUTE AGO. DID ANY OF YOU SEE HER? ANYBODY?!
WELL WHAT GOOD ARE ANY OF YA?!
NEXT TIME YOU LOSE YOUR OWN PROPERTY, DON'T COME LOOKIN' TO US FOR HELP!
SHE COULD BE UNDER ONE OF THESE TABLES, FATHER.
GOOD THINKING, MOTHER.
LYN, DEAR! WHERE ARE YOU, GIRL?
WE WASN'T REALLY GONNA...TAKE... YER HANDS!
IT WAS JUST A BIT O' FUN! NOW COME ON OUT, POPPET!

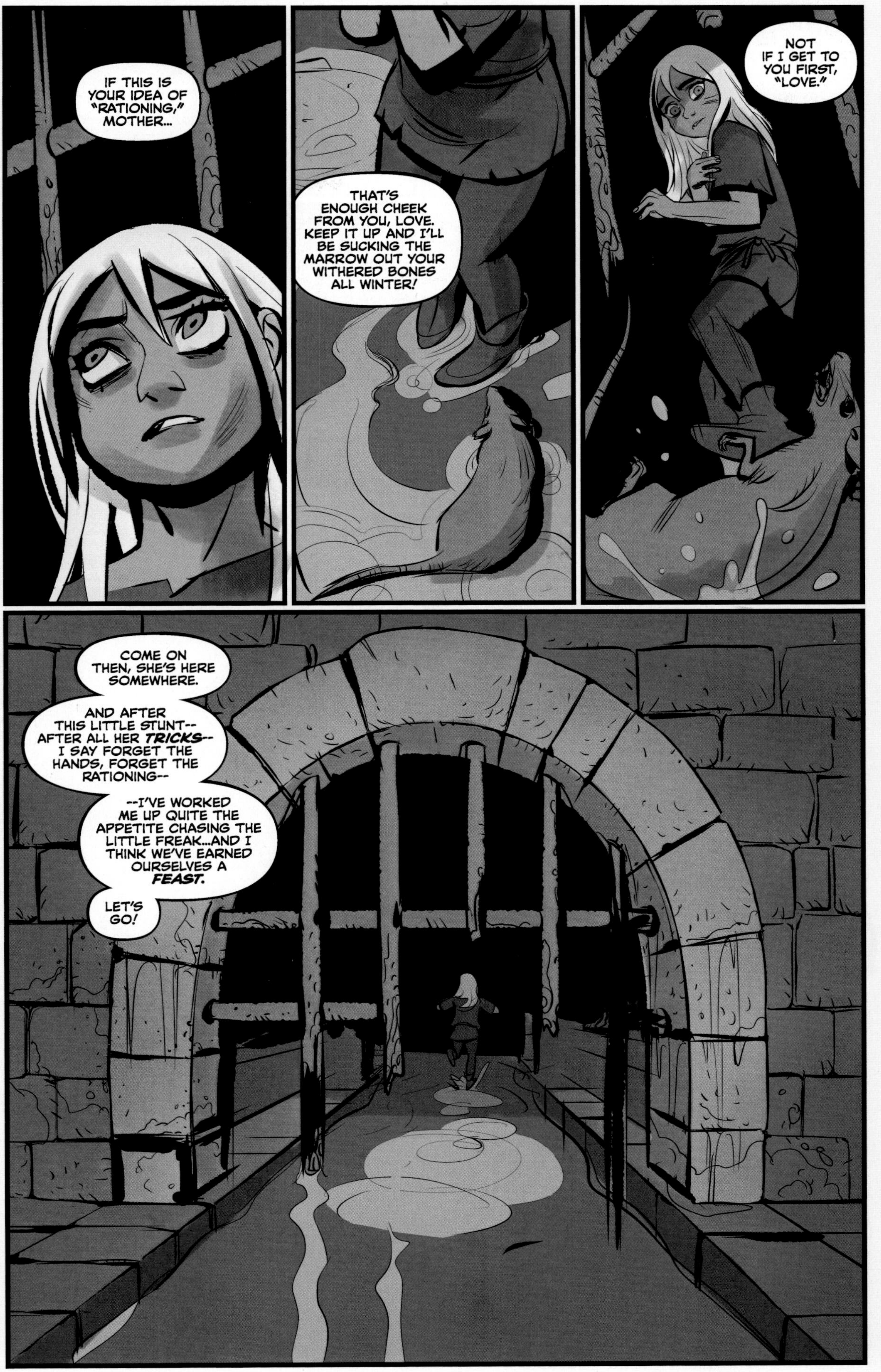
IF THIS IS YOUR IDEA OF "RATIONING," MOTHER...
THAT'S ENOUGH CHEEK FROM YOU, LOVE. KEEP IT UP AND I'LL BE SUCKING THE MARROW OUT YOUR WITHERED BONES ALL WINTER!
NOT IF I GET TO YOU FIRST, "LOVE."
COME ON THEN, SHE'S HERE SOMEWHERE.
AND AFTER THIS LITTLE STUNT-- AFTER ALL HER *TRICKS*-- I SAY FORGET THE HANDS, FORGET THE RATIONING--
--I'VE WORKED ME UP QUITE THE APPETITE CHASING THE LITTLE FREAK...AND I THINK WE'VE EARNED OURSELVES A *FEAST*.
LET'S GO!

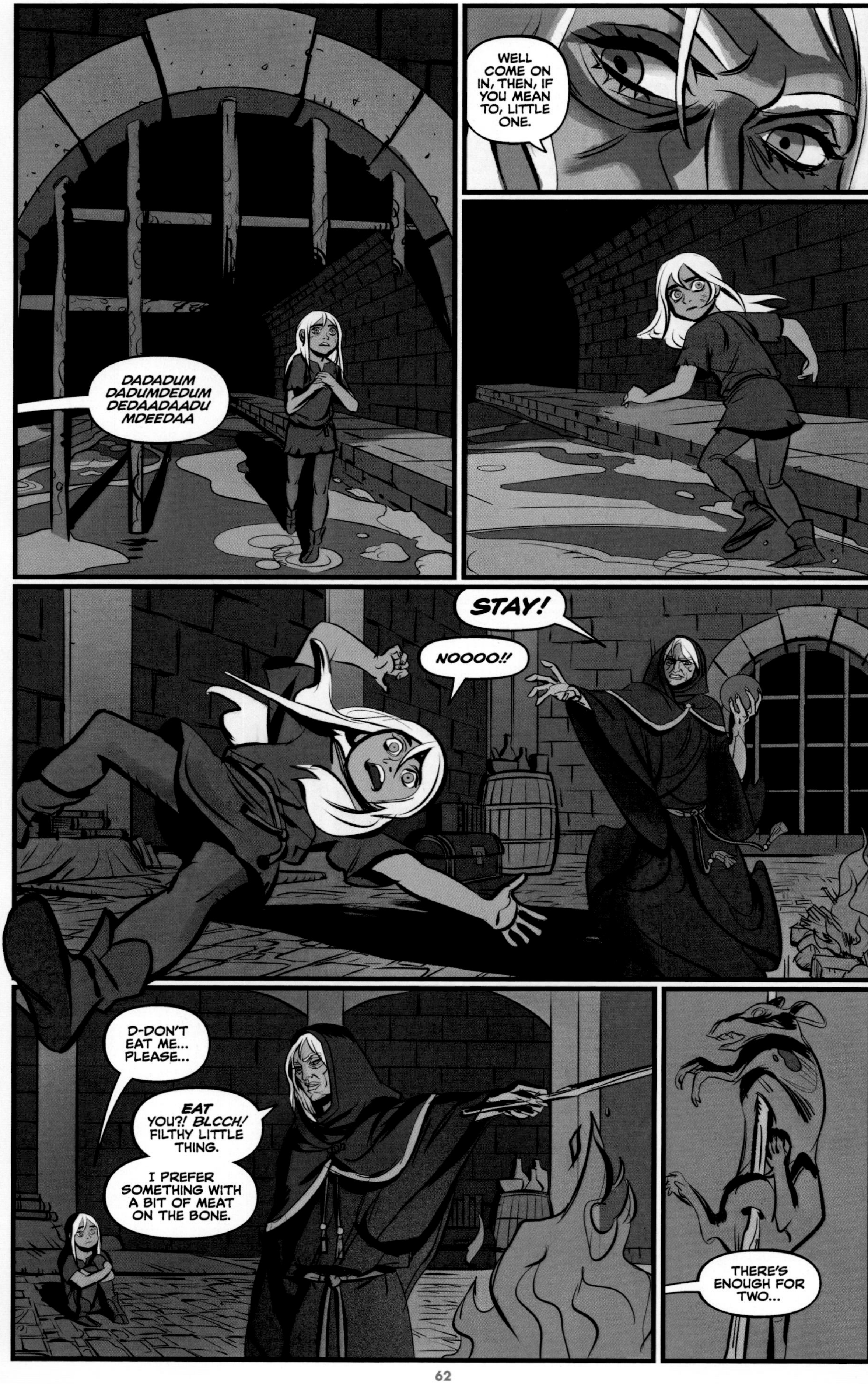
WELL COME ON IN, THEN, IF YOU MEAN TO, LITTLE ONE.
DADADUM DADUMDEDUM DEDAADAADU MDEEDAA
STAY!
NOOOO!!
D-DON'T EAT ME... PLEASE...
EAT YOU?! BLCCH! FILTHY LITTLE THING.
I PREFER SOMETHING WITH A BIT OF MEAT ON THE BONE.
THERE'S ENOUGH FOR TWO...

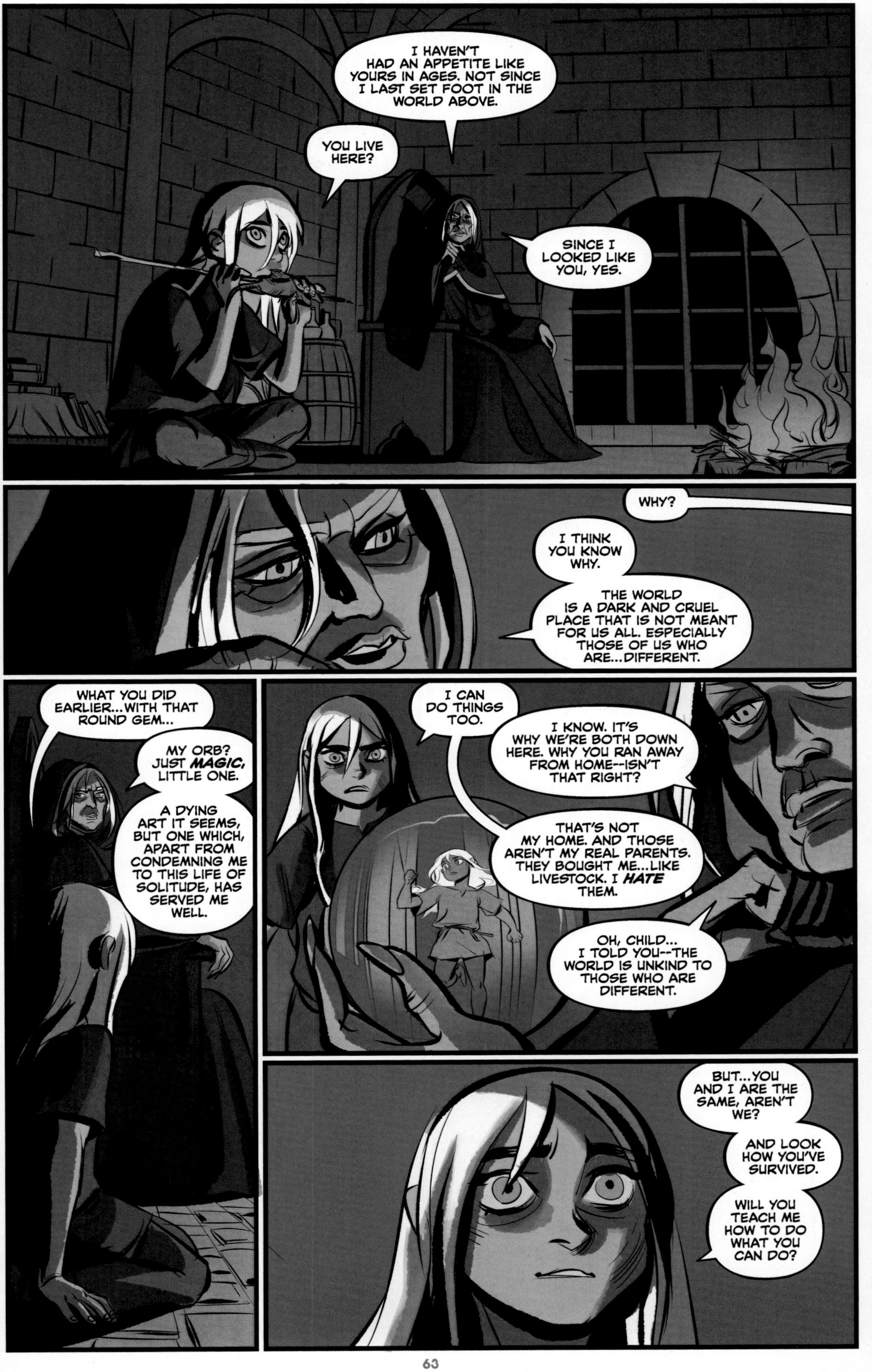
I HAVEN'T HAD AN APPETITE LIKE YOURS IN AGES. NOT SINCE I LAST SET FOOT IN THE WORLD ABOVE.
YOU LIVE HERE?
SINCE I LOOKED LIKE YOU, YES.
WHY?
I THINK YOU KNOW WHY.
THE WORLD IS A DARK AND CRUEL PLACE THAT IS NOT MEANT FOR US ALL. ESPECIALLY THOSE OF US WHO ARE...DIFFERENT.
WHAT YOU DID EARLIER...WITH THAT ROUND GEM...
MY ORB? JUST ***MAGIC,*** LITTLE ONE.
A DYING ART IT SEEMS, BUT ONE WHICH, APART FROM CONDEMNING ME TO THIS LIFE OF SOLITUDE, HAS SERVED ME WELL.
I CAN DO THINGS TOO.
I KNOW. IT'S WHY WE'RE BOTH DOWN HERE. WHY YOU RAN AWAY FROM HOME--ISN'T THAT RIGHT?
THAT'S NOT MY HOME. AND THOSE AREN'T MY REAL PARENTS. THEY BOUGHT ME...LIKE LIVESTOCK. I ***HATE*** THEM.
OH, CHILD... I TOLD YOU--THE WORLD IS UNKIND TO THOSE WHO ARE DIFFERENT.
BUT...YOU AND I ARE THE SAME, AREN'T WE?
AND LOOK HOW YOU'VE SURVIVED.
WILL YOU TEACH ME HOW TO DO WHAT YOU CAN DO?

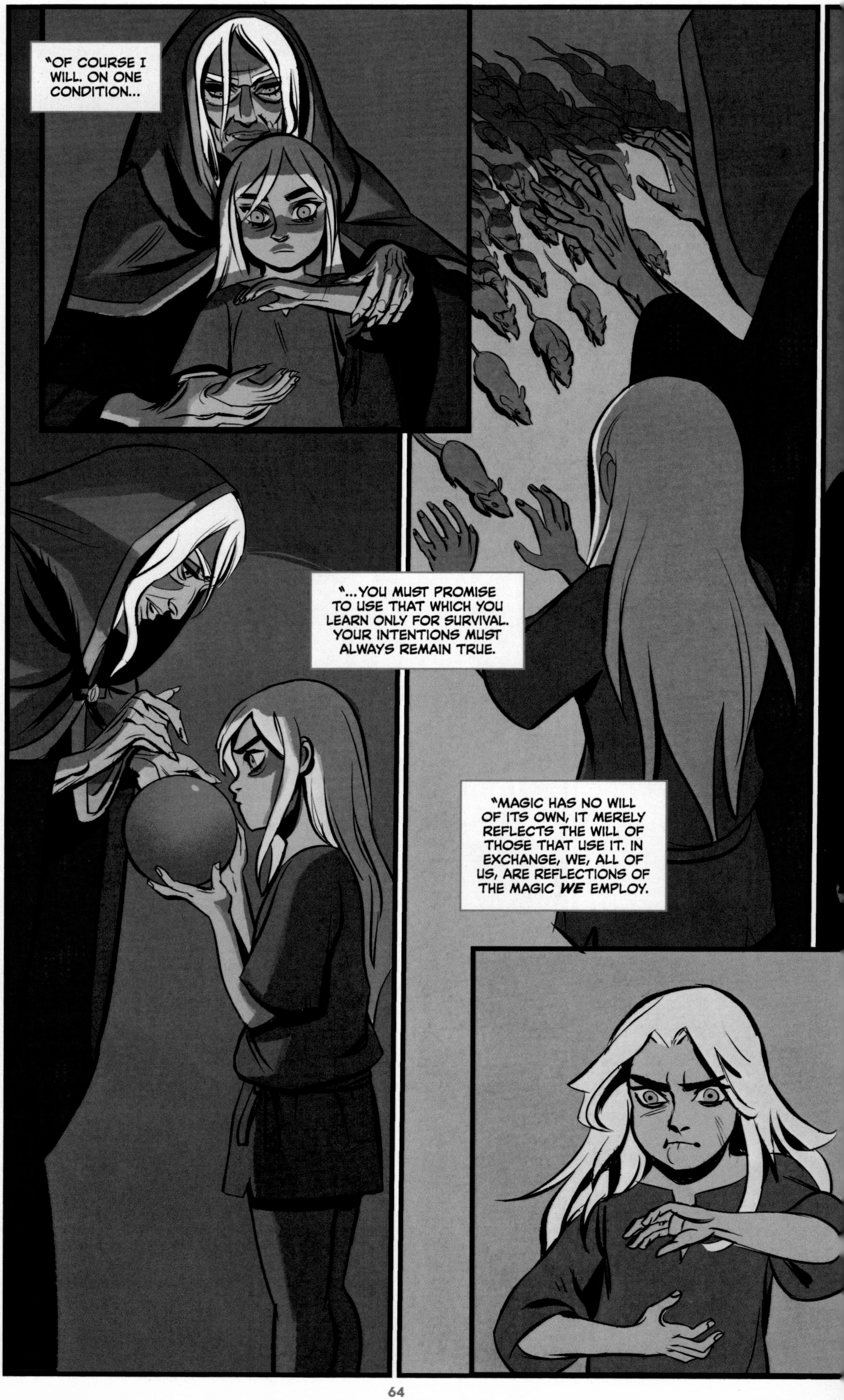
"OF COURSE I WILL. ON ONE CONDITION...
"...YOU MUST PROMISE TO USE THAT WHICH YOU LEARN ONLY FOR SURVIVAL. YOUR INTENTIONS MUST ALWAYS REMAIN TRUE.
"MAGIC HAS NO WILL OF ITS OWN, IT MERELY REFLECTS THE WILL OF THOSE THAT USE IT. IN EXCHANGE, WE, ALL OF US, ARE REFLECTIONS OF THE MAGIC *WE* EMPLOY.

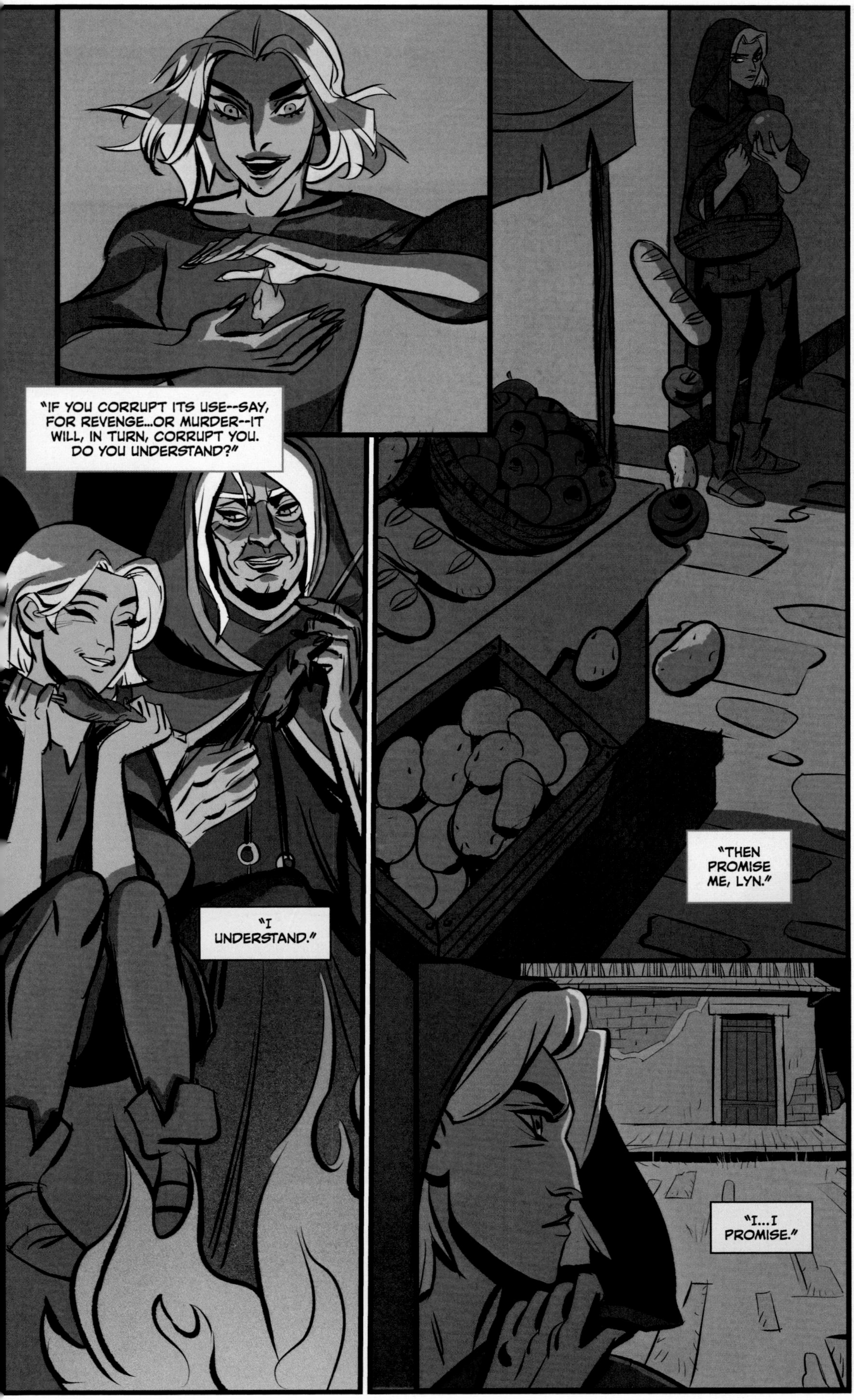
"IF YOU CORRUPT ITS USE--SAY, FOR REVENGE...OR MURDER--IT WILL, IN TURN, CORRUPT YOU. DO YOU UNDERSTAND?"
"I UNDERSTAND."
"THEN PROMISE ME, LYN."
"I...I PROMISE."

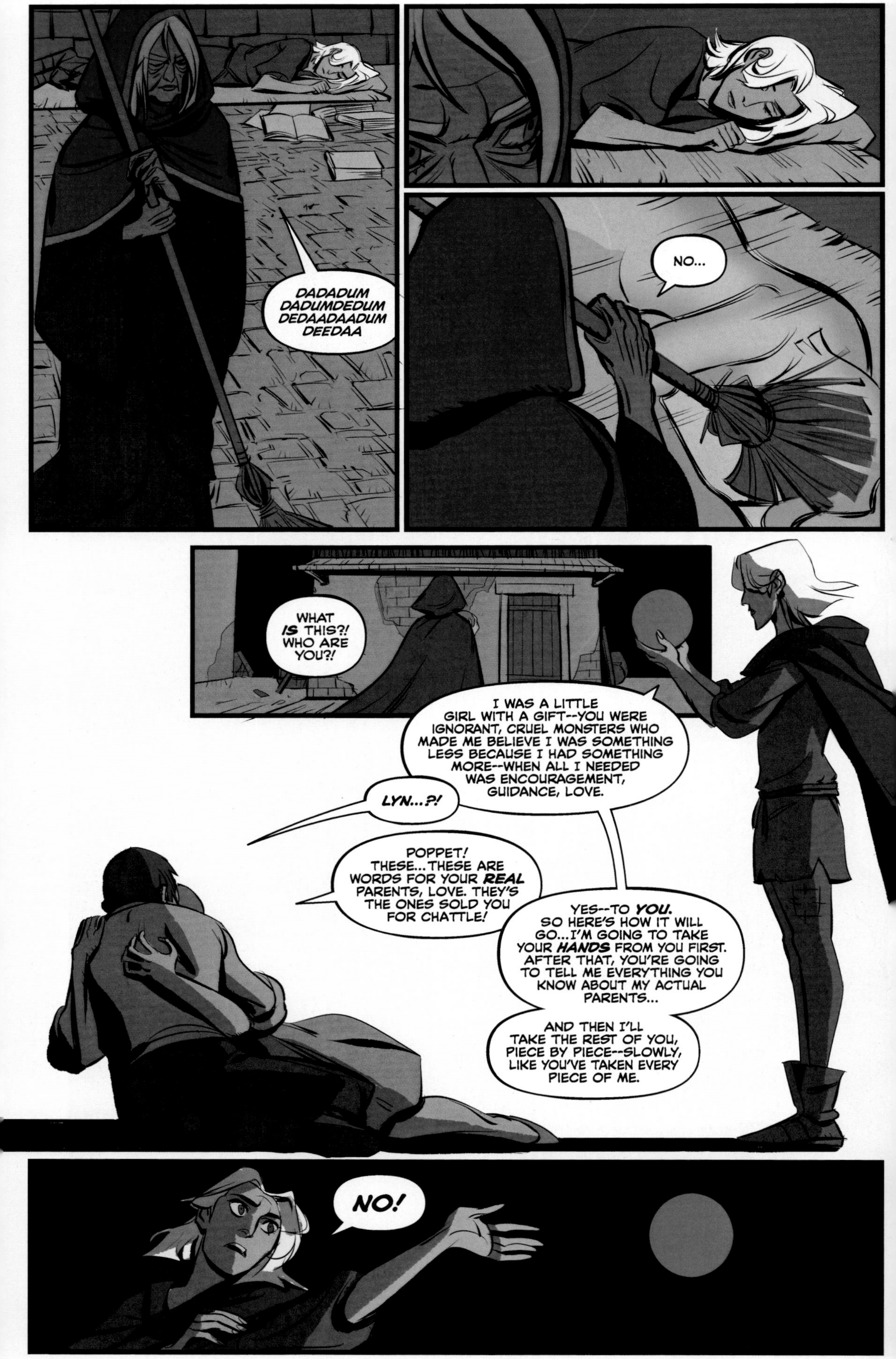
DADADUM DADUMDEDUM DEDAADAADUM DEEDAA
NO...
WHAT IS THIS?! WHO ARE YOU?!
I WAS A LITTLE GIRL WITH A GIFT--YOU WERE IGNORANT, CRUEL MONSTERS WHO MADE ME BELIEVE I WAS SOMETHING LESS BECAUSE I HAD SOMETHING MORE--WHEN ALL I NEEDED WAS ENCOURAGEMENT, GUIDANCE, LOVE.
LYN...?!
POPPET! THESE...THESE ARE WORDS FOR YOUR REAL PARENTS, LOVE. THEY'S THE ONES SOLD YOU FOR CHATTLE!
YES--TO YOU. SO HERE'S HOW IT WILL GO...I'M GOING TO TAKE YOUR HANDS FROM YOU FIRST. AFTER THAT, YOU'RE GOING TO TELL ME EVERYTHING YOU KNOW ABOUT MY ACTUAL PARENTS...
AND THEN I'LL TAKE THE REST OF YOU, PIECE BY PIECE--SLOWLY, LIKE YOU'VE TAKEN EVERY PIECE OF ME.
NO!

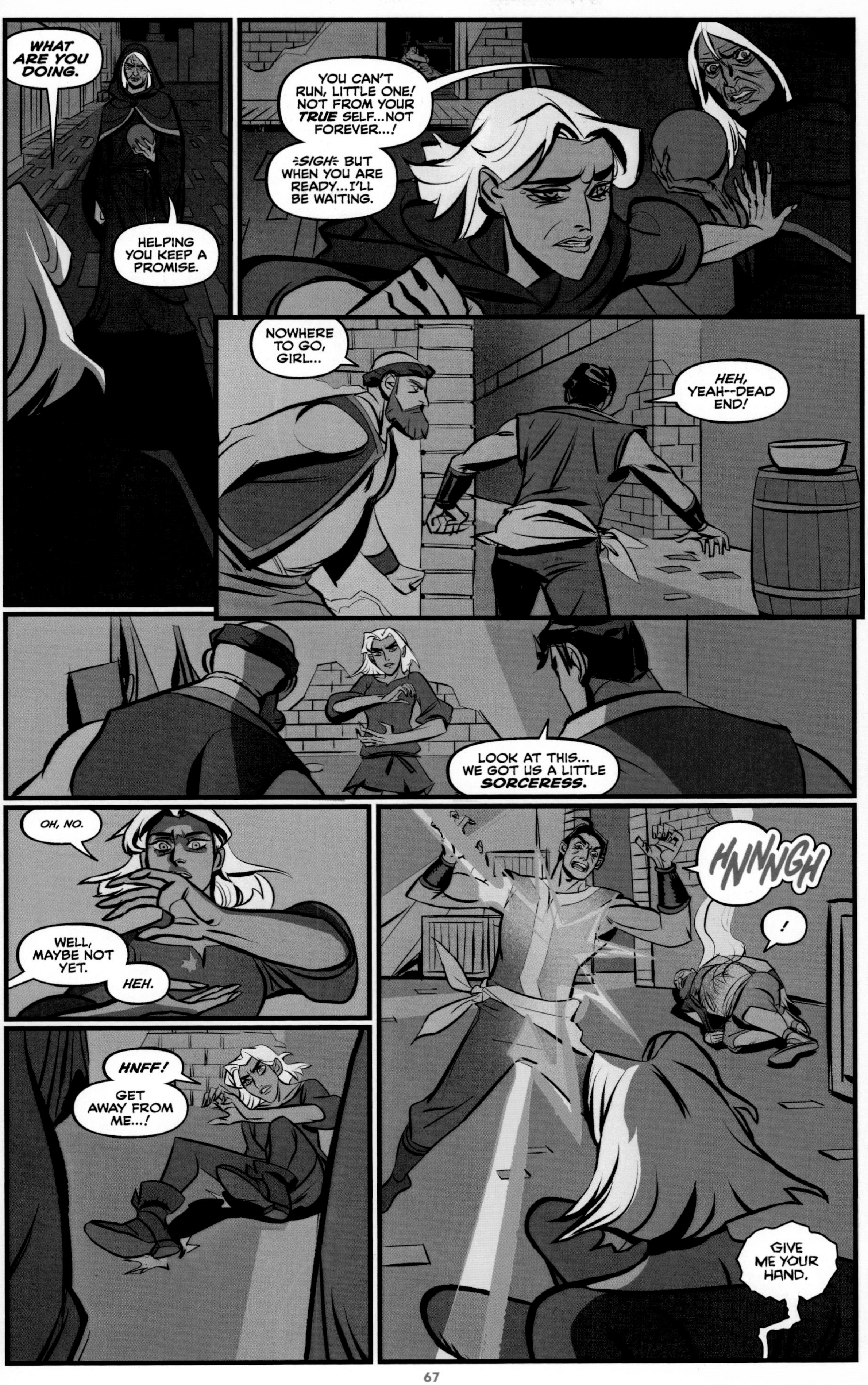
WHAT ARE YOU DOING.
HELPING YOU KEEP A PROMISE.
YOU CAN'T RUN, LITTLE ONE! NOT FROM YOUR TRUE SELF...NOT FOREVER...!
SIGH BUT WHEN YOU ARE READY...I'LL BE WAITING.
NOWHERE TO GO, GIRL...
HEH, YEAH--DEAD END!
LOOK AT THIS... WE GOT US A LITTLE SORCERESS.
OH, NO.
WELL, MAYBE NOT YET.
HEH.
HNNNGH
!
HNFF!
GET AWAY FROM ME...!
GIVE ME YOUR HAND.

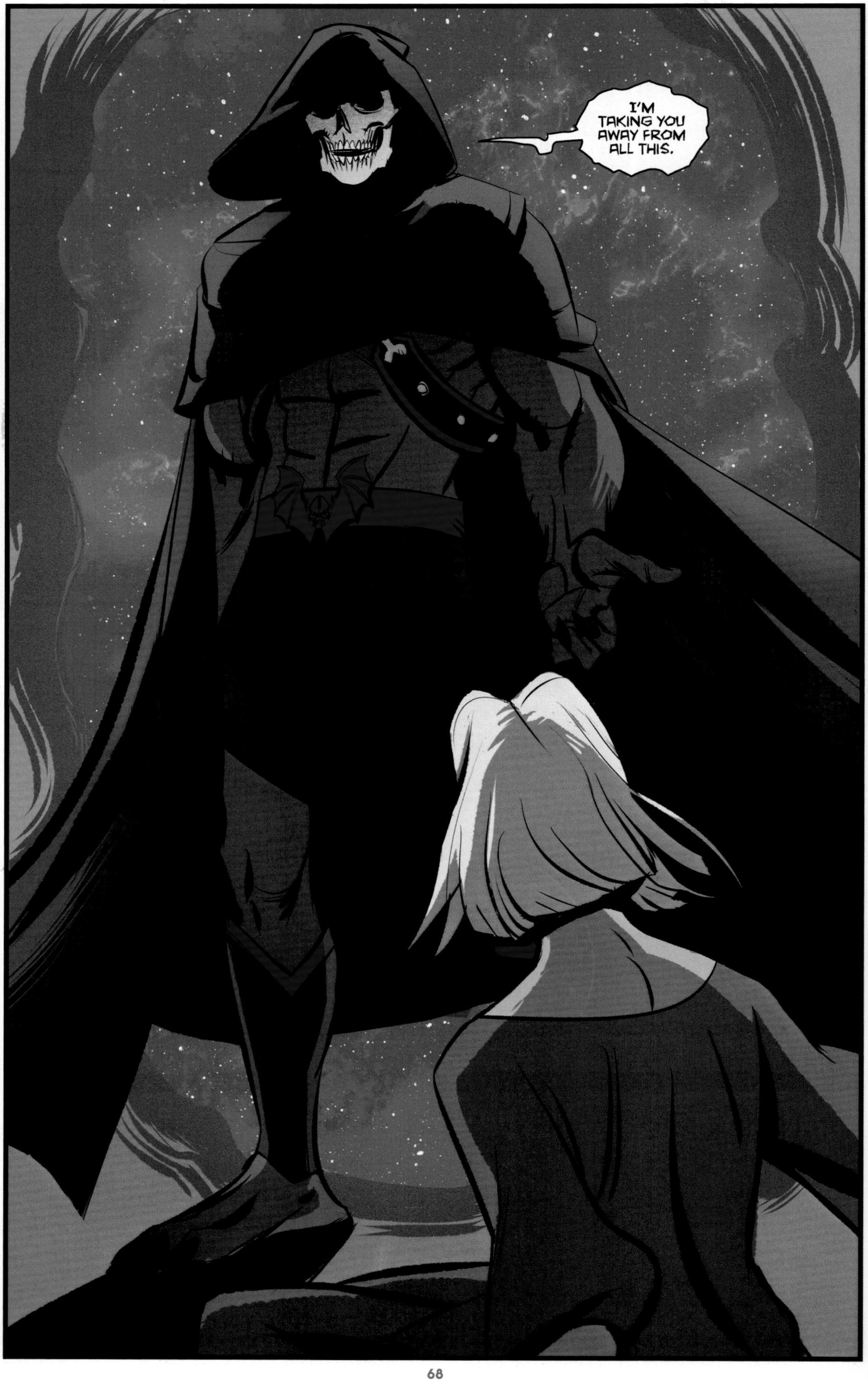
I'M TAKING YOU AWAY FROM ALL THIS.

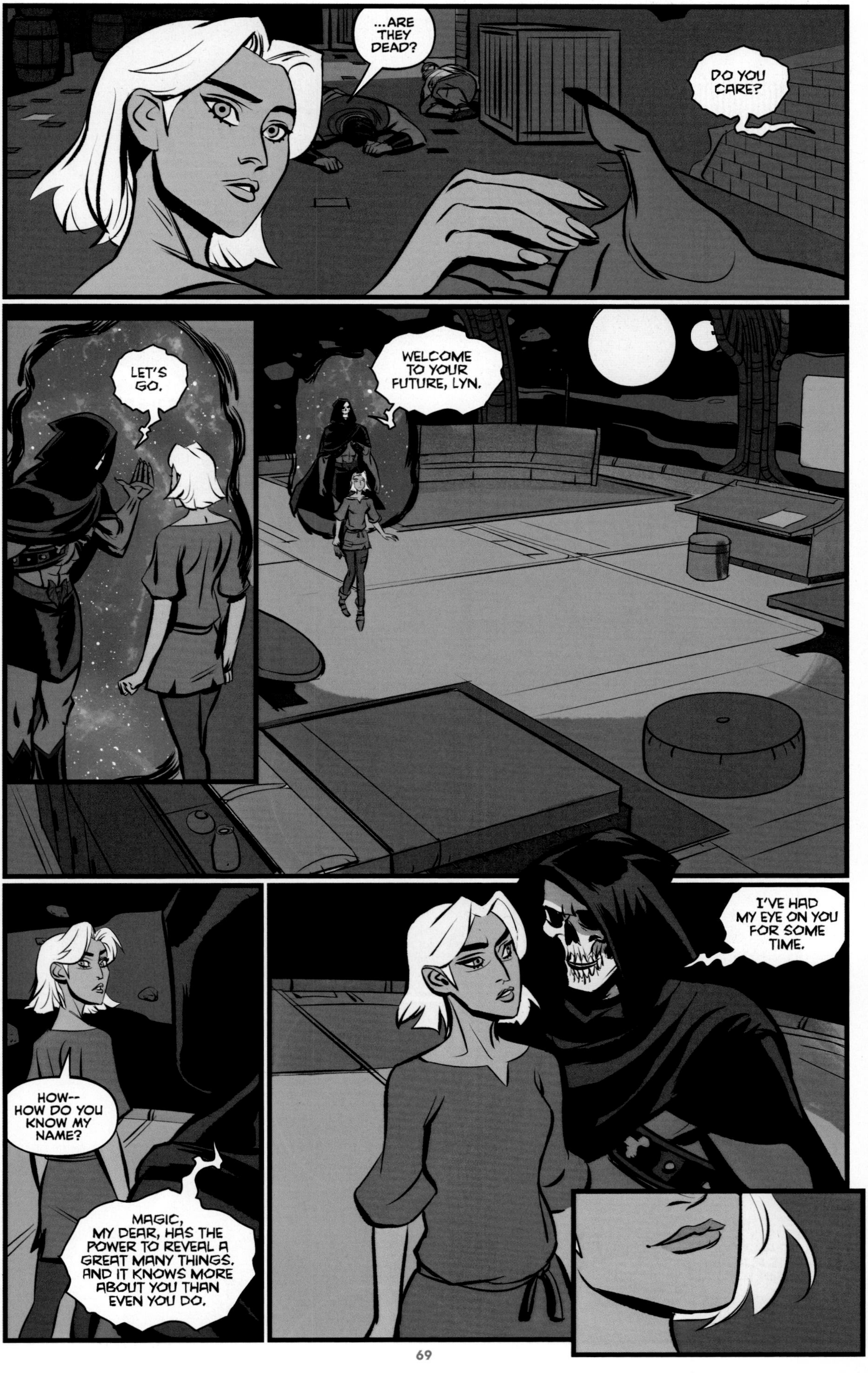
...ARE THEY DEAD?
DO YOU CARE?
LET'S GO.
WELCOME TO YOUR FUTURE, LYN.
HOW-- HOW DO YOU KNOW MY NAME?
I'VE HAD MY EYE ON YOU FOR SOME TIME.
MAGIC, MY DEAR, HAS THE POWER TO REVEAL A GREAT MANY THINGS. AND IT KNOWS MORE ABOUT YOU THAN EVEN YOU DO.

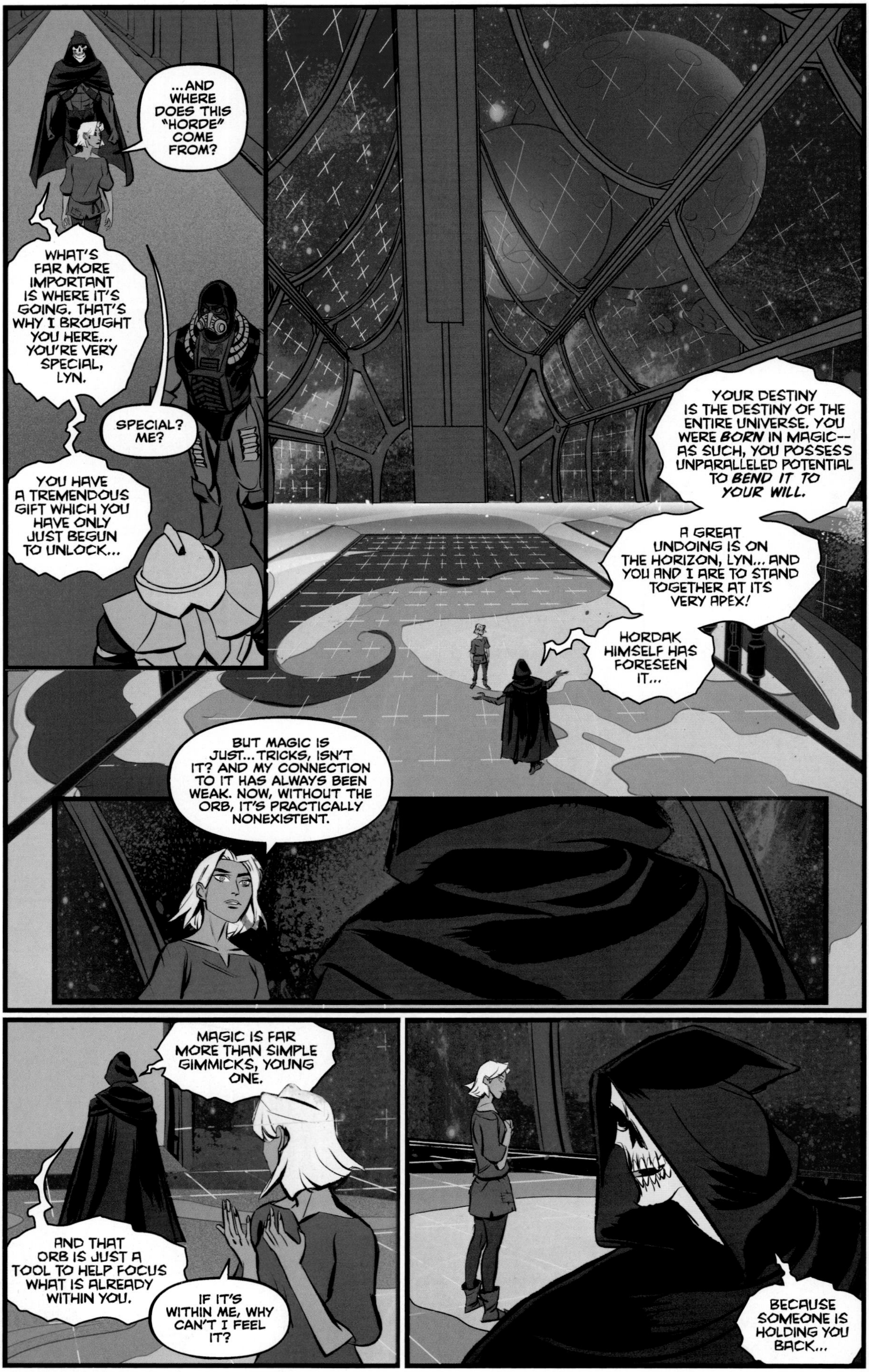
...AND WHERE DOES THIS "HORDE" COME FROM?
WHAT'S FAR MORE IMPORTANT IS WHERE IT'S GOING. THAT'S WHY I BROUGHT YOU HERE... YOU'RE VERY SPECIAL, LYN.
SPECIAL? ME?
YOU HAVE A TREMENDOUS GIFT WHICH YOU HAVE ONLY JUST BEGUN TO UNLOCK...
YOUR DESTINY IS THE DESTINY OF THE ENTIRE UNIVERSE. YOU WERE BORN IN MAGIC-- AS SUCH, YOU POSSESS UNPARALLELED POTENTIAL TO BEND IT TO YOUR WILL.
A GREAT UNDOING IS ON THE HORIZON, LYN... AND YOU AND I ARE TO STAND TOGETHER AT ITS VERY APEX!
HORDAK HIMSELF HAS FORESEEN IT...
BUT MAGIC IS JUST...TRICKS, ISN'T IT? AND MY CONNECTION TO IT HAS ALWAYS BEEN WEAK. NOW, WITHOUT THE ORB, IT'S PRACTICALLY NONEXISTENT.
MAGIC IS FAR MORE THAN SIMPLE GIMMICKS, YOUNG ONE.
AND THAT ORB IS JUST A TOOL TO HELP FOCUS WHAT IS ALREADY WITHIN YOU.
IF IT'S WITHIN ME, WHY CAN'T I FEEL IT?
BECAUSE SOMEONE IS HOLDING YOU BACK...

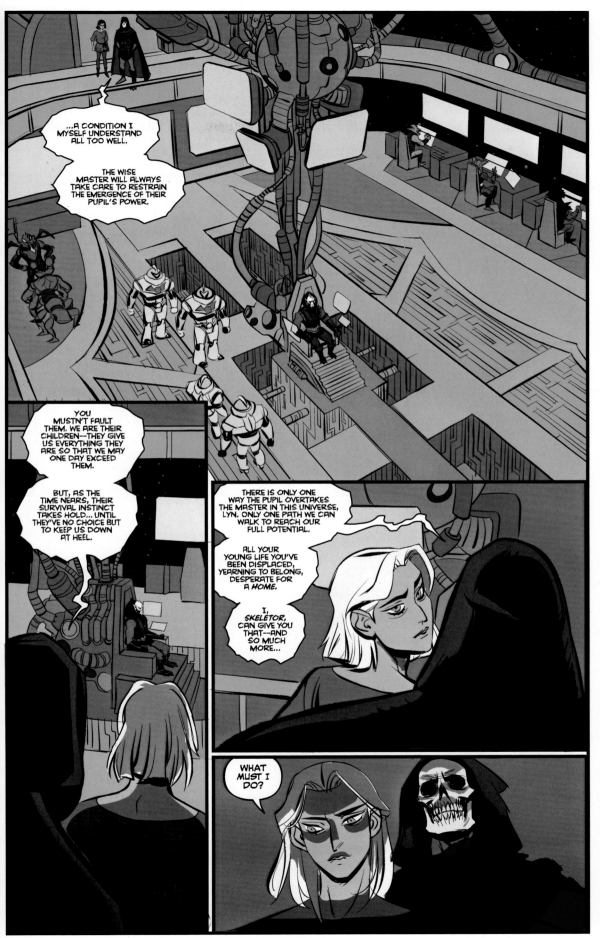

...A CONDITION I MYSELF UNDERSTAND ALL TOO WELL.

THE WISE MASTER WILL ALWAYS TAKE CARE TO RESTRAIN THE EMERGENCE OF THEIR PUPIL'S POWER.

YOU MUSTN'T FAULT THEM. WE ARE THEIR CHILDREN--THEY GIVE US EVERYTHING THEY ARE SO THAT WE MAY ONE DAY EXCEED THEM.

BUT, AS THE TIME NEARS, THEIR SURVIVAL INSTINCT TAKES HOLD... UNTIL THEY'VE NO CHOICE BUT TO KEEP US DOWN AT HEEL.

THERE IS ONLY ONE WAY THE PUPIL OVERTAKES THE MASTER IN THIS UNIVERSE, LYN. ONLY ONE PATH WE CAN WALK TO REACH OUR FULL POTENTIAL.

ALL YOUR YOUNG LIFE YOU'VE BEEN DISPLACED, YEARNING TO BELONG, DESPERATE FOR A *HOME*.

I, *SKELETOR*, CAN GIVE YOU THAT--AND SO MUCH MORE...

WHAT MUST I DO?

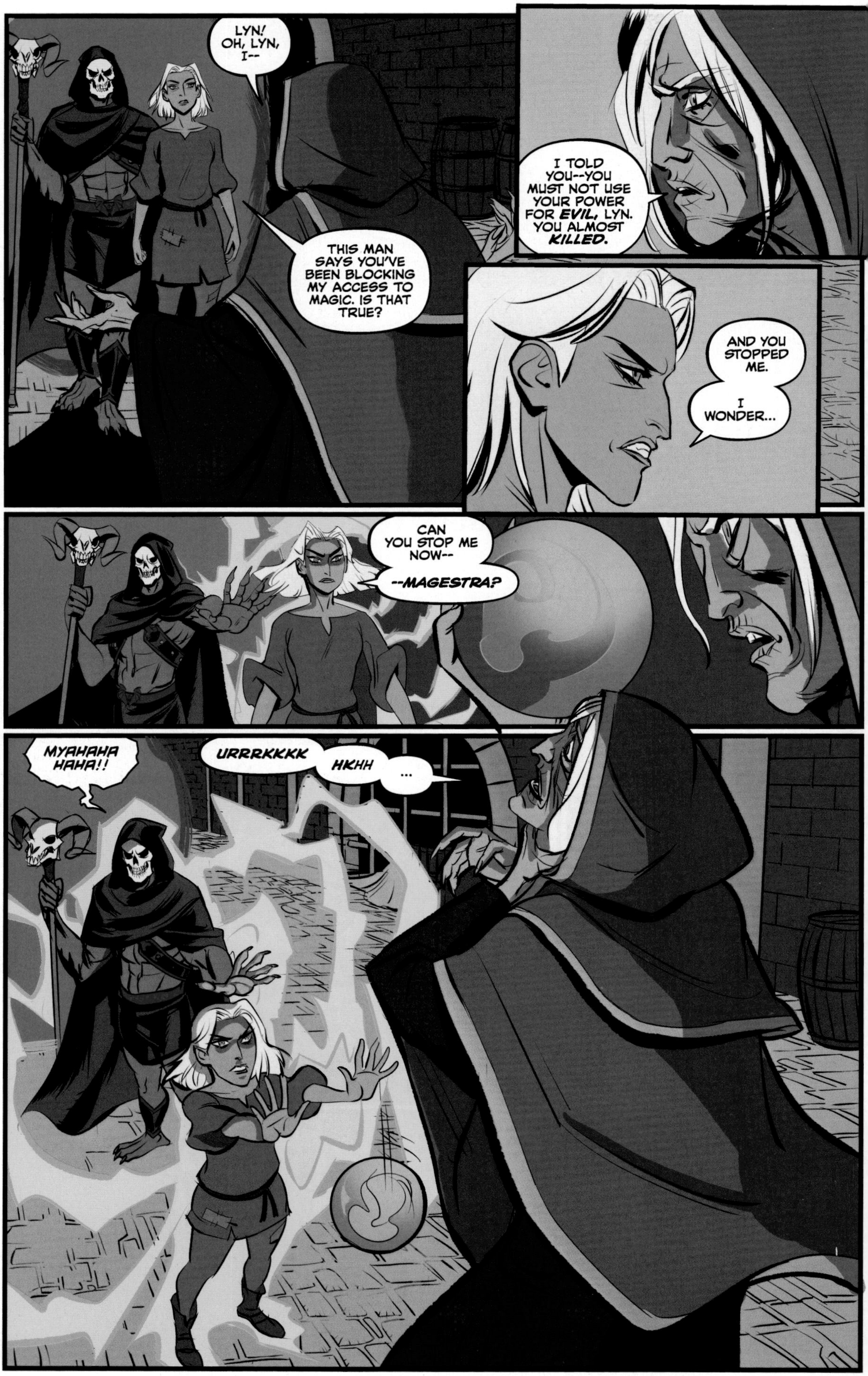
LYN! OH, LYN, I--
THIS MAN SAYS YOU'VE BEEN BLOCKING MY ACCESS TO MAGIC. IS THAT TRUE?
I TOLD YOU--YOU MUST NOT USE YOUR POWER FOR EVIL, LYN. YOU ALMOST KILLED.
AND YOU STOPPED ME.
I WONDER...
CAN YOU STOP ME NOW--
--MAGESTRA?
MYAHAHA HAHA!!
URRRKKKK
HKHH
...

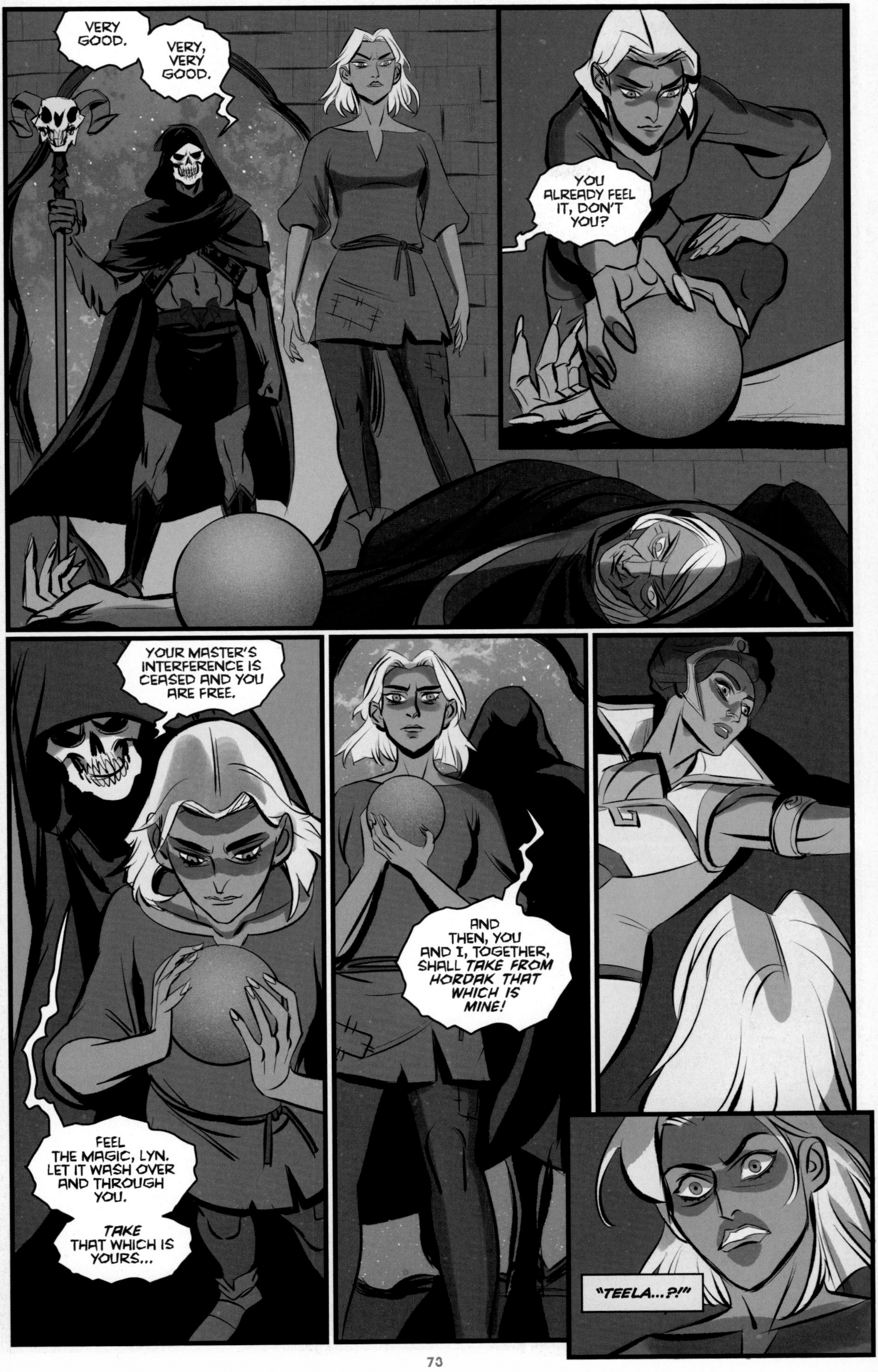
VERY GOOD.
VERY, VERY GOOD.
YOU ALREADY FEEL IT, DON'T YOU?
YOUR MASTER'S INTERFERENCE IS CEASED AND YOU ARE FREE.
FEEL THE MAGIC, LYN. LET IT WASH OVER AND THROUGH YOU.
TAKE THAT WHICH IS YOURS...
AND THEN, YOU AND I, TOGETHER, SHALL TAKE FROM HORDAK THAT WHICH IS MINE!
"TEELA...?!"

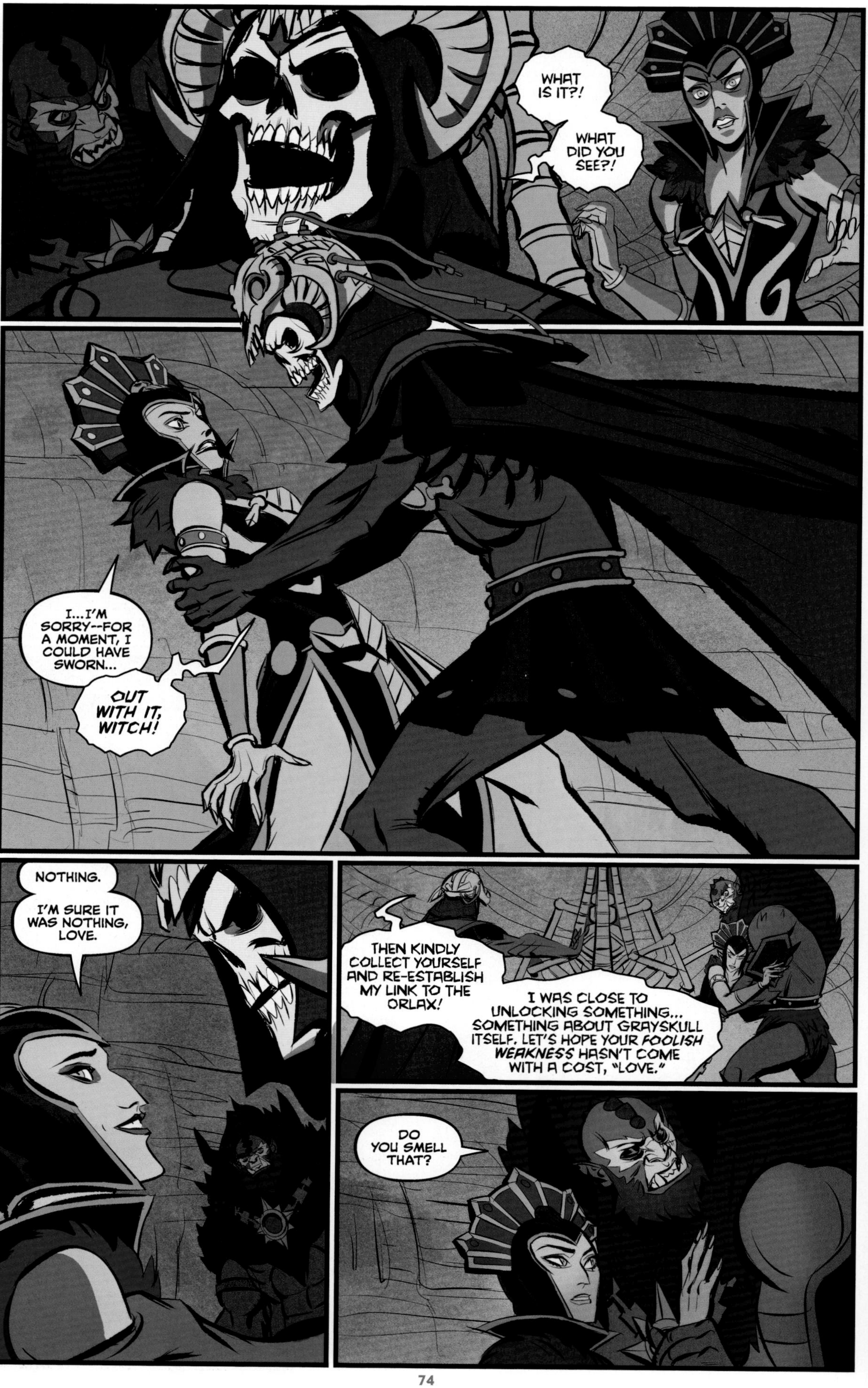
WHAT IS IT?!
WHAT DID YOU SEE?!
I...I'M SORRY--FOR A MOMENT, I COULD HAVE SWORN...
OUT WITH IT, WITCH!
NOTHING.
I'M SURE IT WAS NOTHING, LOVE.
THEN KINDLY COLLECT YOURSELF AND RE-ESTABLISH MY LINK TO THE ORLAX!
I WAS CLOSE TO UNLOCKING SOMETHING... SOMETHING ABOUT GRAYSKULL ITSELF. LET'S HOPE YOUR *FOOLISH WEAKNESS* HASN'T COME WITH A COST, "LOVE."
DO YOU SMELL THAT?

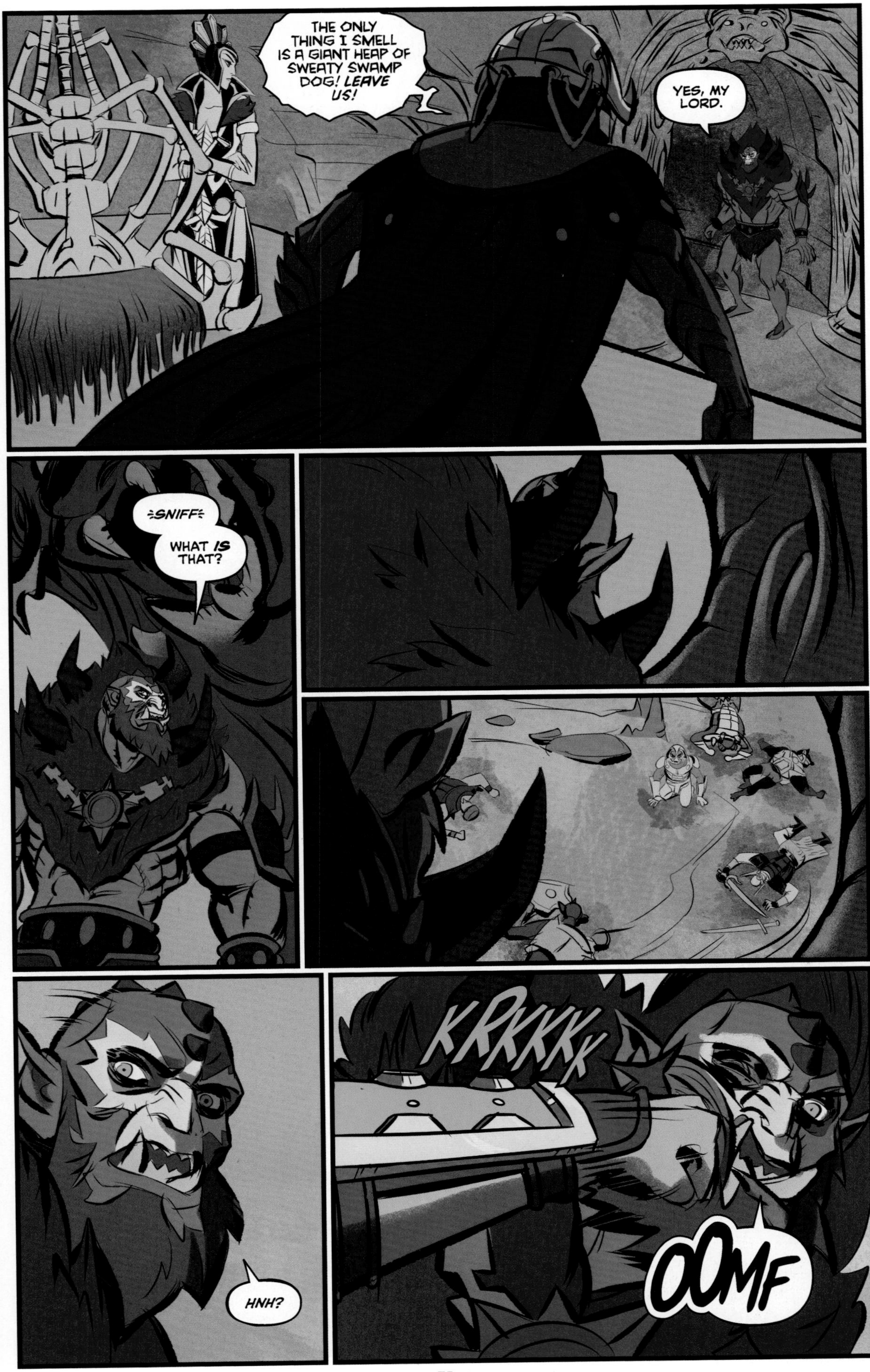

THE ONLY THING I SMELL IS A GIANT HEAP OF SWEATY SWAMP DOG! LEAVE US!
YES, MY LORD.
SNIFF
WHAT IS THAT?
HNH?
KRRKKK
OOMF

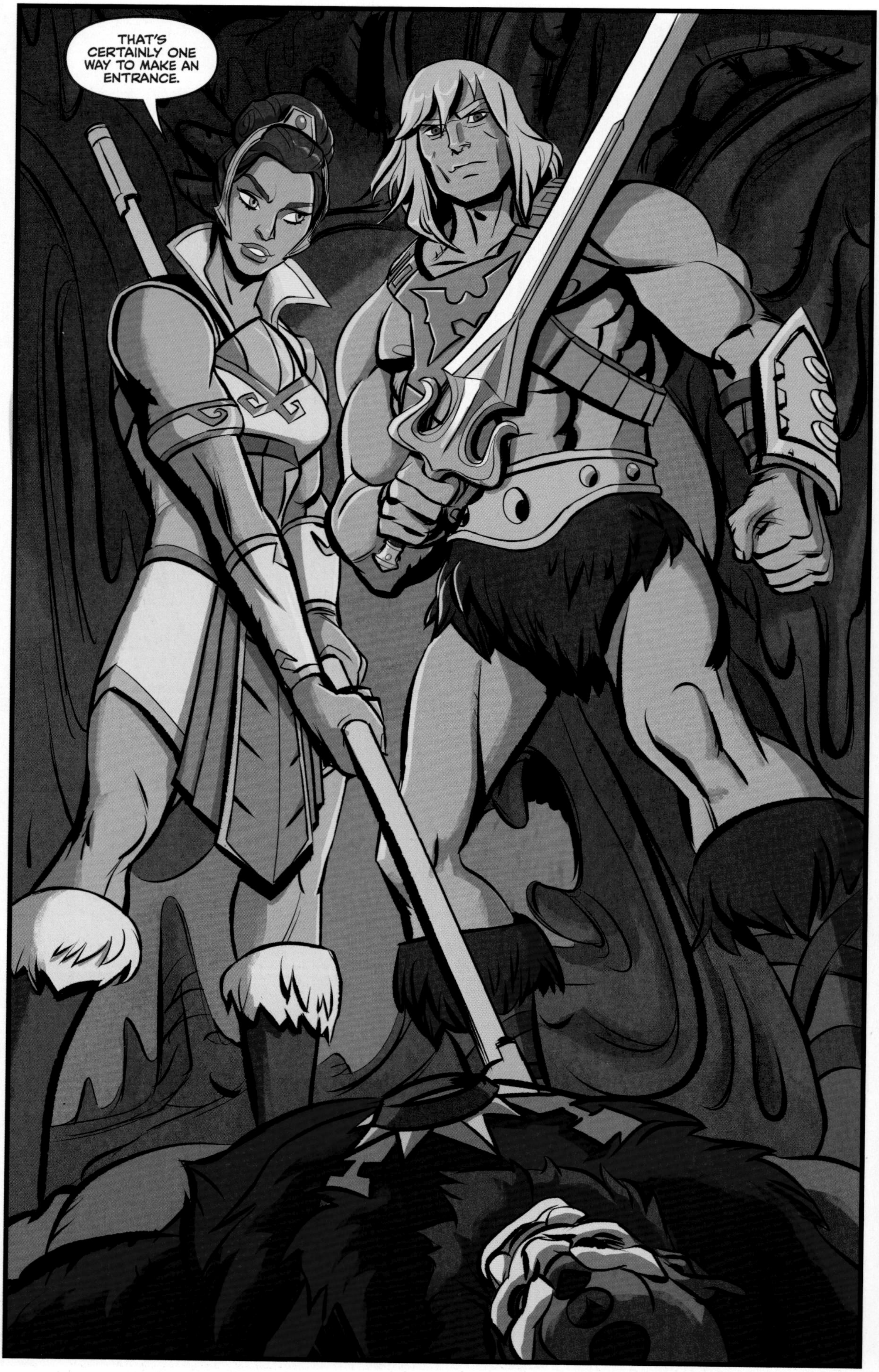
THAT'S CERTAINLY ONE WAY TO MAKE AN ENTRANCE.

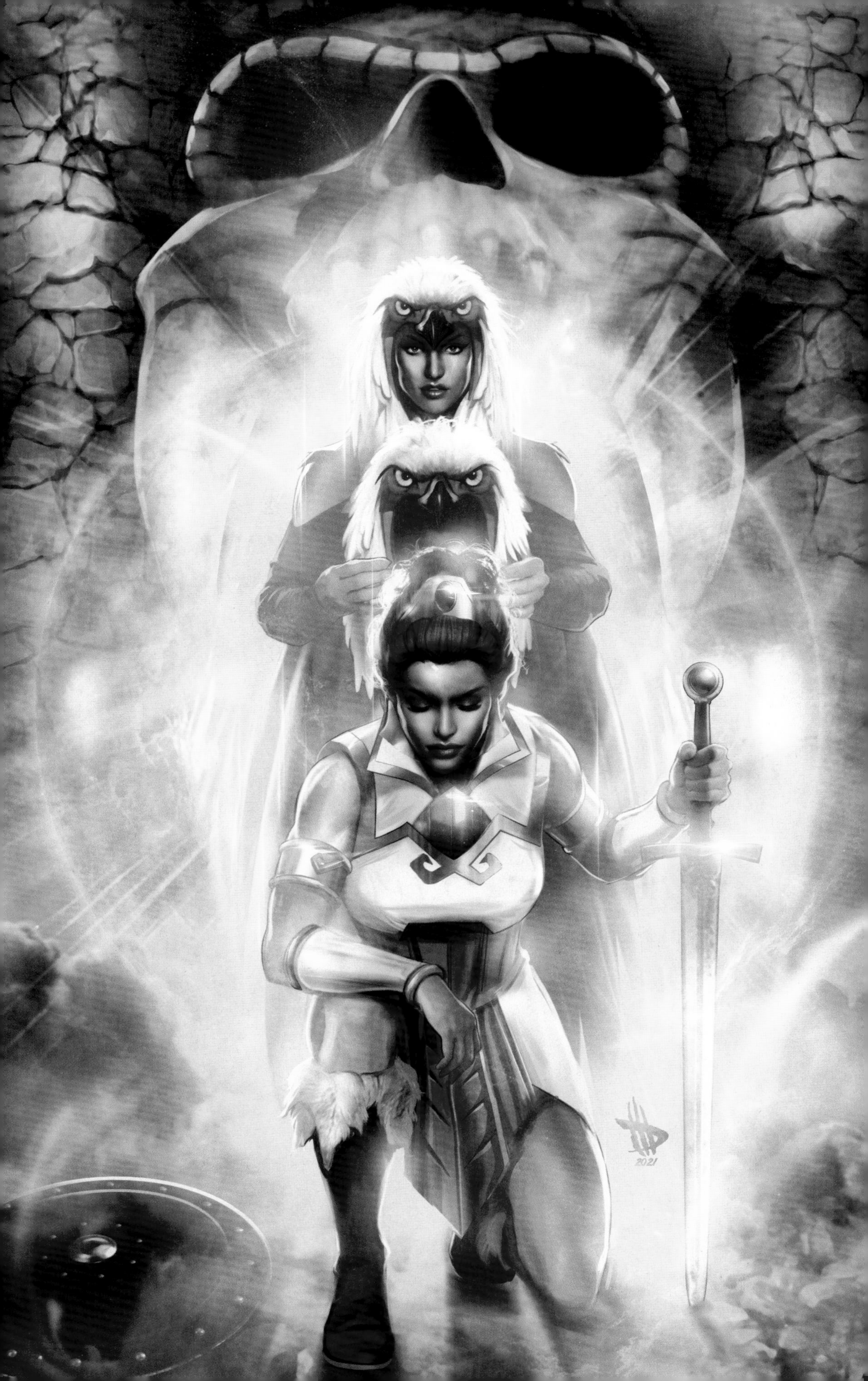
2021

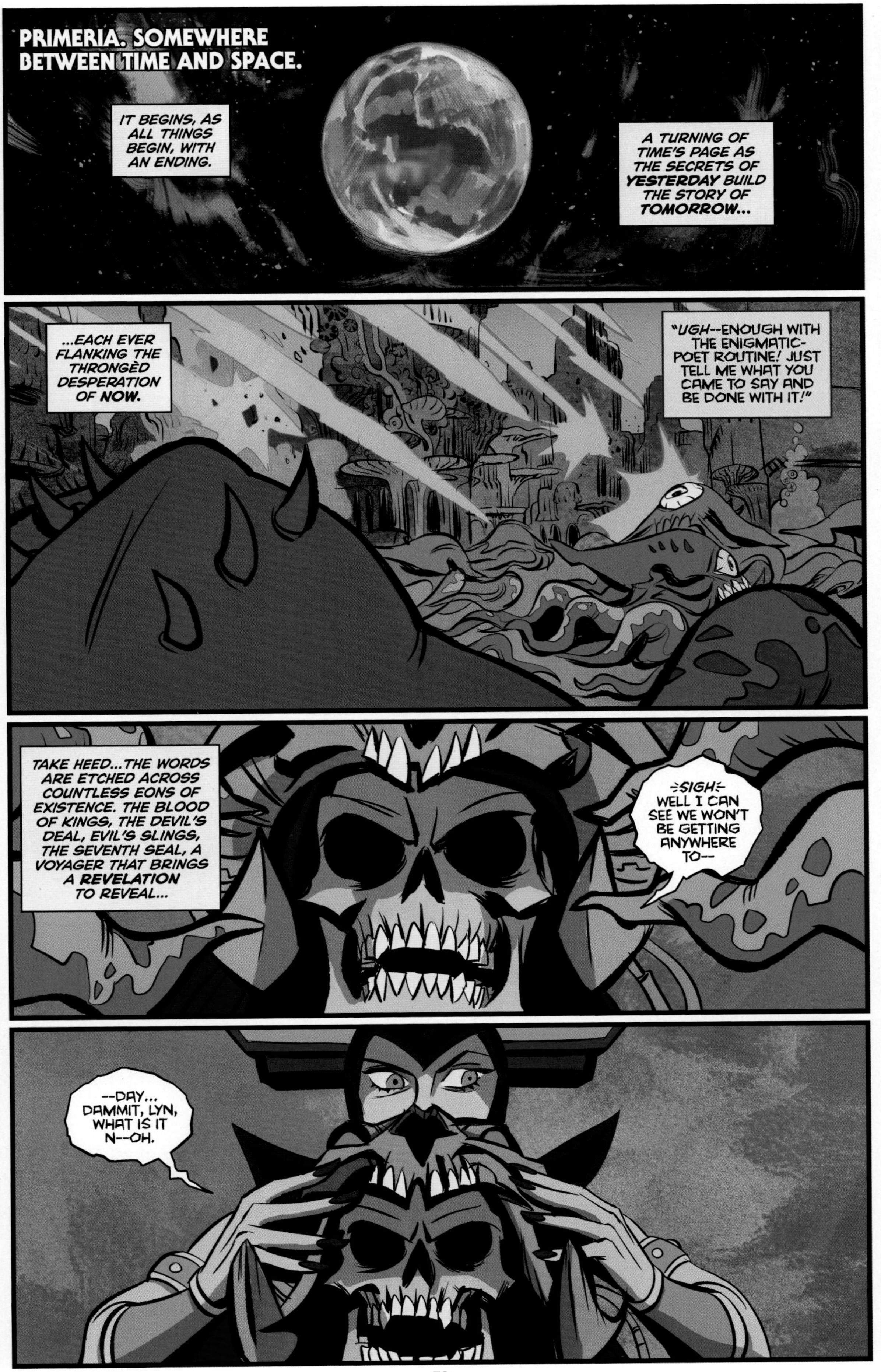
PRIMERIA. SOMEWHERE BETWEEN TIME AND SPACE.
IT BEGINS, AS ALL THINGS BEGIN, WITH AN ENDING.
A TURNING OF TIME'S PAGE AS THE SECRETS OF YESTERDAY BUILD THE STORY OF TOMORROW...
...EACH EVER FLANKING THE THRONGÈD DESPERATION OF NOW.
"UGH--ENOUGH WITH THE ENIGMATIC-POET ROUTINE! JUST TELL ME WHAT YOU CAME TO SAY AND BE DONE WITH IT!"
TAKE HEED...THE WORDS ARE ETCHED ACROSS COUNTLESS EONS OF EXISTENCE. THE BLOOD OF KINGS, THE DEVIL'S DEAL, EVIL'S SLINGS, THE SEVENTH SEAL, A VOYAGER THAT BRINGS A REVELATION TO REVEAL...
SIGH WELL I CAN SEE WE WON'T BE GETTING ANYWHERE TO--
--DAY... DAMMIT, LYN, WHAT IS IT N--OH.

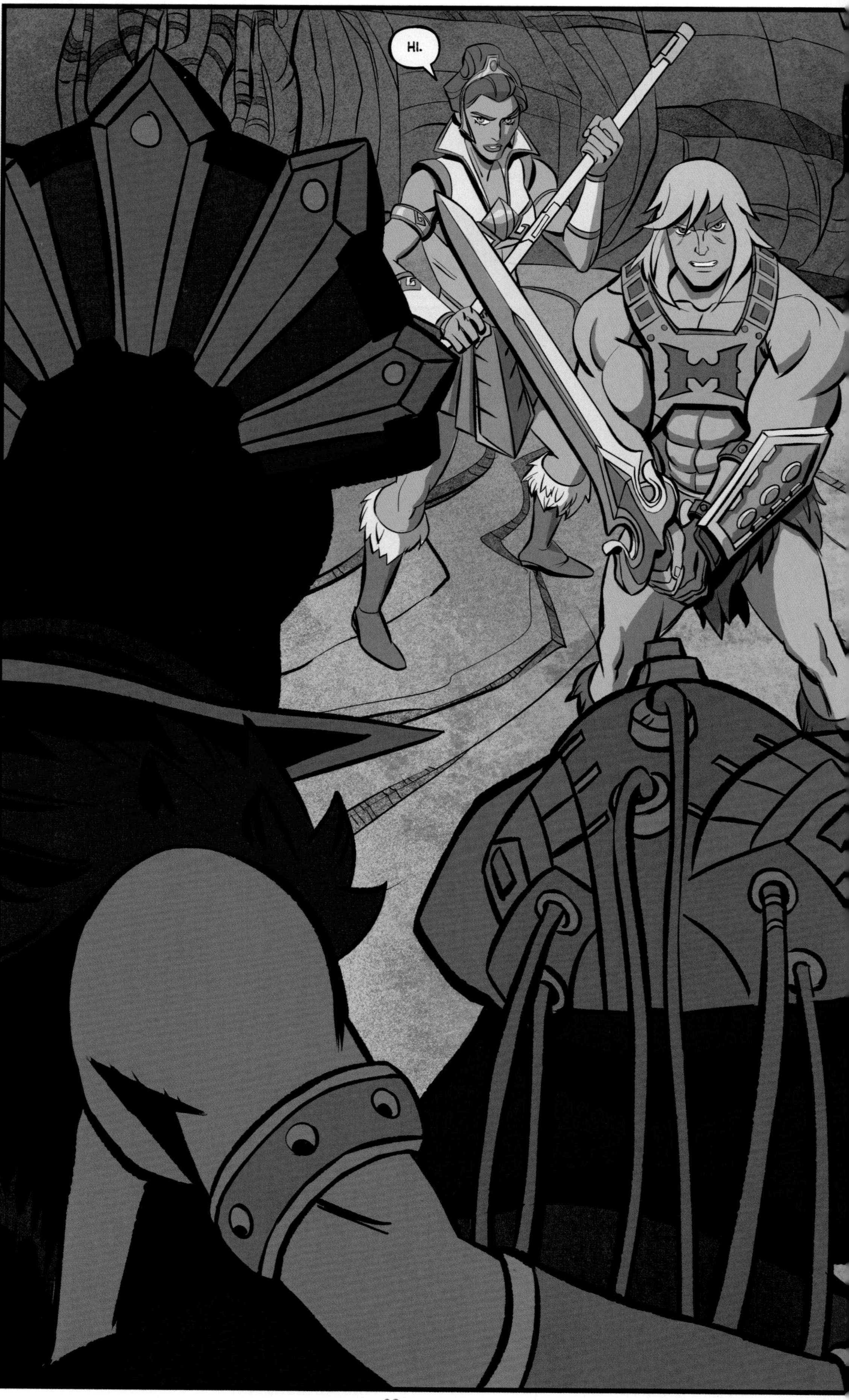
HI.

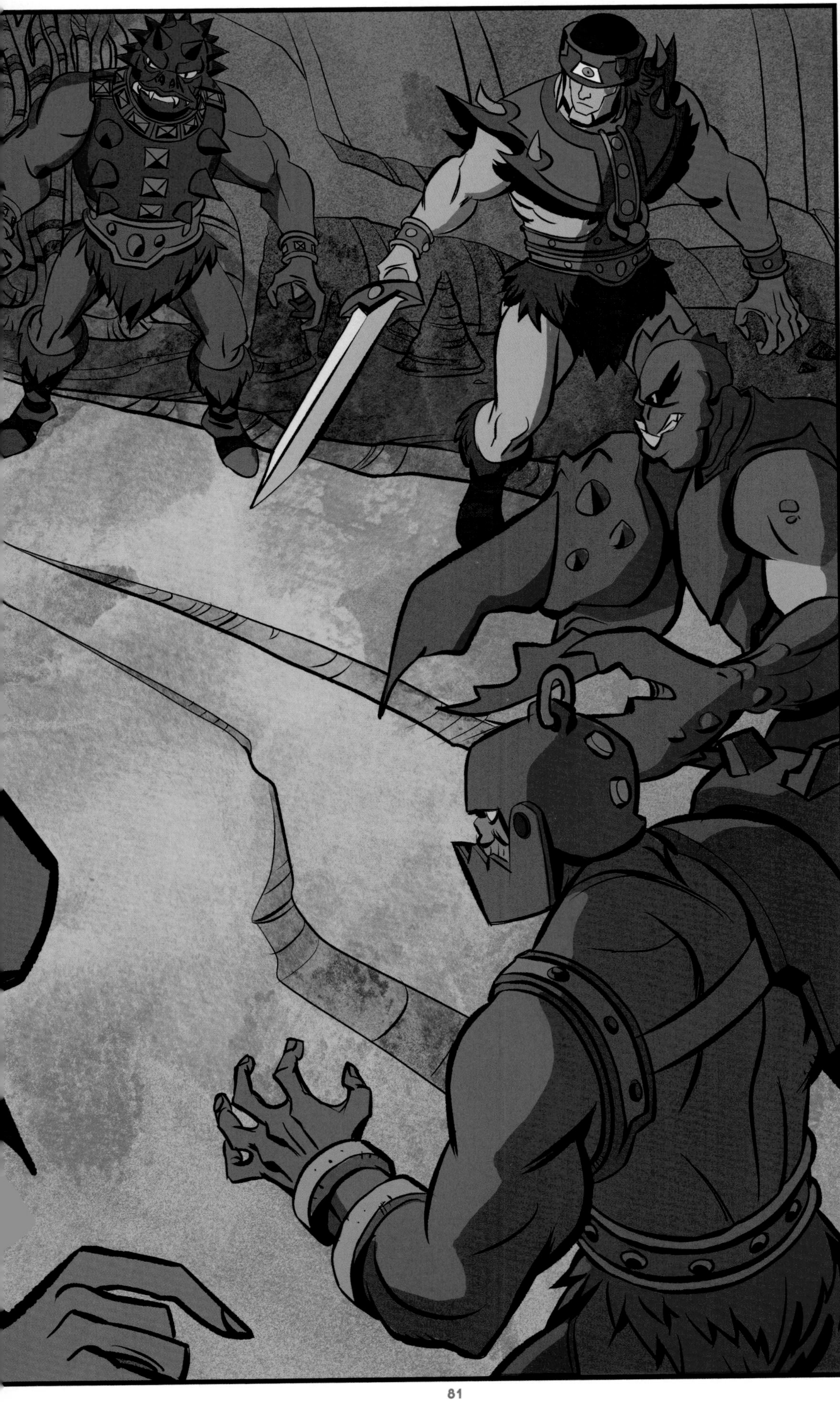

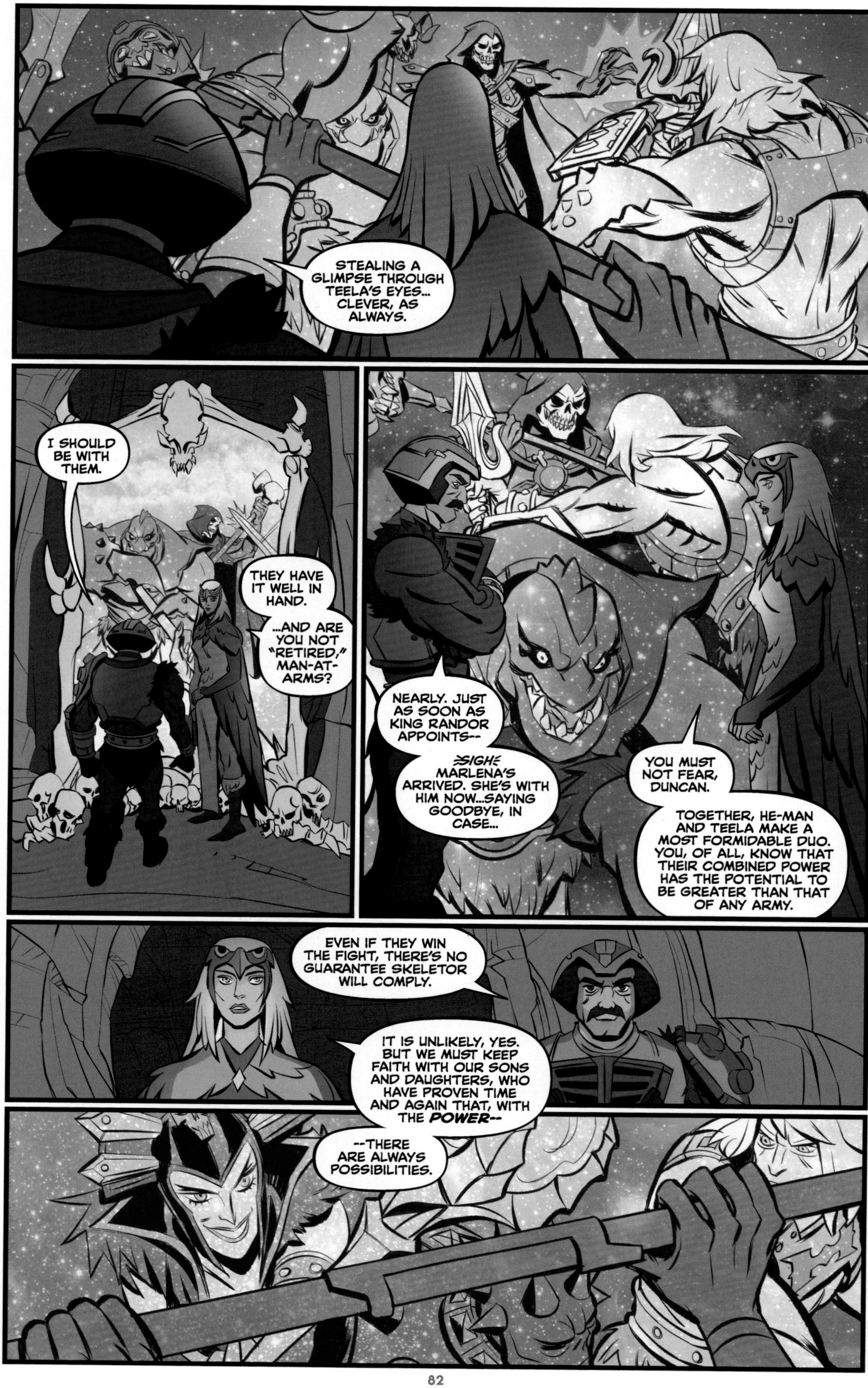
STEALING A GLIMPSE THROUGH TEELA'S EYES... CLEVER, AS ALWAYS.
I SHOULD BE WITH THEM.
THEY HAVE IT WELL IN HAND.
...AND ARE YOU NOT "RETIRED," MAN-AT-ARMS?
NEARLY. JUST AS SOON AS KING RANDOR APPOINTS--
SIGH
MARLENA'S ARRIVED. SHE'S WITH HIM NOW...SAYING GOODBYE, IN CASE...
YOU MUST NOT FEAR, DUNCAN.
TOGETHER, HE-MAN AND TEELA MAKE A MOST FORMIDABLE DUO. YOU, OF ALL, KNOW THAT THEIR COMBINED POWER HAS THE POTENTIAL TO BE GREATER THAN THAT OF ANY ARMY.
EVEN IF THEY WIN THE FIGHT, THERE'S NO GUARANTEE SKELETOR WILL COMPLY.
IT IS UNLIKELY, YES. BUT WE MUST KEEP FAITH WITH OUR SONS AND DAUGHTERS, WHO HAVE PROVEN TIME AND AGAIN THAT, WITH THE POWER--
--THERE ARE ALWAYS POSSIBILITIES.

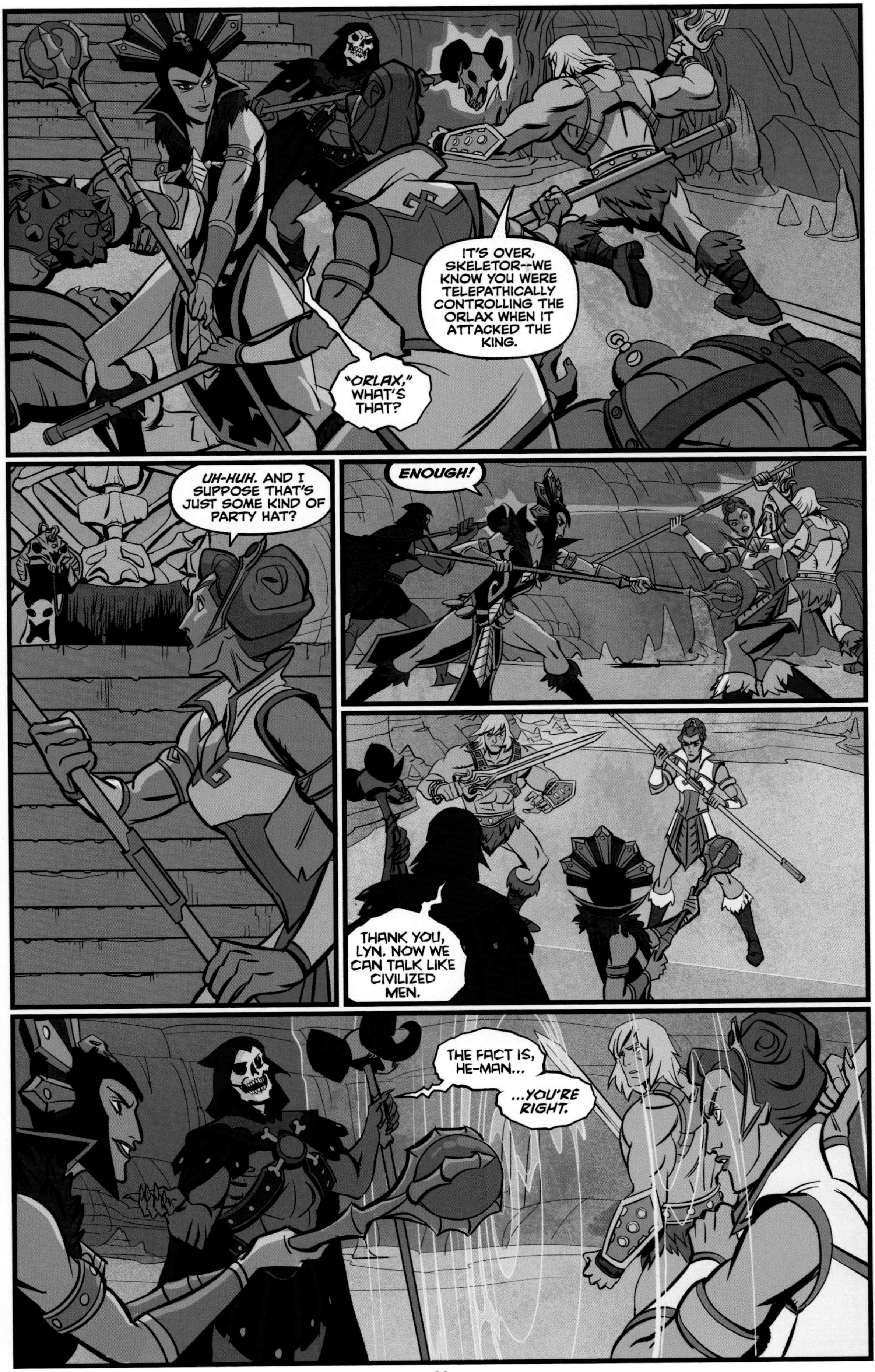
IT'S OVER, SKELETOR--WE KNOW YOU WERE TELEPATHICALLY CONTROLLING THE ORLAX WHEN IT ATTACKED THE KING.
"ORLAX," WHAT'S THAT?
UH-HUH. AND I SUPPOSE THAT'S JUST SOME KIND OF PARTY HAT?
ENOUGH!
THANK YOU, LYN. NOW WE CAN TALK LIKE CIVILIZED MEN.
THE FACT IS, HE-MAN...
...YOU'RE RIGHT.

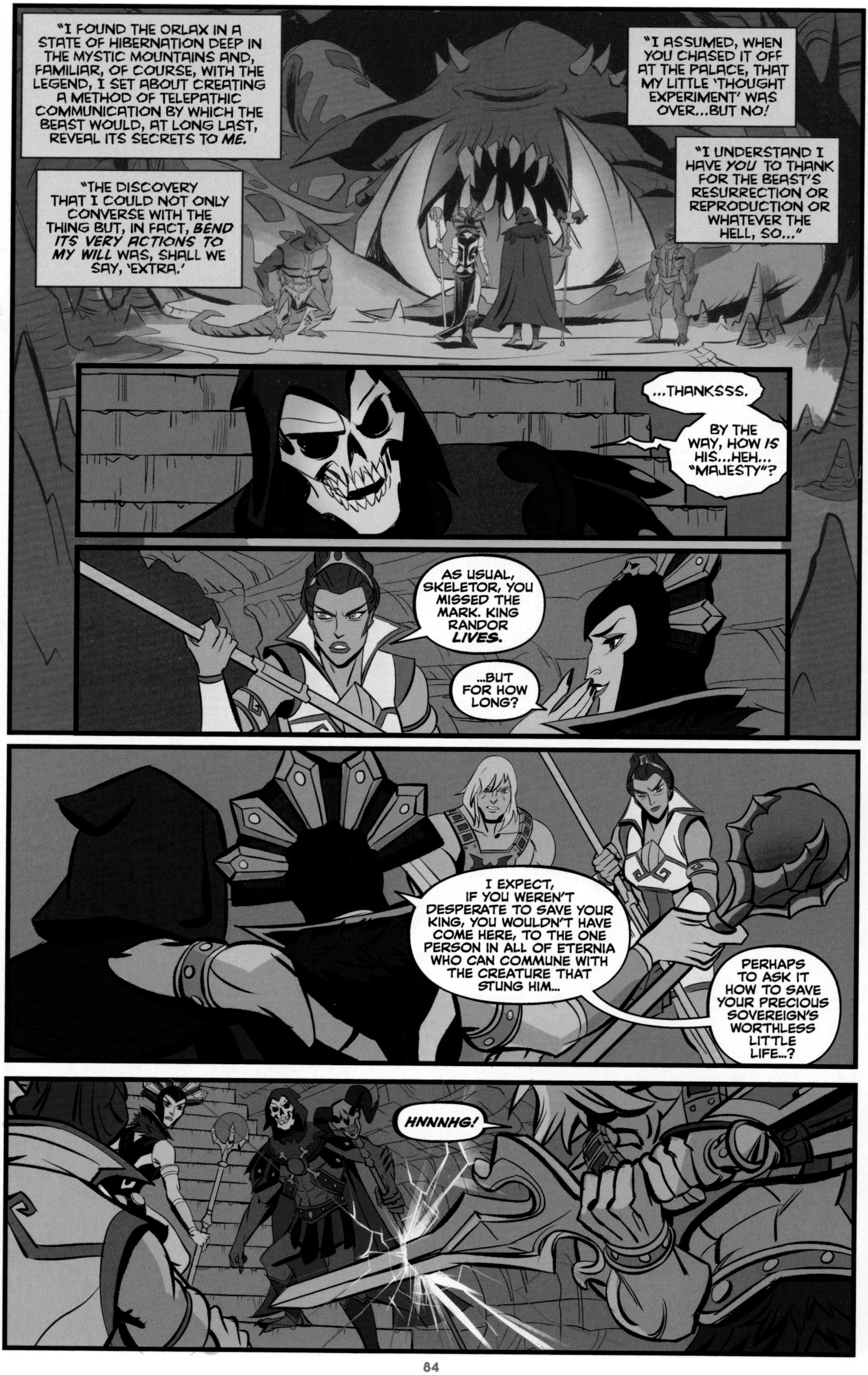
"I FOUND THE ORLAX IN A STATE OF HIBERNATION DEEP IN THE MYSTIC MOUNTAINS AND, FAMILIAR, OF COURSE, WITH THE LEGEND, I SET ABOUT CREATING A METHOD OF TELEPATHIC COMMUNICATION BY WHICH THE BEAST WOULD, AT LONG LAST, REVEAL ITS SECRETS TO *ME.*
"THE DISCOVERY THAT I COULD NOT ONLY CONVERSE WITH THE THING BUT, IN FACT, *BEND ITS VERY ACTIONS TO MY WILL* WAS, SHALL WE SAY, 'EXTRA.'
"I ASSUMED, WHEN YOU CHASED IT OFF AT THE PALACE, THAT MY LITTLE 'THOUGHT EXPERIMENT' WAS OVER...BUT NO!
"I UNDERSTAND I HAVE *YOU* TO THANK FOR THE BEAST'S RESURRECTION OR REPRODUCTION OR WHATEVER THE HELL, SO..."
...THANKSSS.
BY THE WAY, HOW *IS* HIS...HEH... "MAJESTY"?
AS USUAL, SKELETOR, YOU MISSED THE MARK. KING RANDOR ***LIVES.***
...BUT FOR HOW LONG?
I EXPECT, IF YOU WEREN'T DESPERATE TO SAVE YOUR KING, YOU WOULDN'T HAVE COME HERE, TO THE ONE PERSON IN ALL OF ETERNIA WHO CAN COMMUNE WITH THE CREATURE THAT STUNG HIM...
PERHAPS TO ASK IT HOW TO SAVE YOUR PRECIOUS SOVEREIGN'S WORTHLESS LITTLE LIFE...?
HNNNHG!

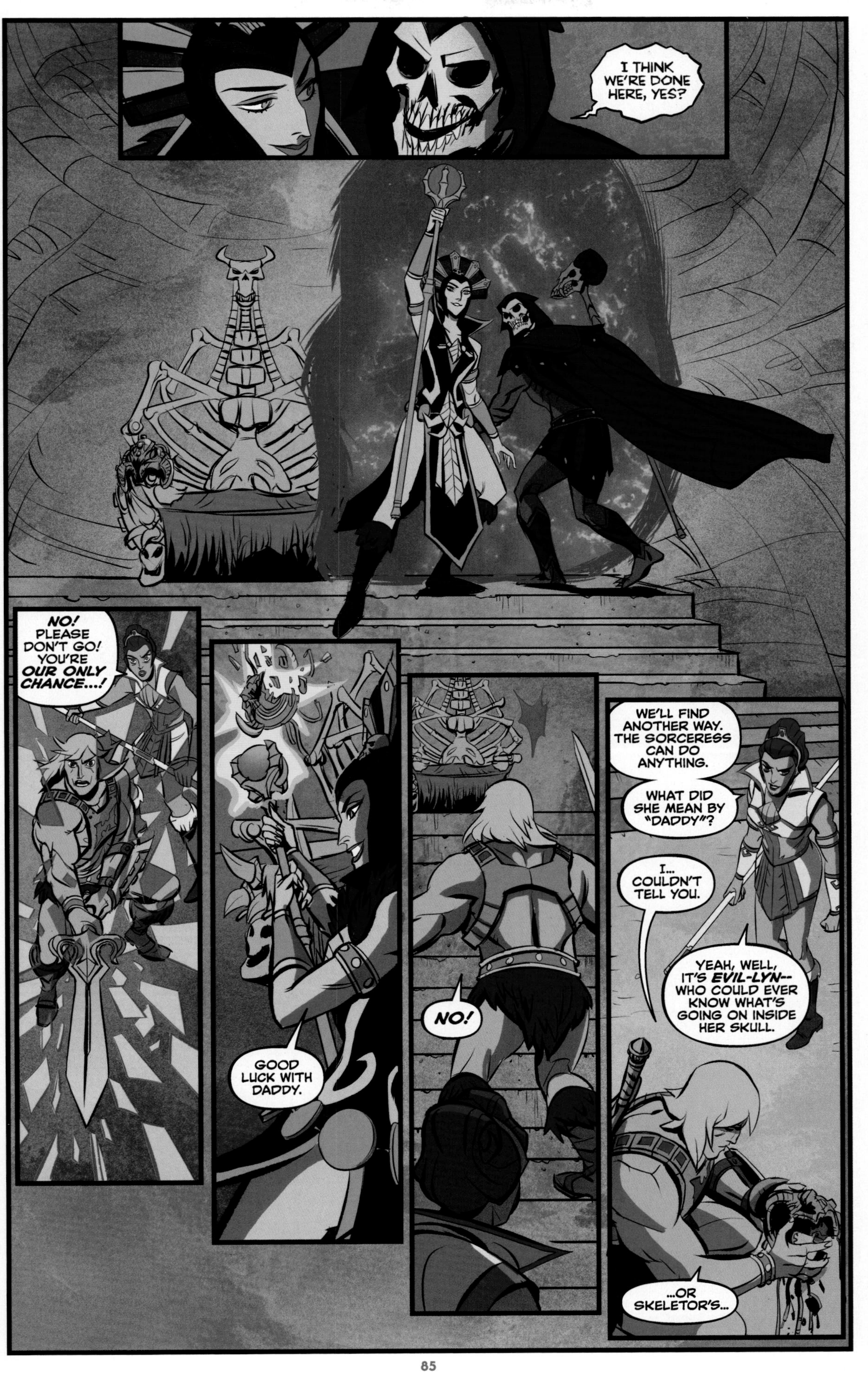
I THINK WE'RE DONE HERE, YES?
NO! PLEASE DON'T GO! YOU'RE OUR ONLY CHANCE...!
GOOD LUCK WITH DADDY.
NO!
WE'LL FIND ANOTHER WAY. THE SORCERESS CAN DO ANYTHING.
WHAT DID SHE MEAN BY "DADDY"?
I... COULDN'T TELL YOU.
YEAH, WELL, IT'S EVIL-LYN-- WHO COULD EVER KNOW WHAT'S GOING ON INSIDE HER SKULL.
...OR SKELETOR'S...

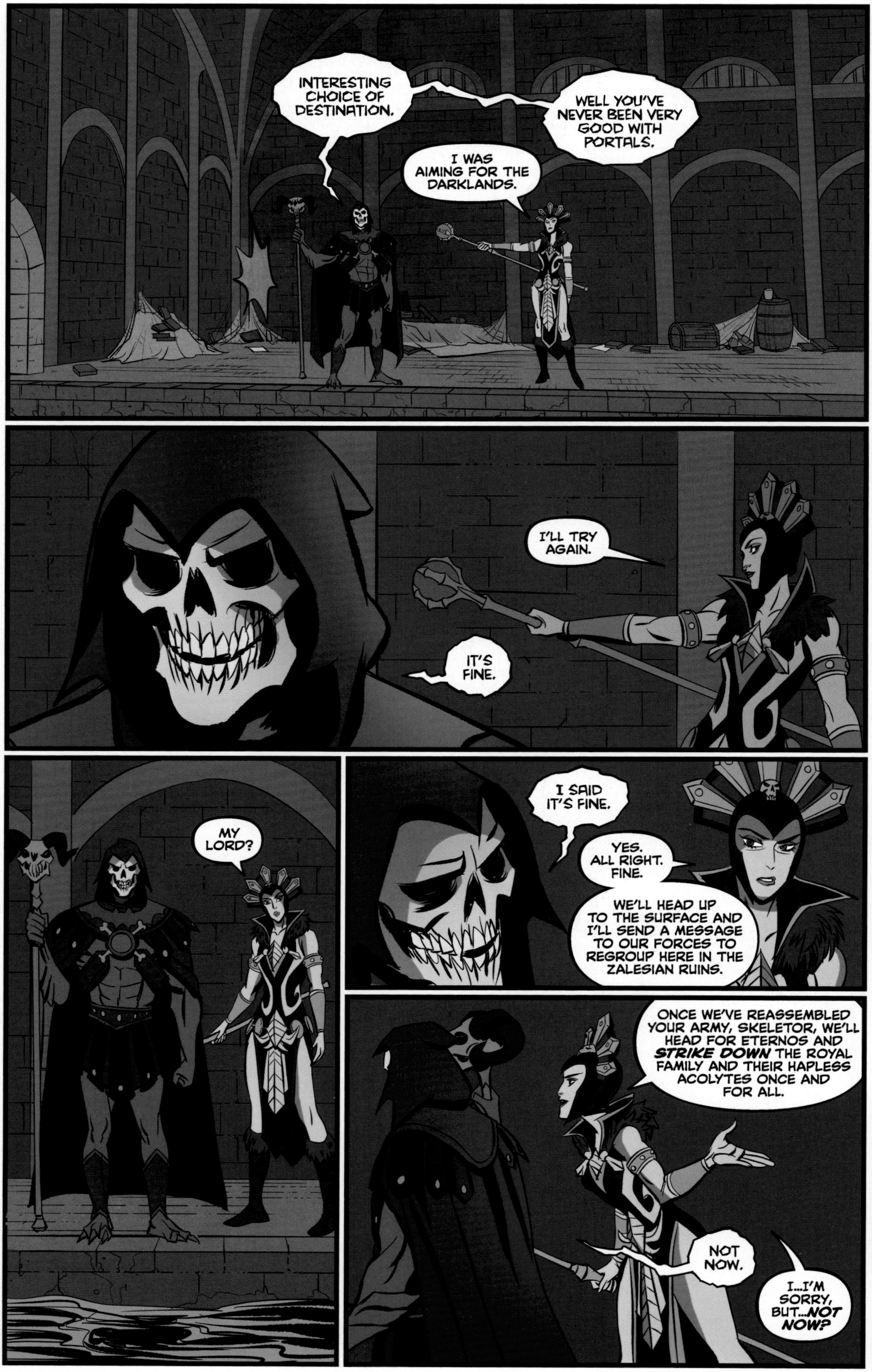
INTERESTING CHOICE OF DESTINATION.
I WAS AIMING FOR THE DARKLANDS.
WELL YOU'VE NEVER BEEN VERY GOOD WITH PORTALS.
I'LL TRY AGAIN.
IT'S FINE.
MY LORD?
I SAID IT'S FINE.
YES. ALL RIGHT. FINE.
WE'LL HEAD UP TO THE SURFACE AND I'LL SEND A MESSAGE TO OUR FORCES TO REGROUP HERE IN THE ZALESIAN RUINS.
ONCE WE'VE REASSEMBLED YOUR ARMY, SKELETOR, WE'LL HEAD FOR ETERNOS AND ***STRIKE DOWN*** THE ROYAL FAMILY AND THEIR HAPLESS ACOLYTES ONCE AND FOR ALL.
NOT NOW.
I...I'M SORRY, BUT...***NOT NOW?***

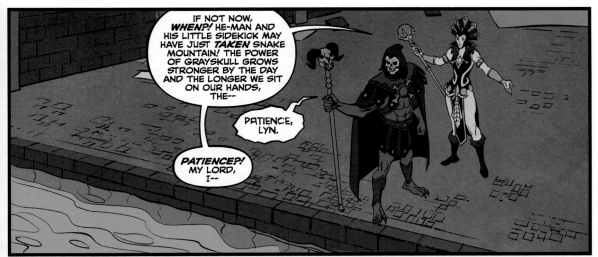

IF NOT NOW, *WHEN?!* HE-MAN AND HIS LITTLE SIDEKICK MAY HAVE JUST *TAKEN* SNAKE MOUNTAIN! THE POWER OF GRAYSKULL GROWS STRONGER BY THE DAY AND THE LONGER WE SIT ON OUR HANDS, THE--

PATIENCE, LYN.

PATIENCE?! MY LORD, I--

DO YOU REMEMBER THE LAST TIME WE WERE HERE?

HOW COULD I NOT?

I MADE YOU A PROMISE, RIGHT HERE, ON THIS SPOT. IF YOU HELPED ME DEFEAT HORDAK, ONE DAY I WOULD GIVE YOU ALL THE POWER YOU COULD EVER THINK TO DESIRE.

THAT DAY HAS, AT LAST, ARRIVED.

I DID IT, LYN. JUST AS WE LOST THE TELEPATHIC CONNECTION, WHEN HE-MAN STORMED IN--THERE WAS A BLINDING LIGHT AND SOMETHING... UNLOCKED...

THE SECRETS OF THE ORLAX...

AND SO MUCH MORE.

SOMETHING IS COMING. SOMETHING TERRIBLE AND DANGEROUS AND...USEFUL.

WHAT A FOOL I'VE BEEN!

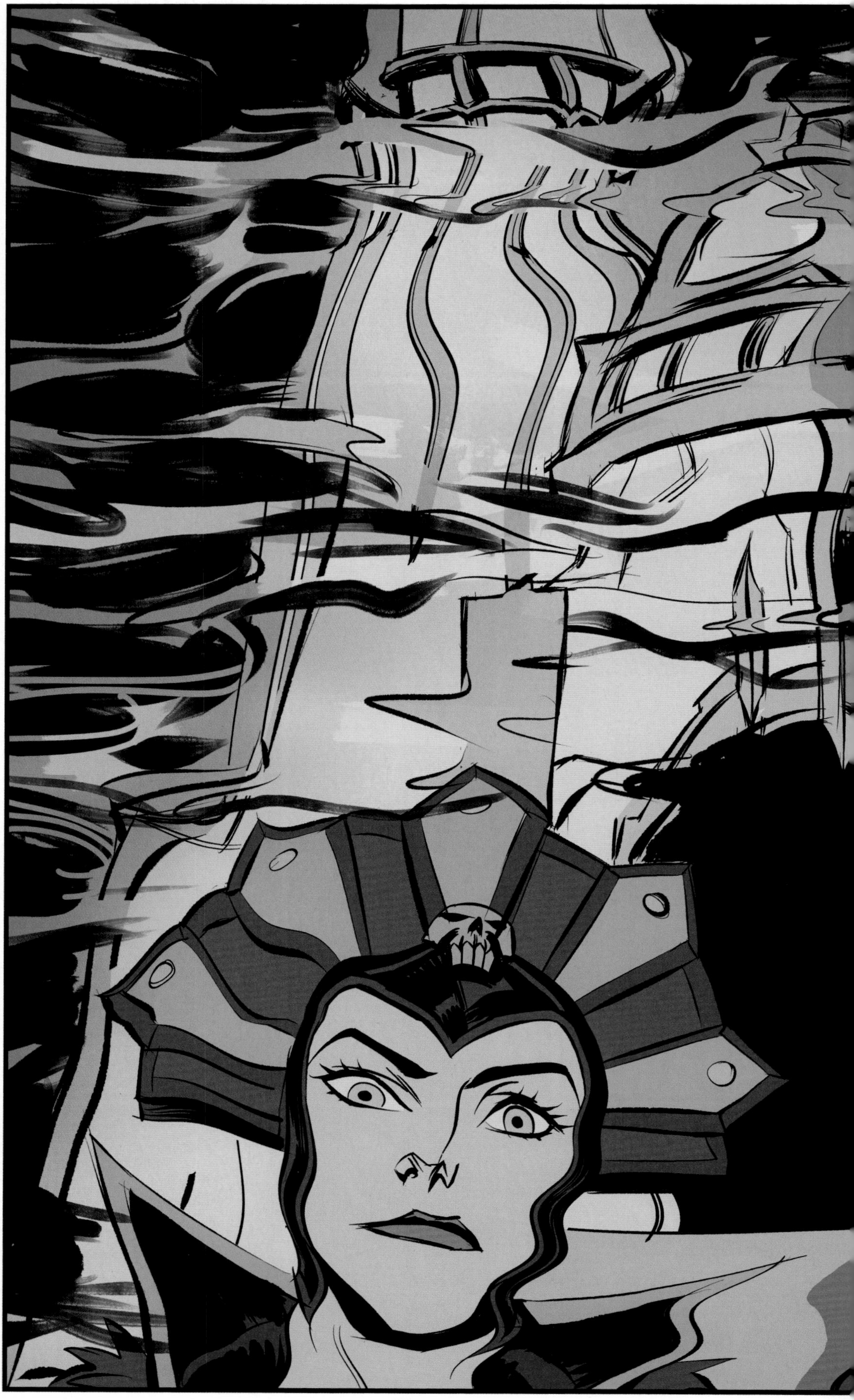

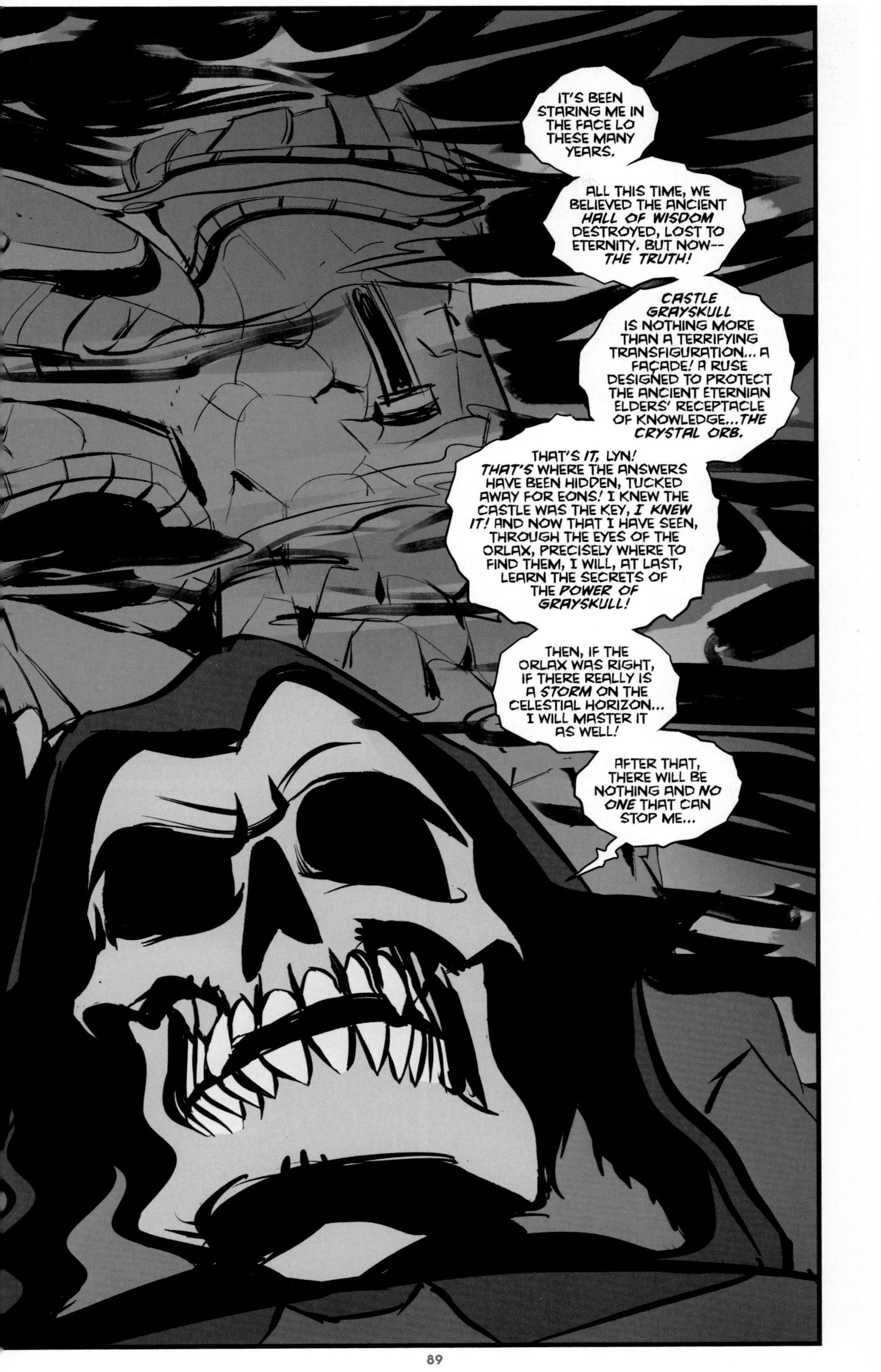
IT'S BEEN STARING ME IN THE FACE LO THESE MANY YEARS.
ALL THIS TIME, WE BELIEVED THE ANCIENT HALL OF WISDOM DESTROYED, LOST TO ETERNITY. BUT NOW-- THE TRUTH!
CASTLE GRAYSKULL IS NOTHING MORE THAN A TERRIFYING TRANSFIGURATION... A FACADE! A RUSE DESIGNED TO PROTECT THE ANCIENT ETERNIAN ELDERS' RECEPTACLE OF KNOWLEDGE...THE CRYSTAL ORB.
THAT'S IT, LYN! THAT'S WHERE THE ANSWERS HAVE BEEN HIDDEN, TUCKED AWAY FOR EONS! I KNEW THE CASTLE WAS THE KEY, I KNEW IT! AND NOW THAT I HAVE SEEN, THROUGH THE EYES OF THE ORLAX, PRECISELY WHERE TO FIND THEM, I WILL, AT LAST, LEARN THE SECRETS OF THE POWER OF GRAYSKULL!
THEN, IF THE ORLAX WAS RIGHT, IF THERE REALLY IS A STORM ON THE CELESTIAL HORIZON... I WILL MASTER IT AS WELL!
AFTER THAT, THERE WILL BE NOTHING AND NO ONE THAT CAN STOP ME...

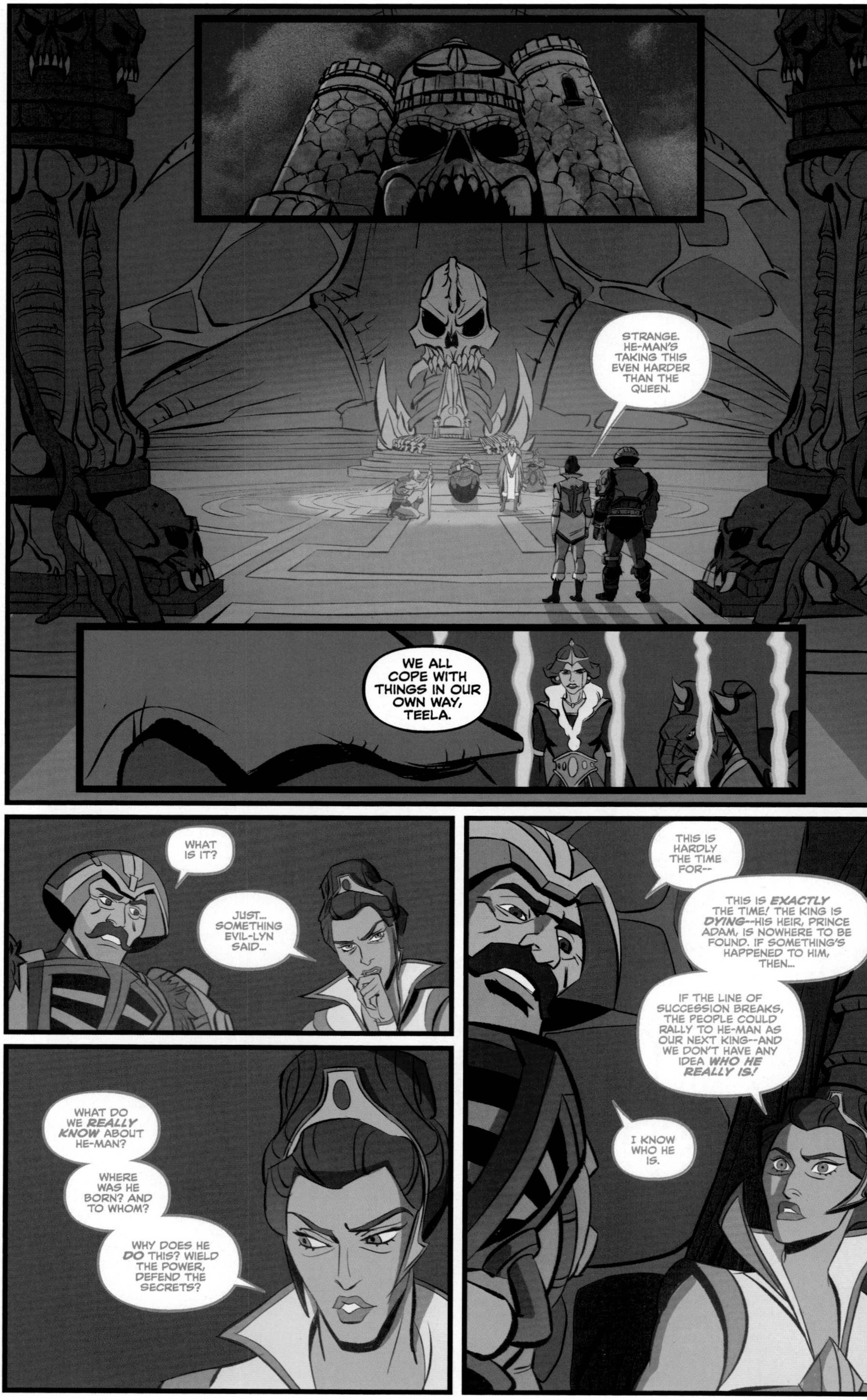
STRANGE. HE-MAN'S TAKING THIS EVEN HARDER THAN THE QUEEN.
WE ALL COPE WITH THINGS IN OUR OWN WAY, TEELA.
WHAT IS IT?
JUST... SOMETHING EVIL-LYN SAID...
WHAT DO WE REALLY KNOW ABOUT HE-MAN?
WHERE WAS HE BORN? AND TO WHOM?
WHY DOES HE DO THIS? WIELD THE POWER, DEFEND THE SECRETS?
THIS IS HARDLY THE TIME FOR--
THIS IS EXACTLY THE TIME! THE KING IS DYING--HIS HEIR, PRINCE ADAM, IS NOWHERE TO BE FOUND. IF SOMETHING'S HAPPENED TO HIM, THEN...
IF THE LINE OF SUCCESSION BREAKS, THE PEOPLE COULD RALLY TO HE-MAN AS OUR NEXT KING--AND WE DON'T HAVE ANY IDEA WHO HE REALLY IS!
I KNOW WHO HE IS.

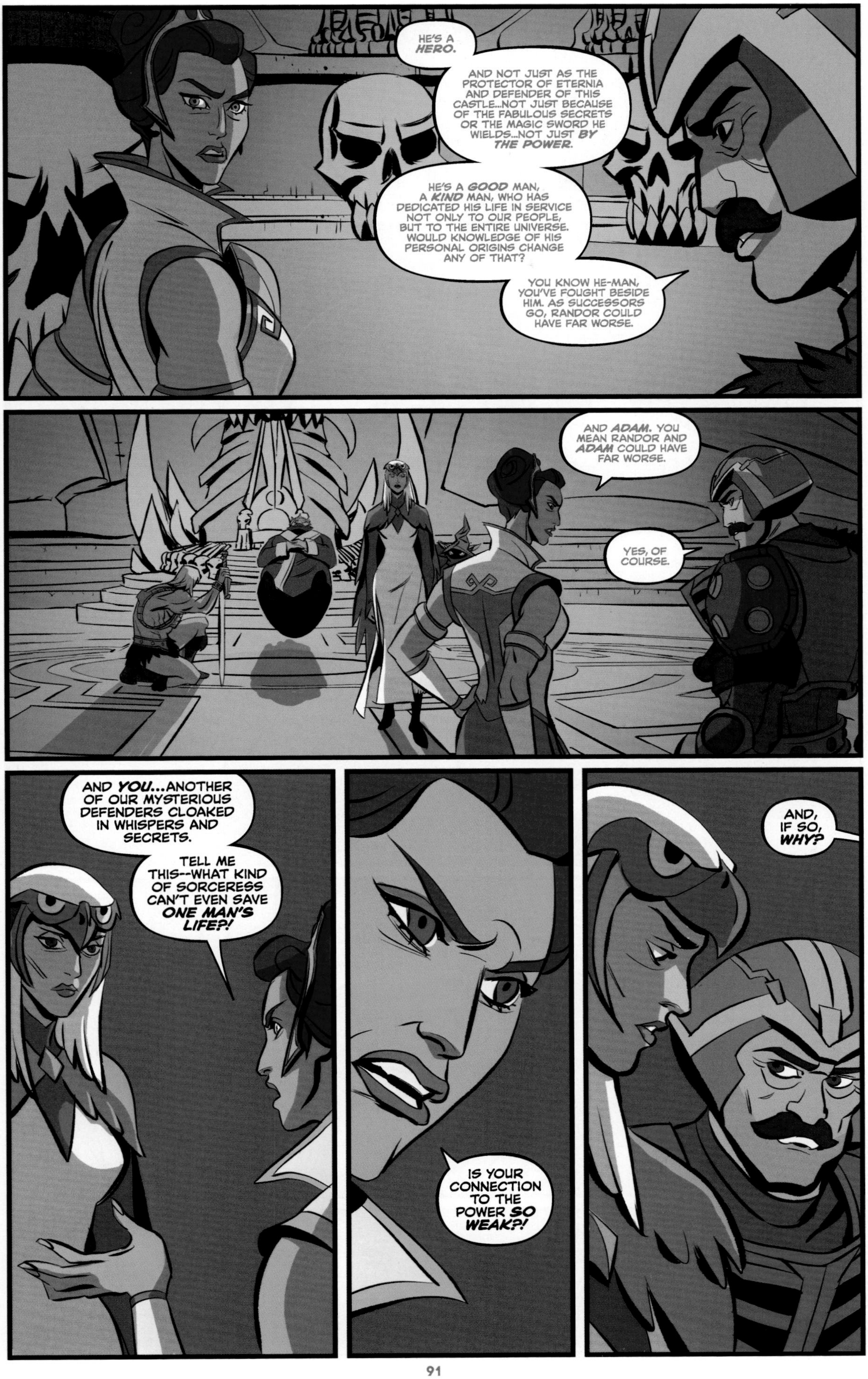
HE'S A **HERO**.
AND NOT JUST AS THE PROTECTOR OF ETERNIA AND DEFENDER OF THIS CASTLE...NOT JUST BECAUSE OF THE FABULOUS SECRETS OR THE MAGIC SWORD HE WIELDS...NOT JUST **BY THE POWER**.
HE'S A **GOOD** MAN, A **KIND** MAN, WHO HAS DEDICATED HIS LIFE IN SERVICE NOT ONLY TO OUR PEOPLE, BUT TO THE ENTIRE UNIVERSE. WOULD KNOWLEDGE OF HIS PERSONAL ORIGINS CHANGE ANY OF THAT?
YOU KNOW HE-MAN, YOU'VE FOUGHT BESIDE HIM. AS SUCCESSORS GO, RANDOR COULD HAVE FAR WORSE.
AND **ADAM**. YOU MEAN RANDOR AND **ADAM** COULD HAVE FAR WORSE.
YES, OF COURSE.
AND **YOU**...ANOTHER OF OUR MYSTERIOUS DEFENDERS CLOAKED IN WHISPERS AND SECRETS.
TELL ME THIS--WHAT KIND OF SORCERESS CAN'T EVEN SAVE **ONE MAN'S LIFE?!**
IS YOUR CONNECTION TO THE POWER **SO WEAK?!**
AND, IF SO, **WHY?**

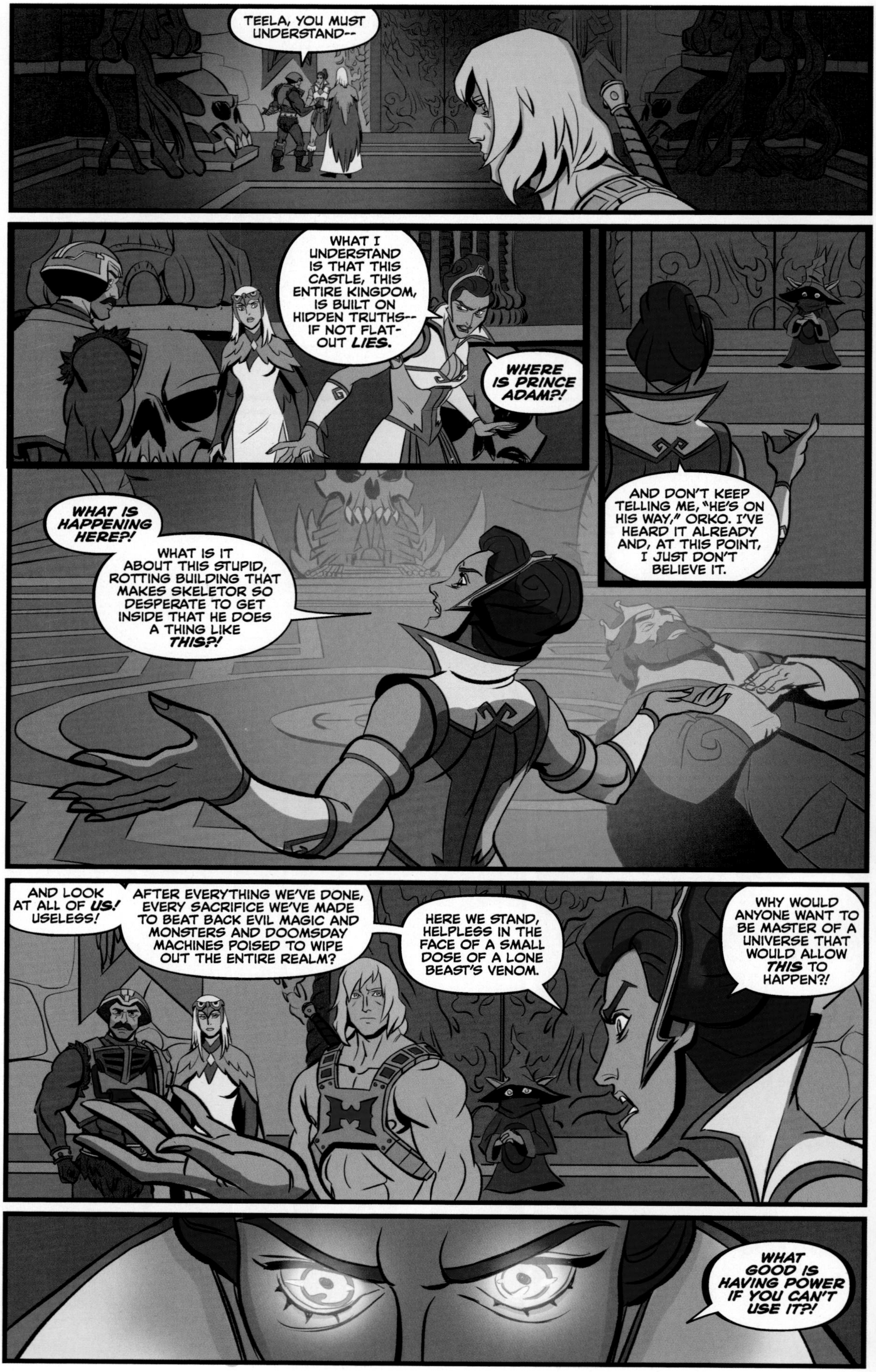
TEELA, YOU MUST UNDERSTAND--
WHAT I UNDERSTAND IS THAT THIS CASTLE, THIS ENTIRE KINGDOM, IS BUILT ON HIDDEN TRUTHS-- IF NOT FLAT-OUT LIES.
WHERE IS PRINCE ADAM?!
AND DON'T KEEP TELLING ME, "HE'S ON HIS WAY," ORKO. I'VE HEARD IT ALREADY AND, AT THIS POINT, I JUST DON'T BELIEVE IT.
WHAT IS HAPPENING HERE?!
WHAT IS IT ABOUT THIS STUPID, ROTTING BUILDING THAT MAKES SKELETOR SO DESPERATE TO GET INSIDE THAT HE DOES A THING LIKE THIS?!
AND LOOK AT ALL OF US! USELESS!
AFTER EVERYTHING WE'VE DONE, EVERY SACRIFICE WE'VE MADE TO BEAT BACK EVIL MAGIC AND MONSTERS AND DOOMSDAY MACHINES POISED TO WIPE OUT THE ENTIRE REALM?
HERE WE STAND, HELPLESS IN THE FACE OF A SMALL DOSE OF A LONE BEAST'S VENOM.
WHY WOULD ANYONE WANT TO BE MASTER OF A UNIVERSE THAT WOULD ALLOW THIS TO HAPPEN?!
WHAT GOOD IS HAVING POWER IF YOU CAN'T USE IT?!

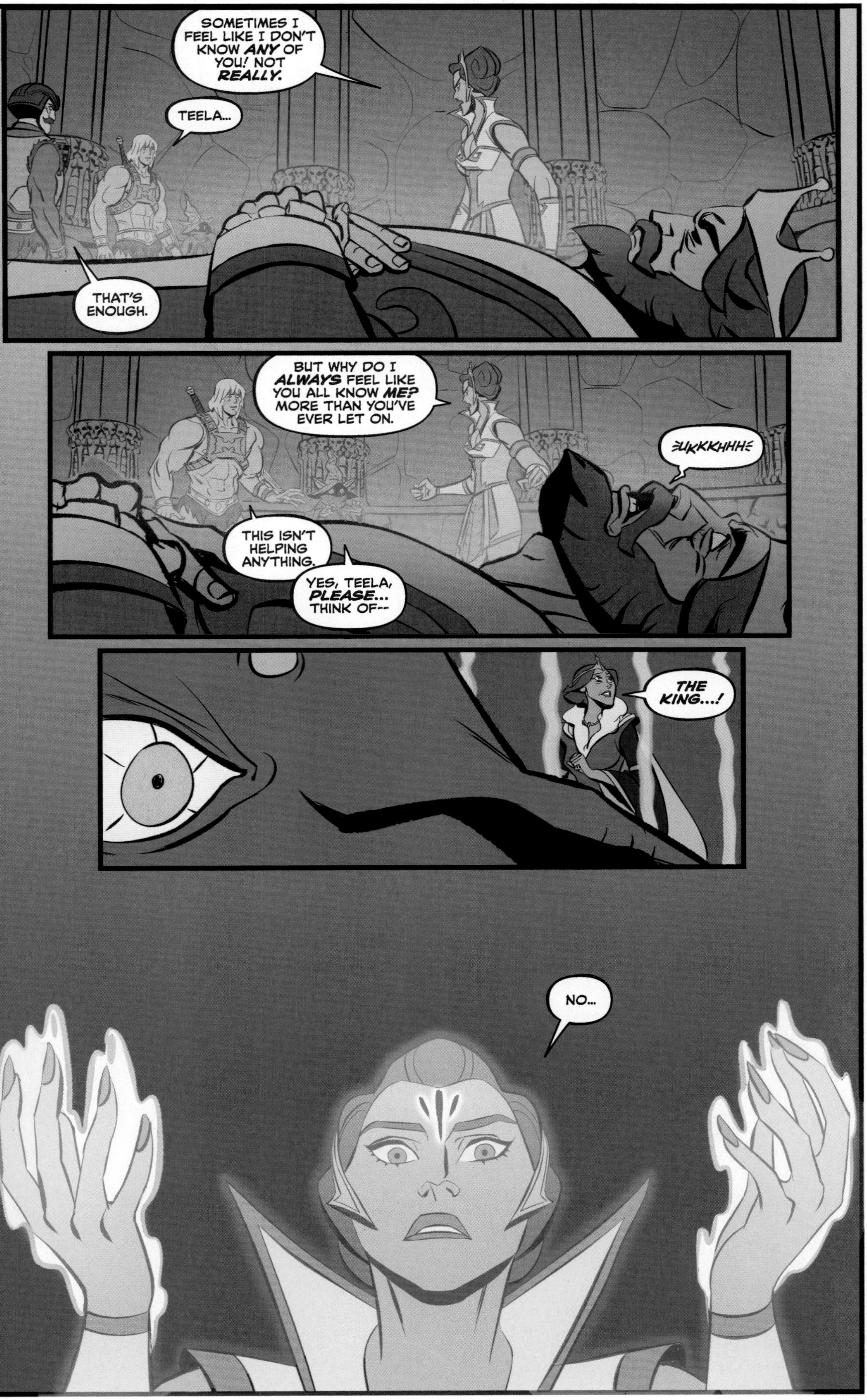
SOMETIMES I FEEL LIKE I DON'T KNOW ANY OF YOU! NOT REALLY.
TEELA...
THAT'S ENOUGH.
BUT WHY DO I ALWAYS FEEL LIKE YOU ALL KNOW ME? MORE THAN YOU'VE EVER LET ON.
UKKKHHH
THIS ISN'T HELPING ANYTHING.
YES, TEELA, PLEASE... THINK OF--
THE KING...!
NO...

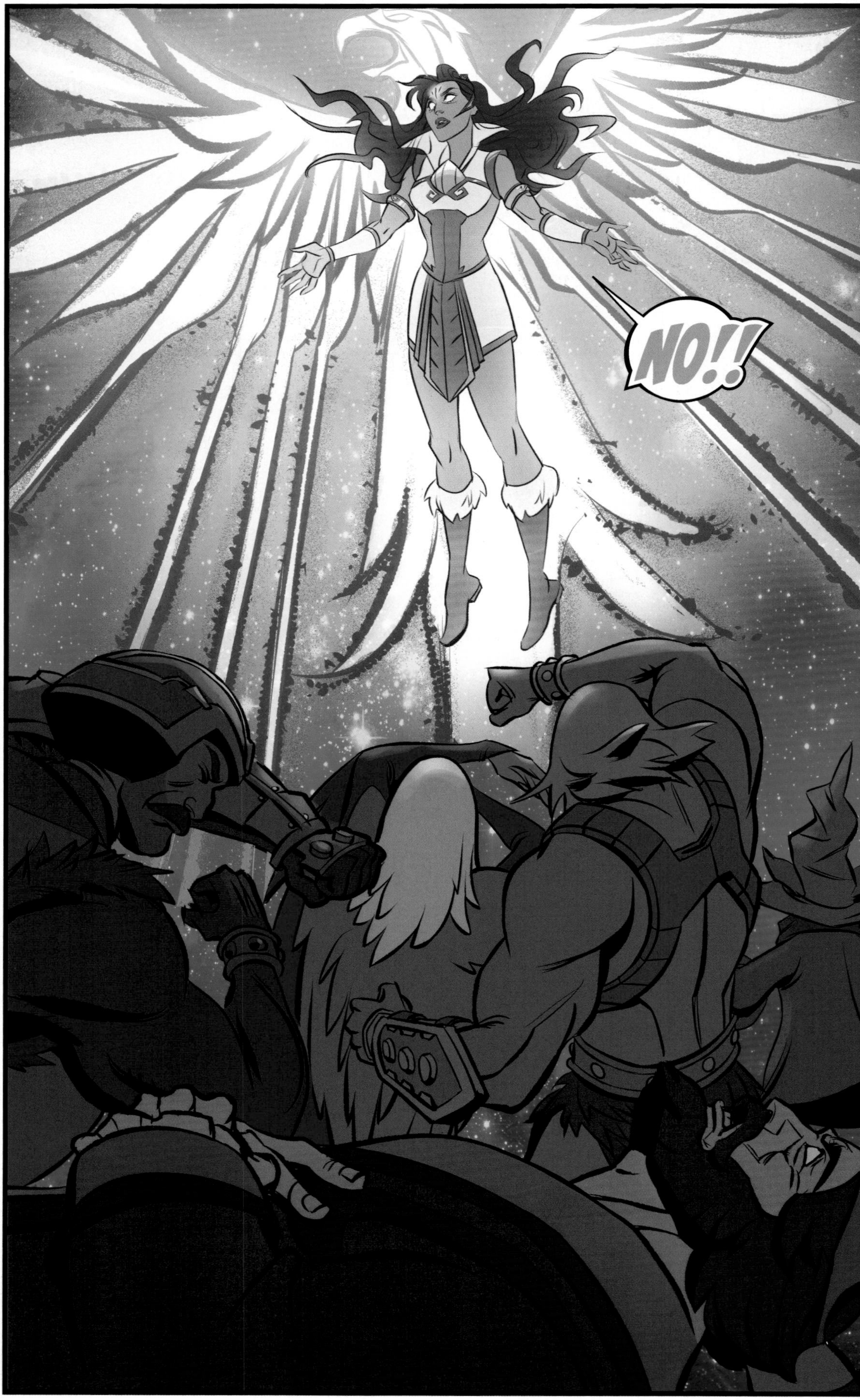
NO!!

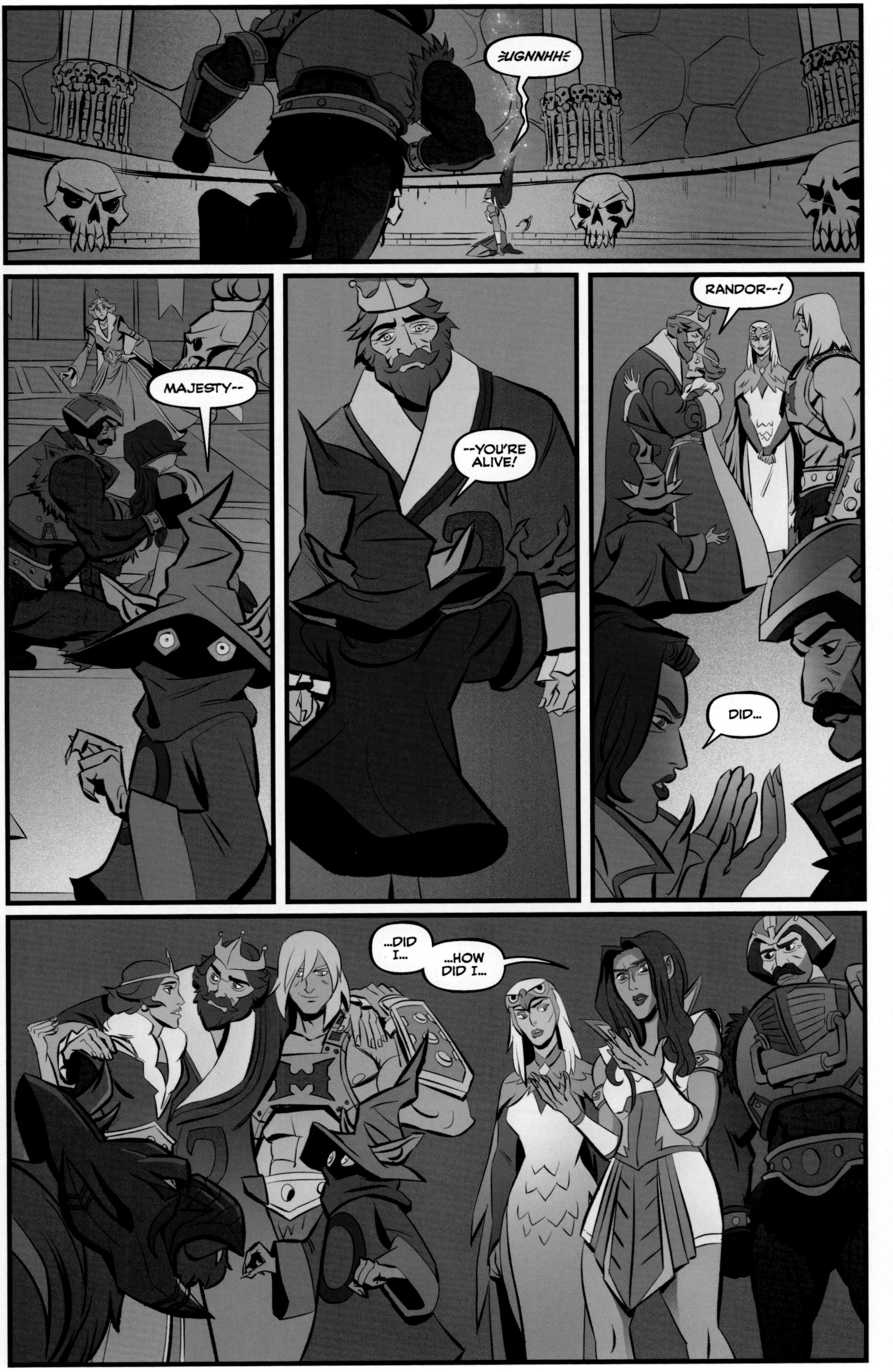
UGNNHH
MAJESTY--
--YOU'RE ALIVE!
RANDOR--!
DID...
...DID I...
...HOW DID I...

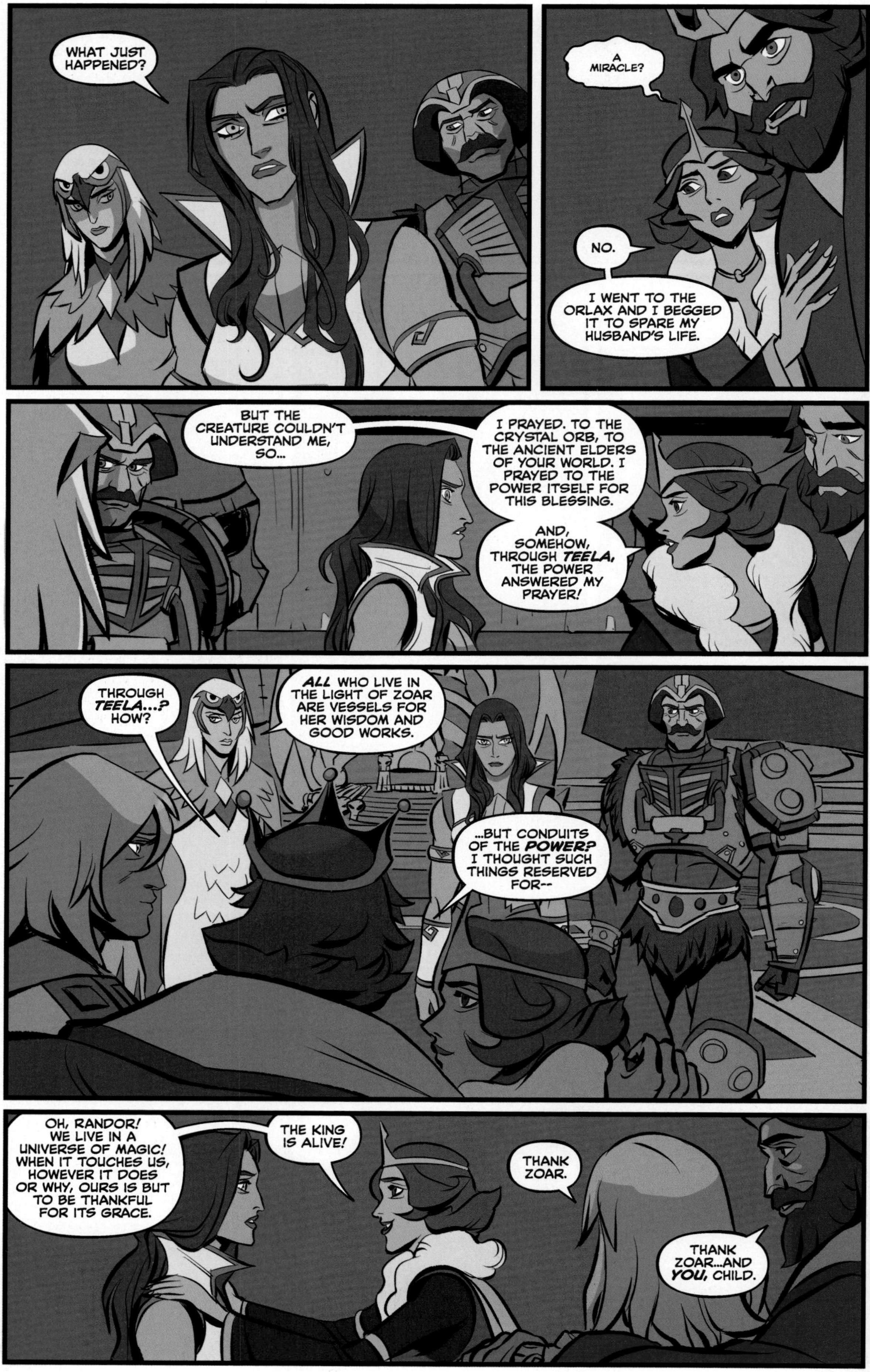
WHAT JUST HAPPENED?
A MIRACLE?
NO.
I WENT TO THE ORLAX AND I BEGGED IT TO SPARE MY HUSBAND'S LIFE.
BUT THE CREATURE COULDN'T UNDERSTAND ME, SO...
I PRAYED. TO THE CRYSTAL ORB, TO THE ANCIENT ELDERS OF YOUR WORLD. I PRAYED TO THE POWER ITSELF FOR THIS BLESSING.
AND, SOMEHOW, THROUGH *TEELA*, THE POWER ANSWERED MY PRAYER!
THROUGH *TEELA...?* HOW?
ALL WHO LIVE IN THE LIGHT OF ZOAR ARE VESSELS FOR HER WISDOM AND GOOD WORKS.
...BUT CONDUITS OF THE *POWER?* I THOUGHT SUCH THINGS RESERVED FOR--
OH, RANDOR! WE LIVE IN A UNIVERSE OF MAGIC! WHEN IT TOUCHES US, HOWEVER IT DOES OR WHY, OURS IS BUT TO BE THANKFUL FOR ITS GRACE.
THE KING IS ALIVE!
THANK ZOAR.
THANK ZOAR...AND *YOU,* CHILD.

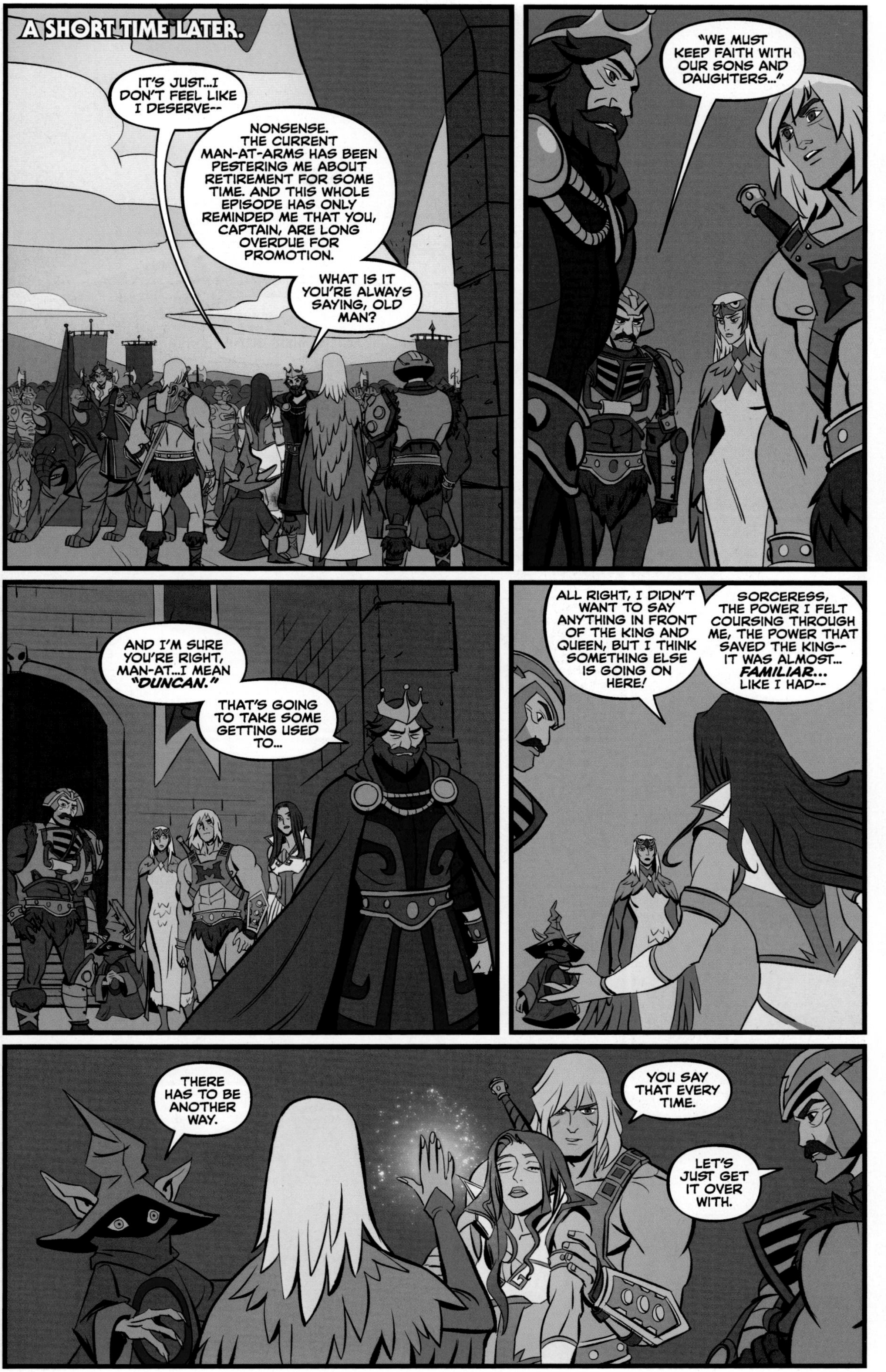
A SHORT TIME LATER.
IT'S JUST...I DON'T FEEL LIKE I DESERVE--
NONSENSE. THE CURRENT MAN-AT-ARMS HAS BEEN PESTERING ME ABOUT RETIREMENT FOR SOME TIME. AND THIS WHOLE EPISODE HAS ONLY REMINDED ME THAT YOU, CAPTAIN, ARE LONG OVERDUE FOR PROMOTION.
WHAT IS IT YOU'RE ALWAYS SAYING, OLD MAN?
"WE MUST KEEP FAITH WITH OUR SONS AND DAUGHTERS..."
AND I'M SURE YOU'RE RIGHT, MAN-AT...I MEAN *"DUNCAN."*
THAT'S GOING TO TAKE SOME GETTING USED TO...
ALL RIGHT, I DIDN'T WANT TO SAY ANYTHING IN FRONT OF THE KING AND QUEEN, BUT I THINK SOMETHING ELSE IS GOING ON HERE!
SORCERESS, THE POWER I FELT COURSING THROUGH ME, THE POWER THAT SAVED THE KING-- IT WAS ALMOST... *FAMILIAR...* LIKE I HAD--
THERE HAS TO BE ANOTHER WAY.
YOU SAY THAT EVERY TIME.
LET'S JUST GET IT OVER WITH.

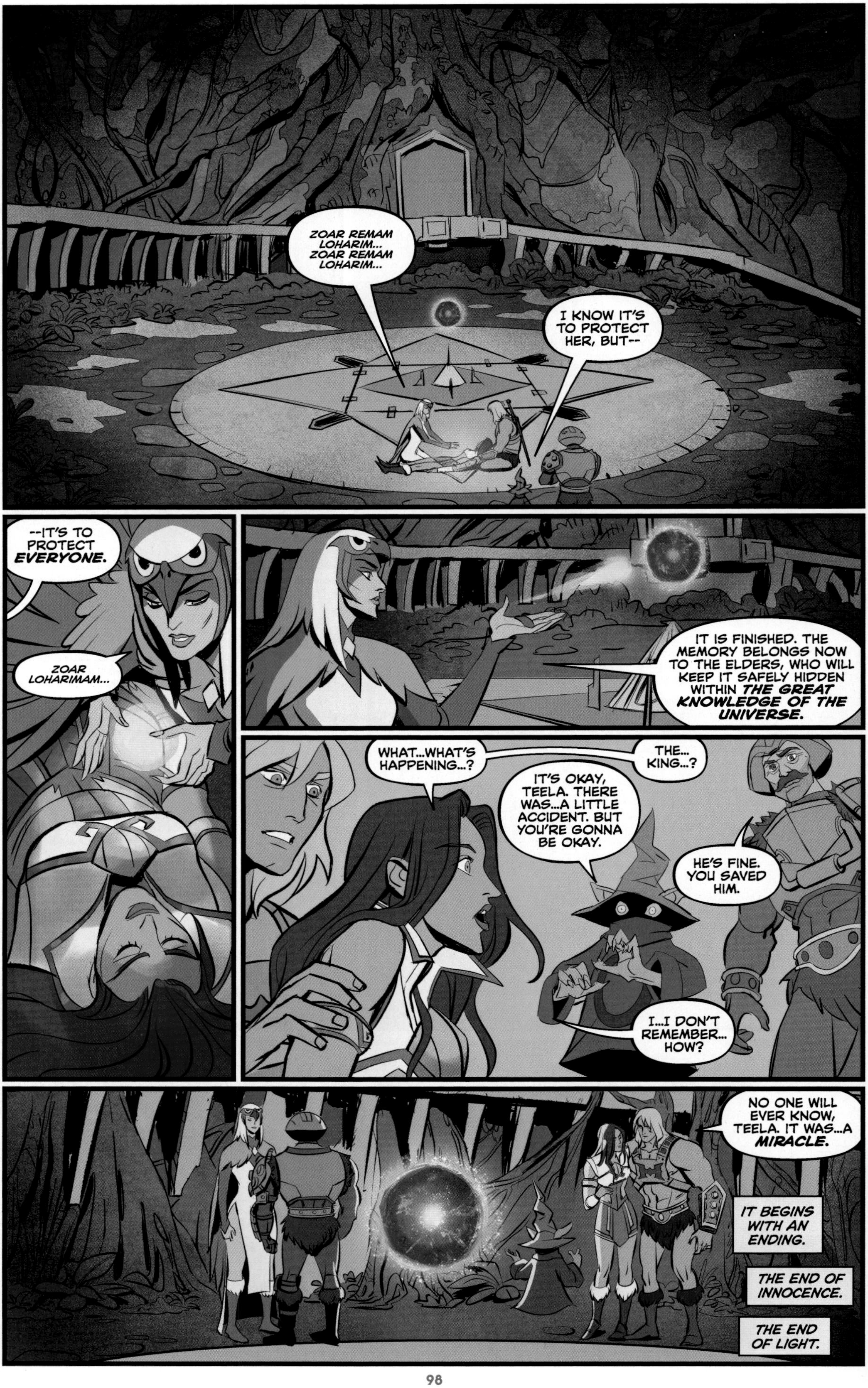
ZOAR REMAM LOHARIM... ZOAR REMAM LOHARIM...
I KNOW IT'S TO PROTECT HER, BUT--
--IT'S TO PROTECT EVERYONE.
ZOAR LOHARIMAM...
IT IS FINISHED. THE MEMORY BELONGS NOW TO THE ELDERS, WHO WILL KEEP IT SAFELY HIDDEN WITHIN THE GREAT KNOWLEDGE OF THE UNIVERSE.
WHAT...WHAT'S HAPPENING...?
THE... KING...?
IT'S OKAY, TEELA. THERE WAS...A LITTLE ACCIDENT. BUT YOU'RE GONNA BE OKAY.
HE'S FINE. YOU SAVED HIM.
I...I DON'T REMEMBER... HOW?
NO ONE WILL EVER KNOW, TEELA. IT WAS...A MIRACLE.
IT BEGINS WITH AN ENDING.
THE END OF INNOCENCE.
THE END OF LIGHT.

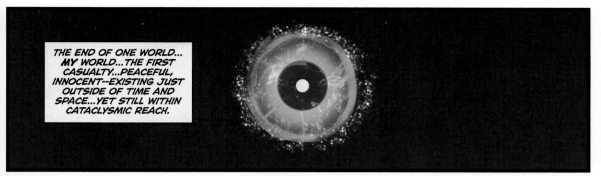

THE END OF ONE WORLD... *MY* WORLD...THE FIRST CASUALTY...PEACEFUL, INNOCENT--EXISTING JUST OUTSIDE OF TIME AND SPACE...YET STILL WITHIN CATACLYSMIC REACH.

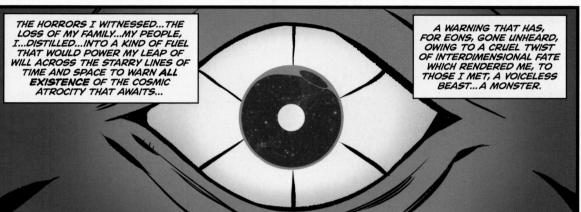

THE HORRORS I WITNESSED...THE LOSS OF MY FAMILY...MY PEOPLE, I...DISTILLED...INTO A KIND OF FUEL THAT WOULD POWER MY LEAP OF WILL ACROSS THE STARRY LINES OF TIME AND SPACE TO WARN *ALL EXISTENCE* OF THE COSMIC ATROCITY THAT AWAITS...

A WARNING THAT HAS, FOR EONS, GONE UNHEARD, OWING TO A CRUEL TWIST OF INTERDIMENSIONAL FATE WHICH RENDERED ME, TO THOSE I MET, A VOICELESS BEAST...A MONSTER.

UNTIL NOW.

MY MESSAGE, MY WARNING CRY, MY *REVELATION*, HAS AT LONG LAST RUNG OUT!

MAY ITS HEARERS *TAKE HEED* AND *CHANGE COURSE* TO AVOID WHAT HAS BEEN WRITTEN IN THE STARS...TO THWART THE HORROR THAT HAS SET ITS SIGHTS ON CREATION...TO SOMEHOW STAY THE HAND OF IMMORTAL DESTINY BEFORE IT CAN BRING TO THEM AS IT BROUGHT TO ME--

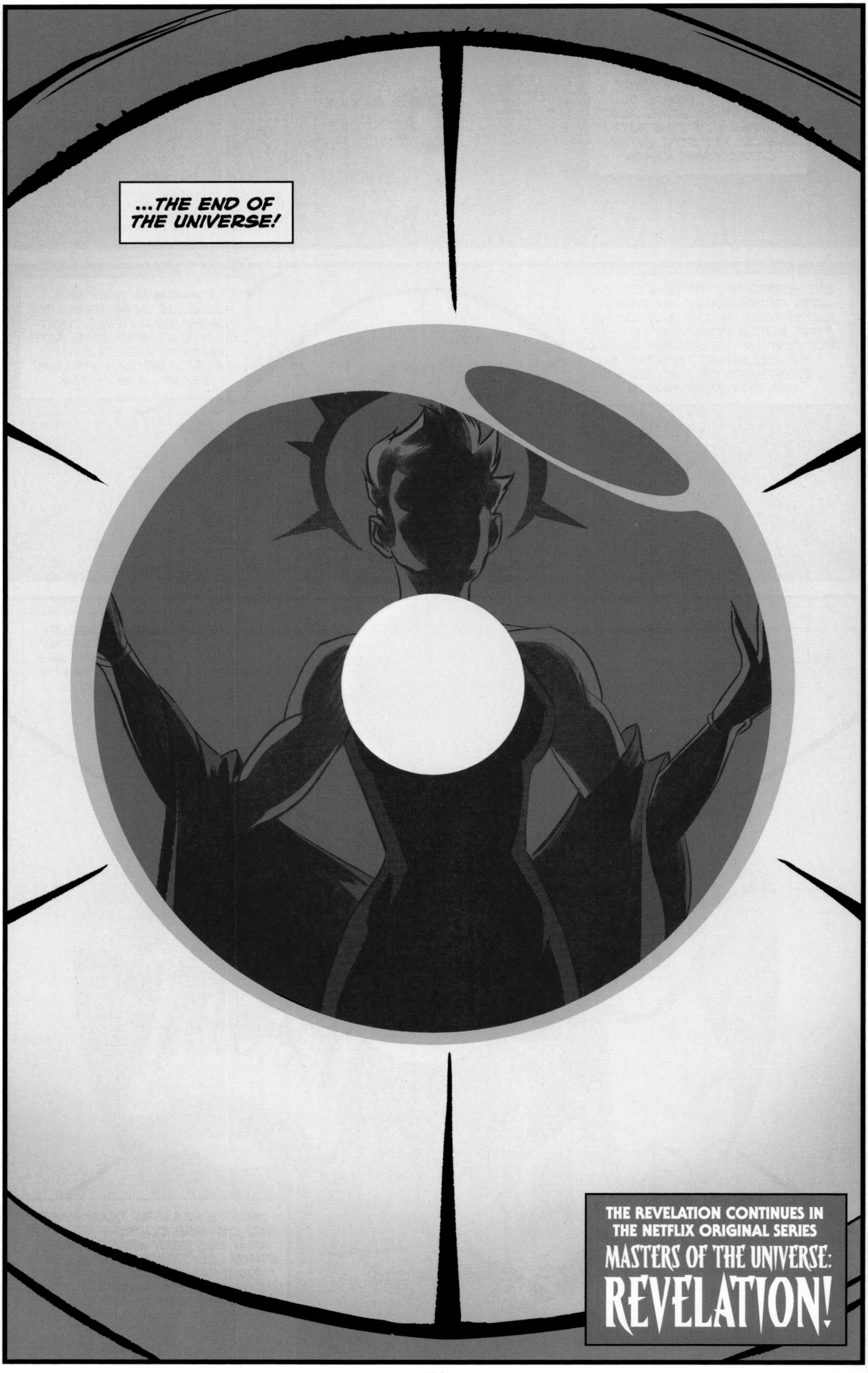
...THE END OF THE UNIVERSE!
THE REVELATION CONTINUES IN THE NETFLIX ORIGINAL SERIES
MASTERS OF THE UNIVERSE: REVELATION!

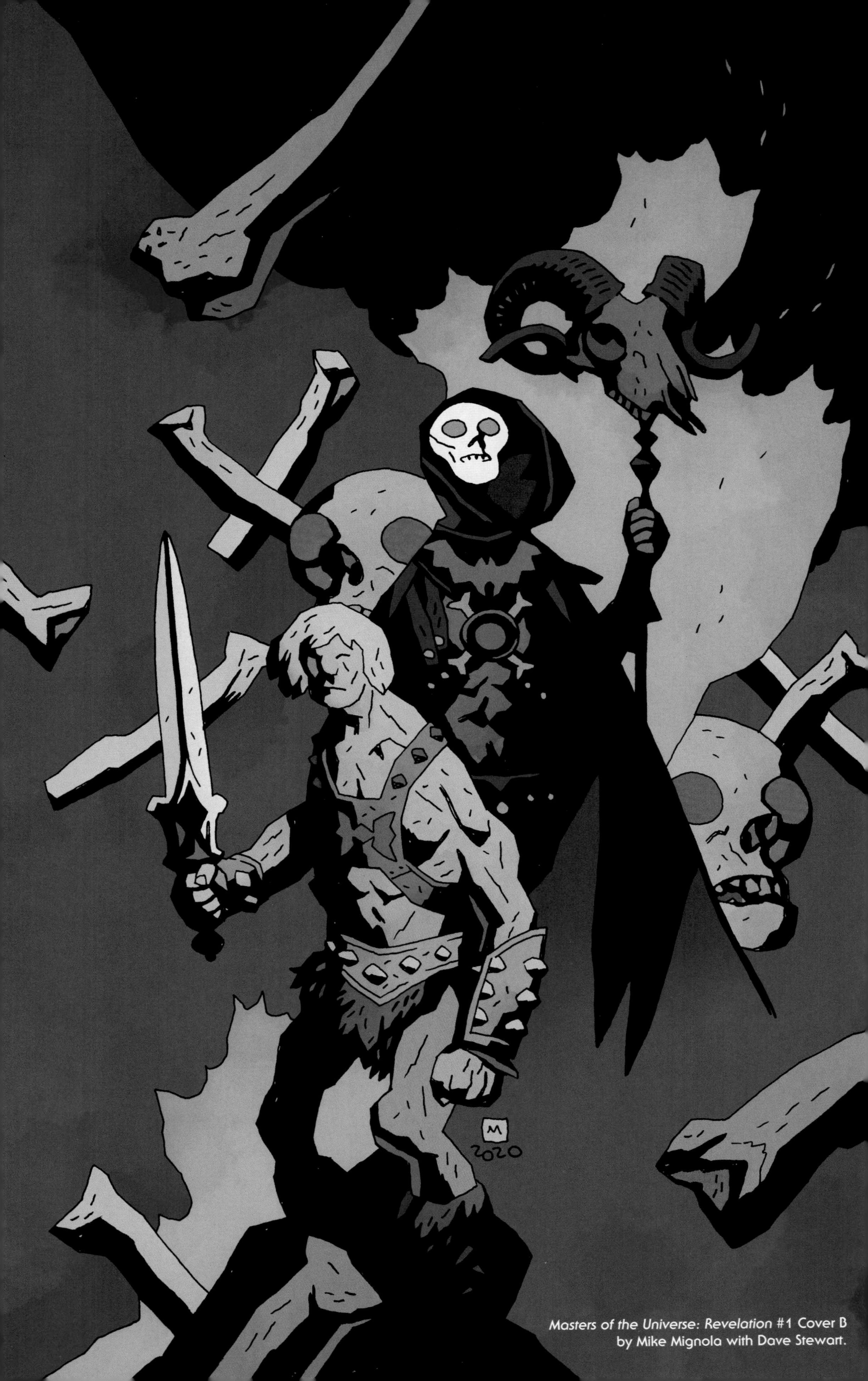

Masters of the Universe: Revelation #1 Cover B
by Mike Mignola with Dave Stewart.

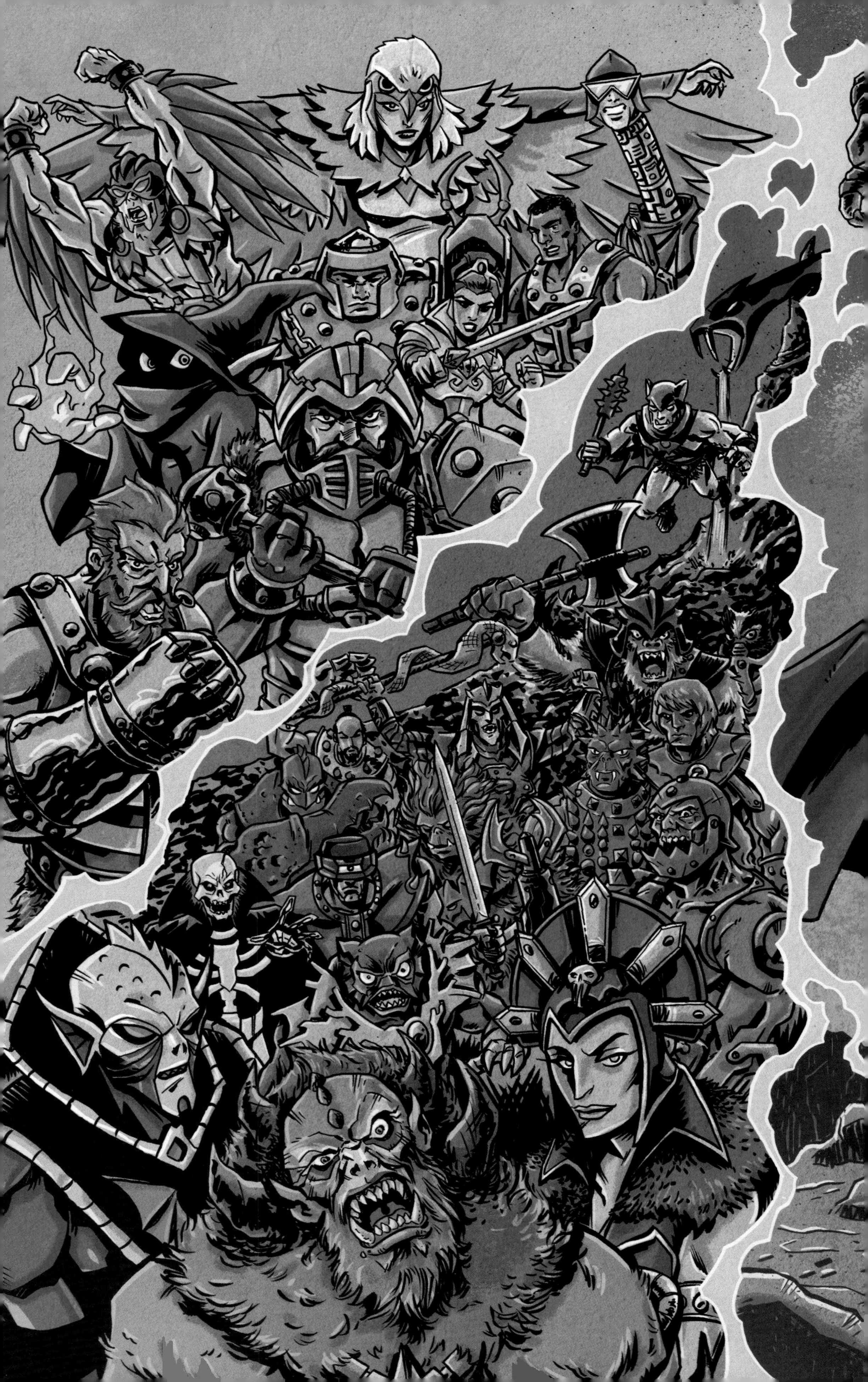

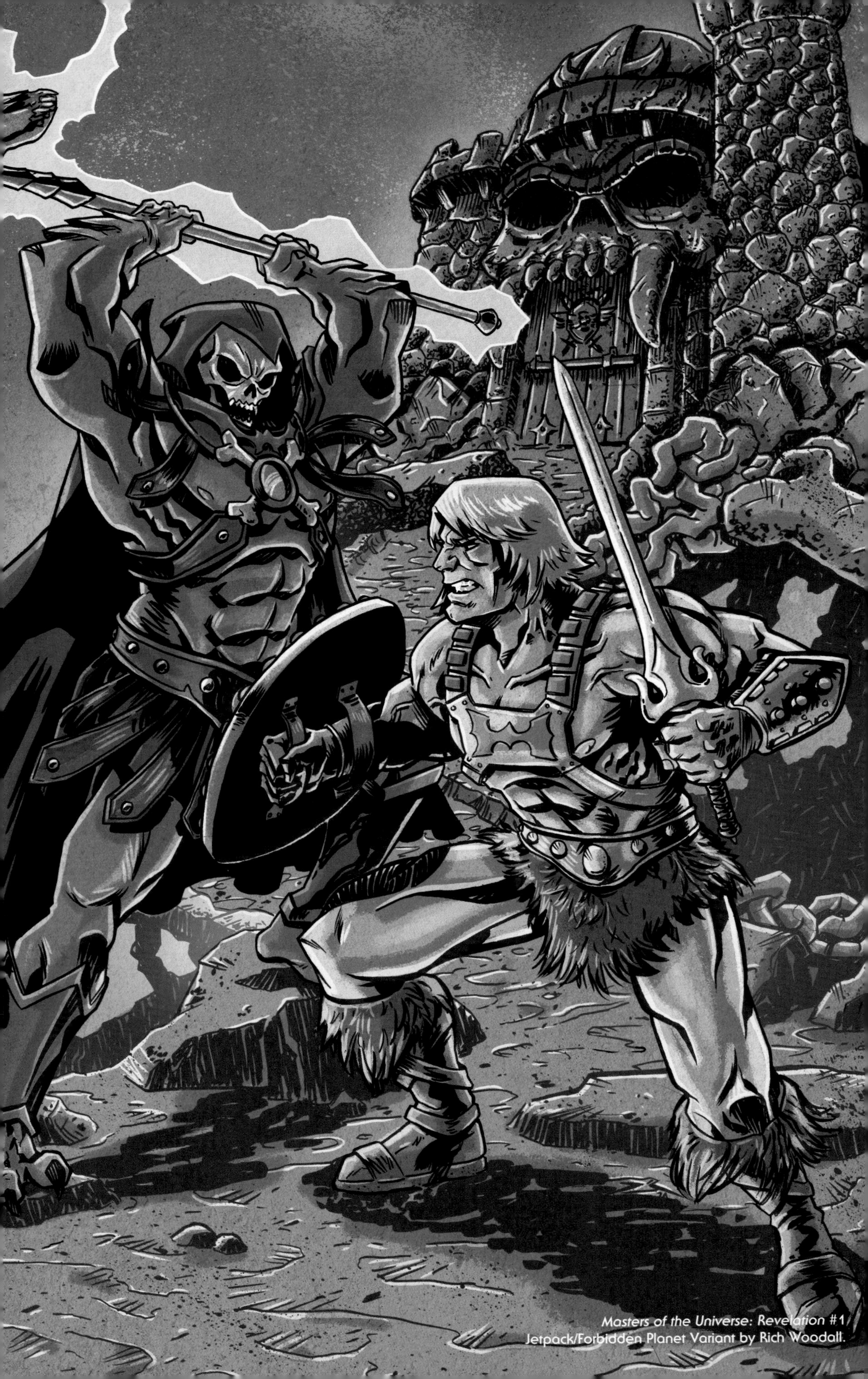

Masters of the Universe: Revelation #1
Jetpack/Forbidden Planet Variant by Rich Woodall.

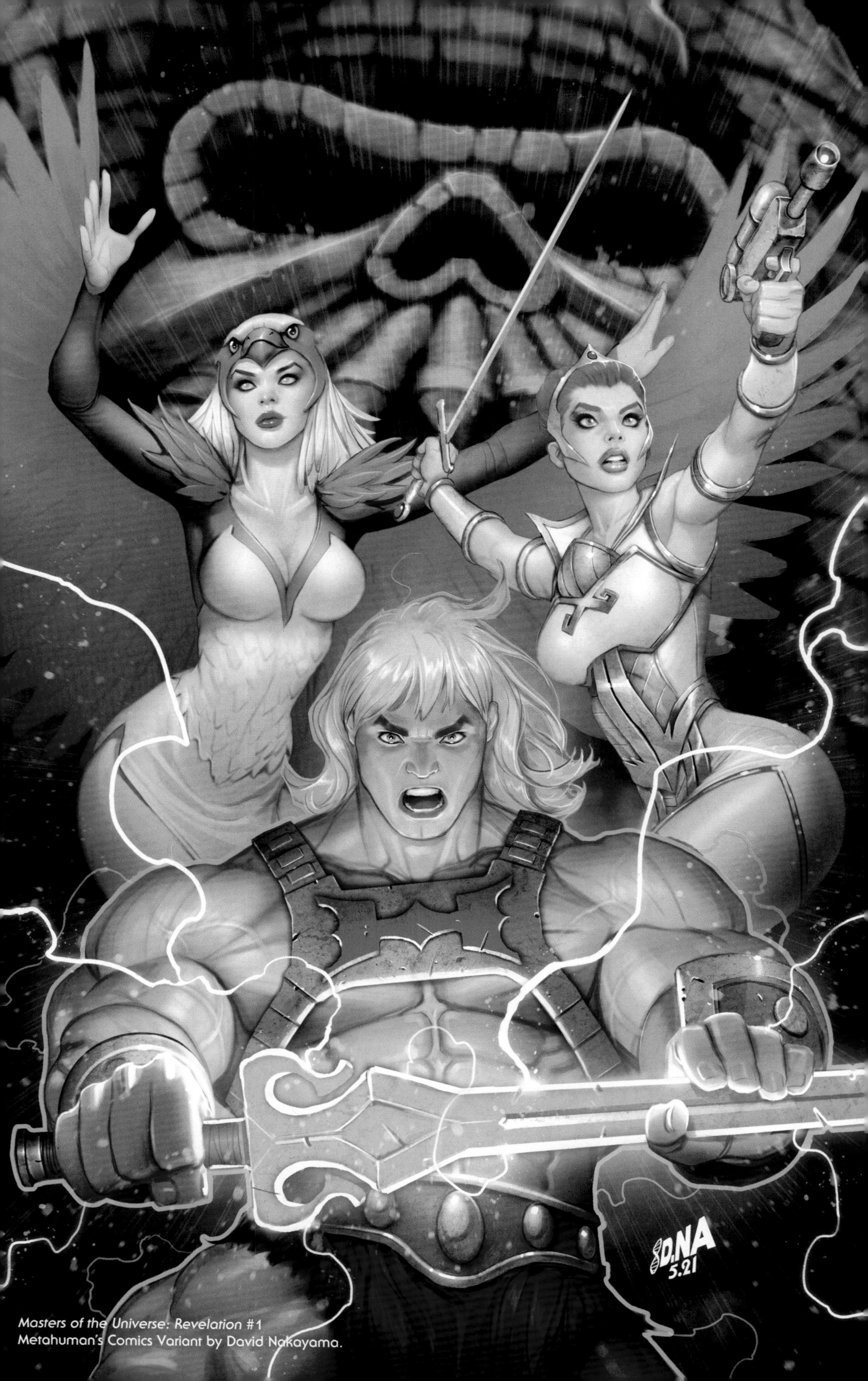
D.NA
5.21

Masters of the Universe: Revelation #1
Metahuman's Comics Variant by David Nakayama.

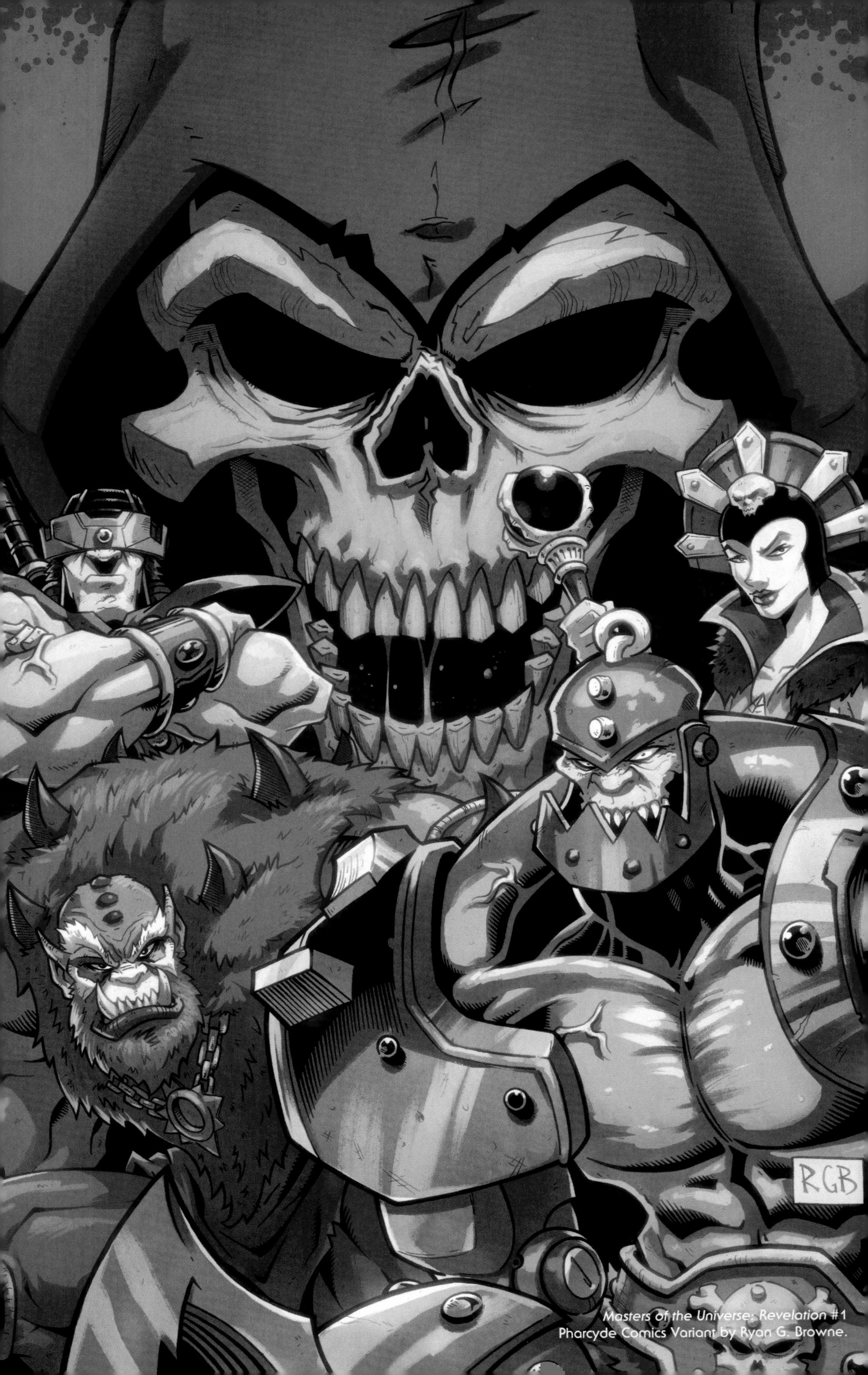
RGB

Masters of the Universe: Revelation #1
Pharcyde Comics Variant by Ryan G. Browne.

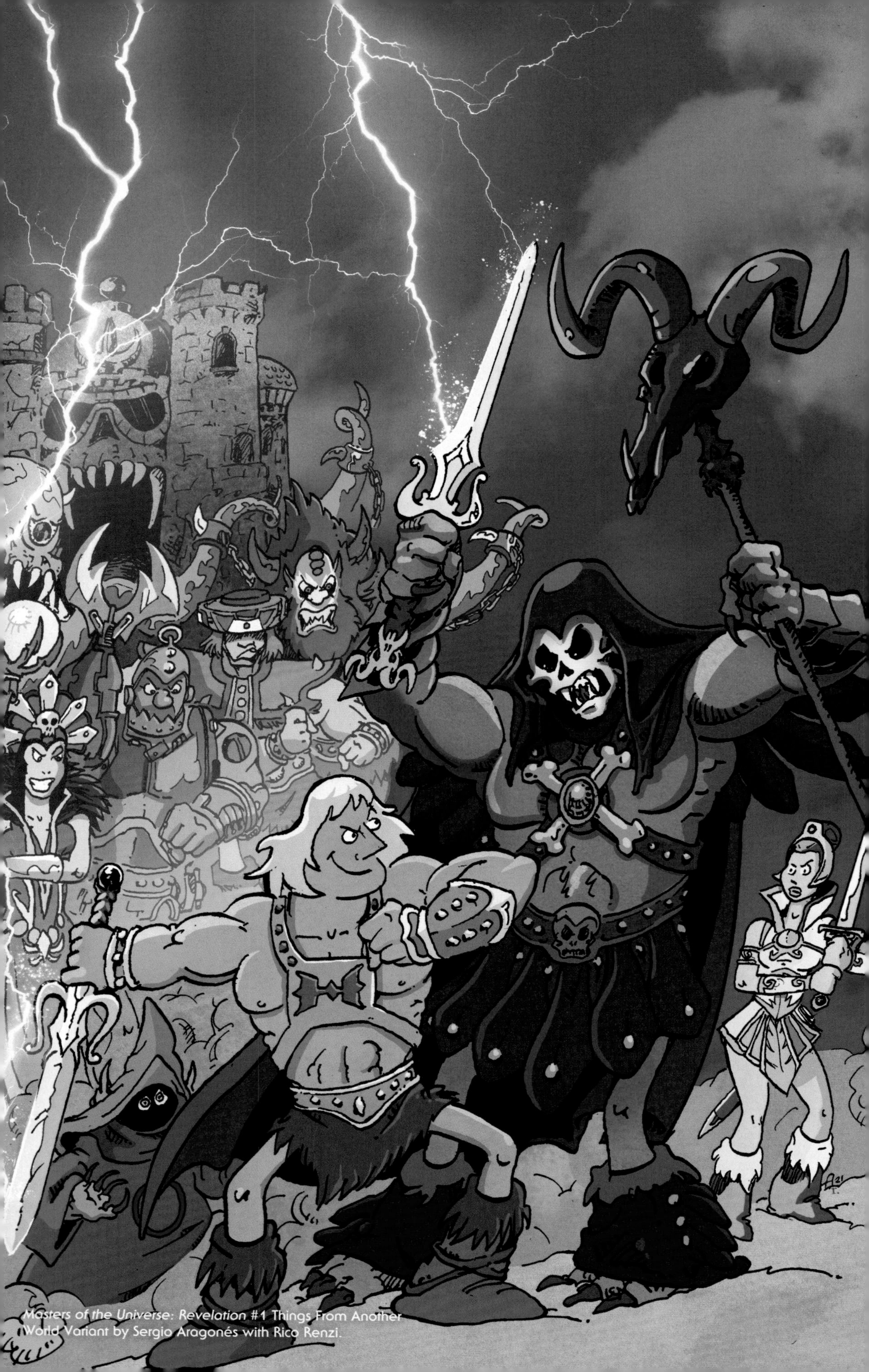

Masters of the Universe: Revelation #1 Things From Another World Variant by Sergio Aragonés with Rico Renzi.

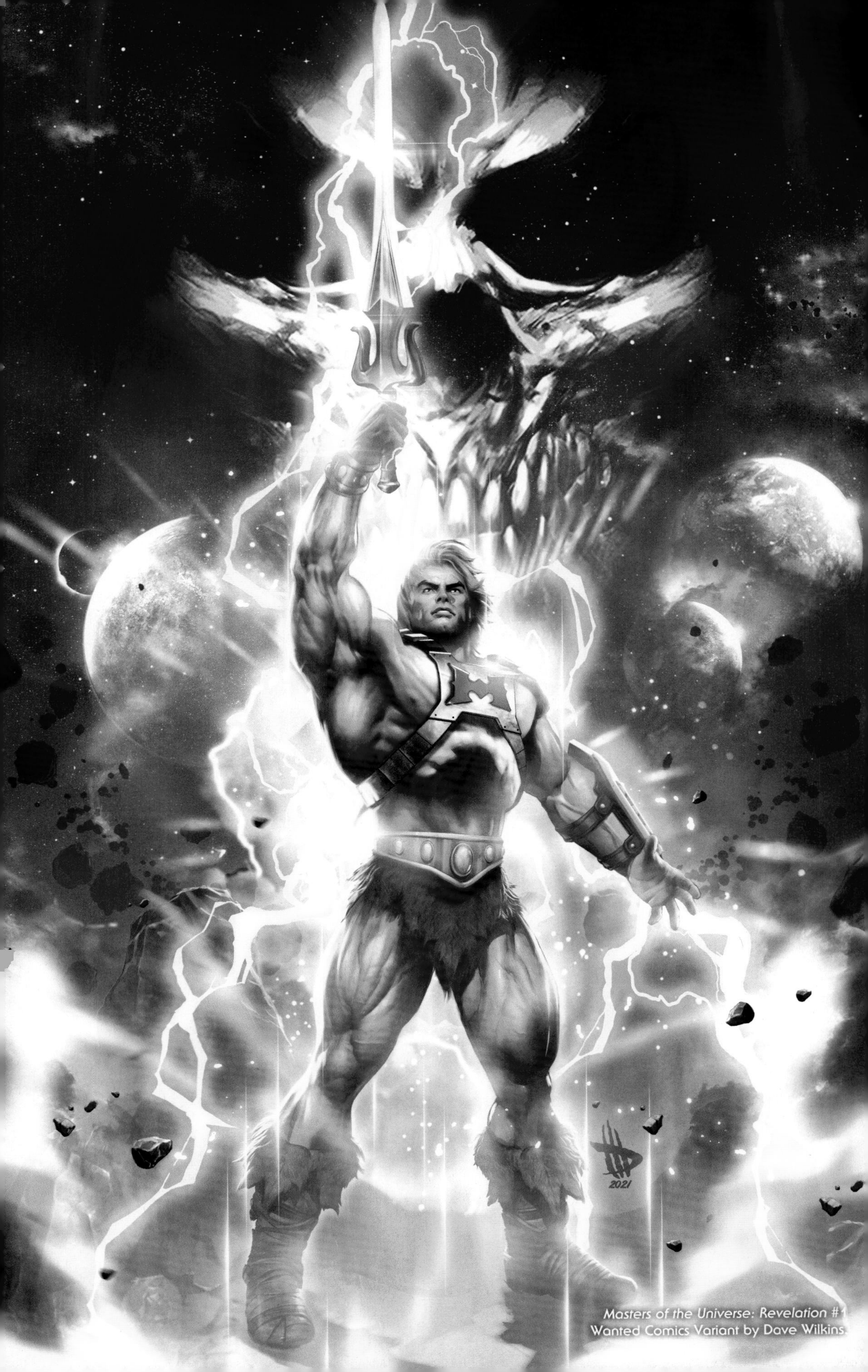
2021

Masters of the Universe: Revelation #1
Wanted Comics Variant by Dave Wilkins

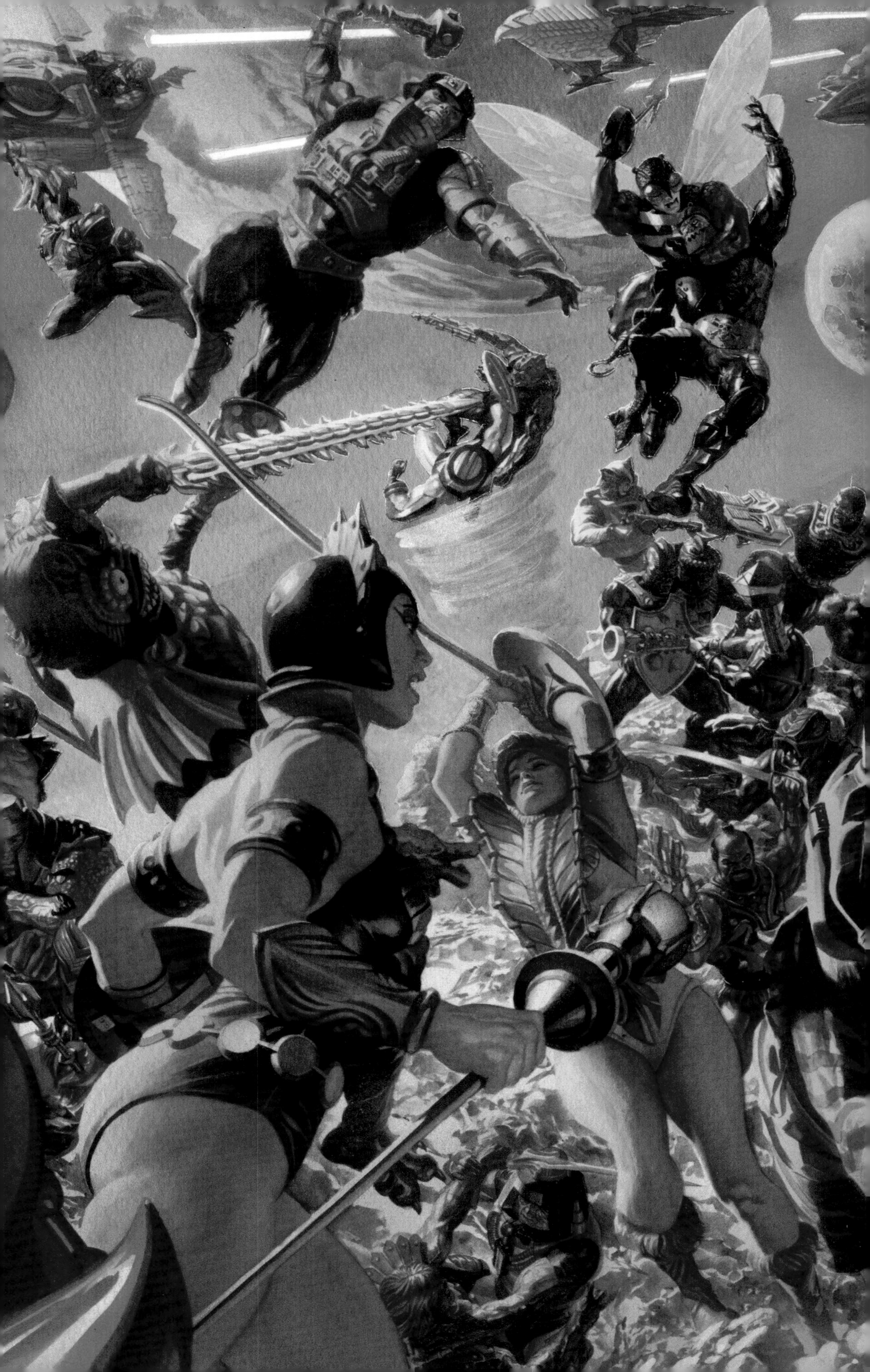

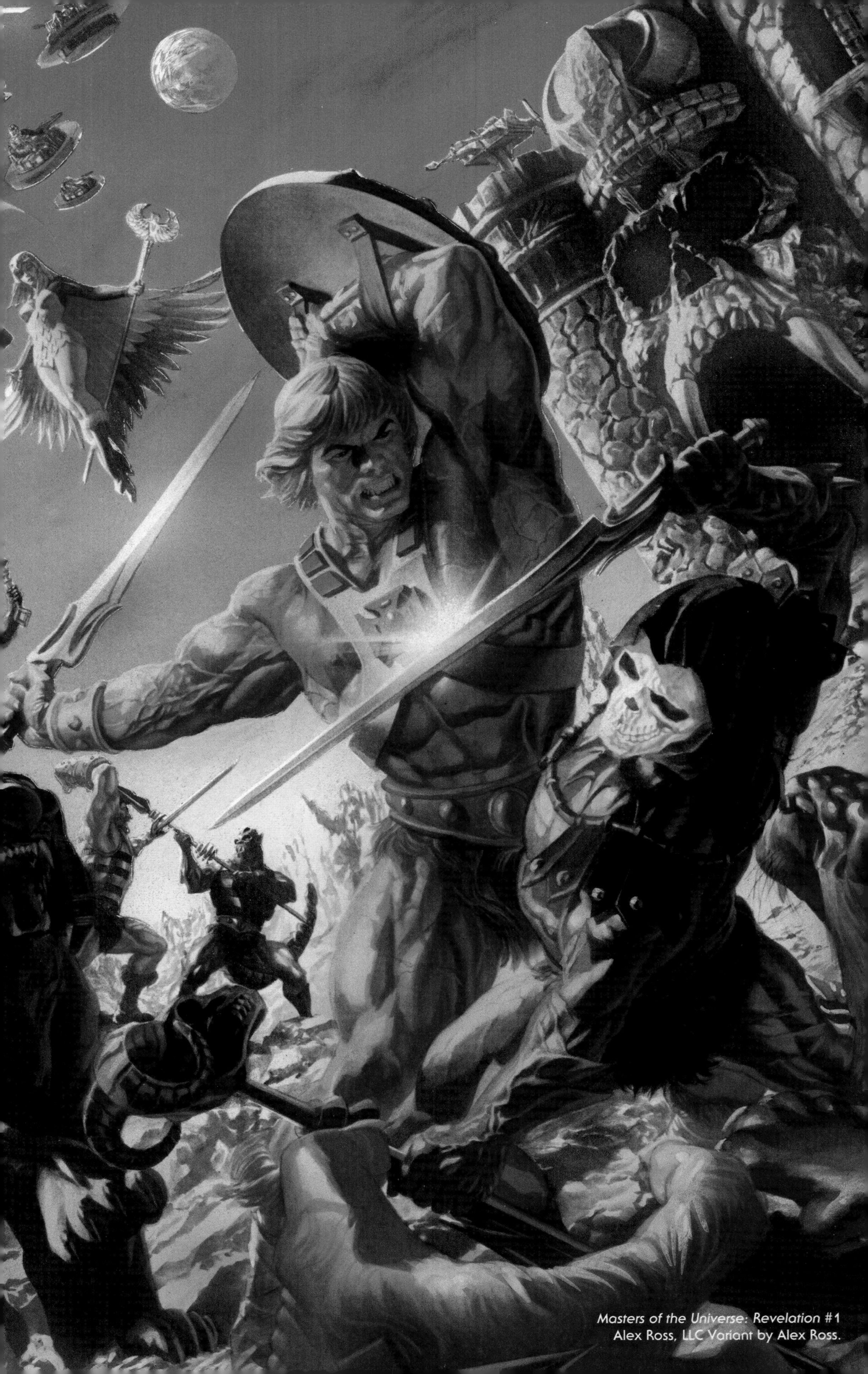

Masters of the Universe: Revelation #1
Alex Ross, LLC Variant by Alex Ross.

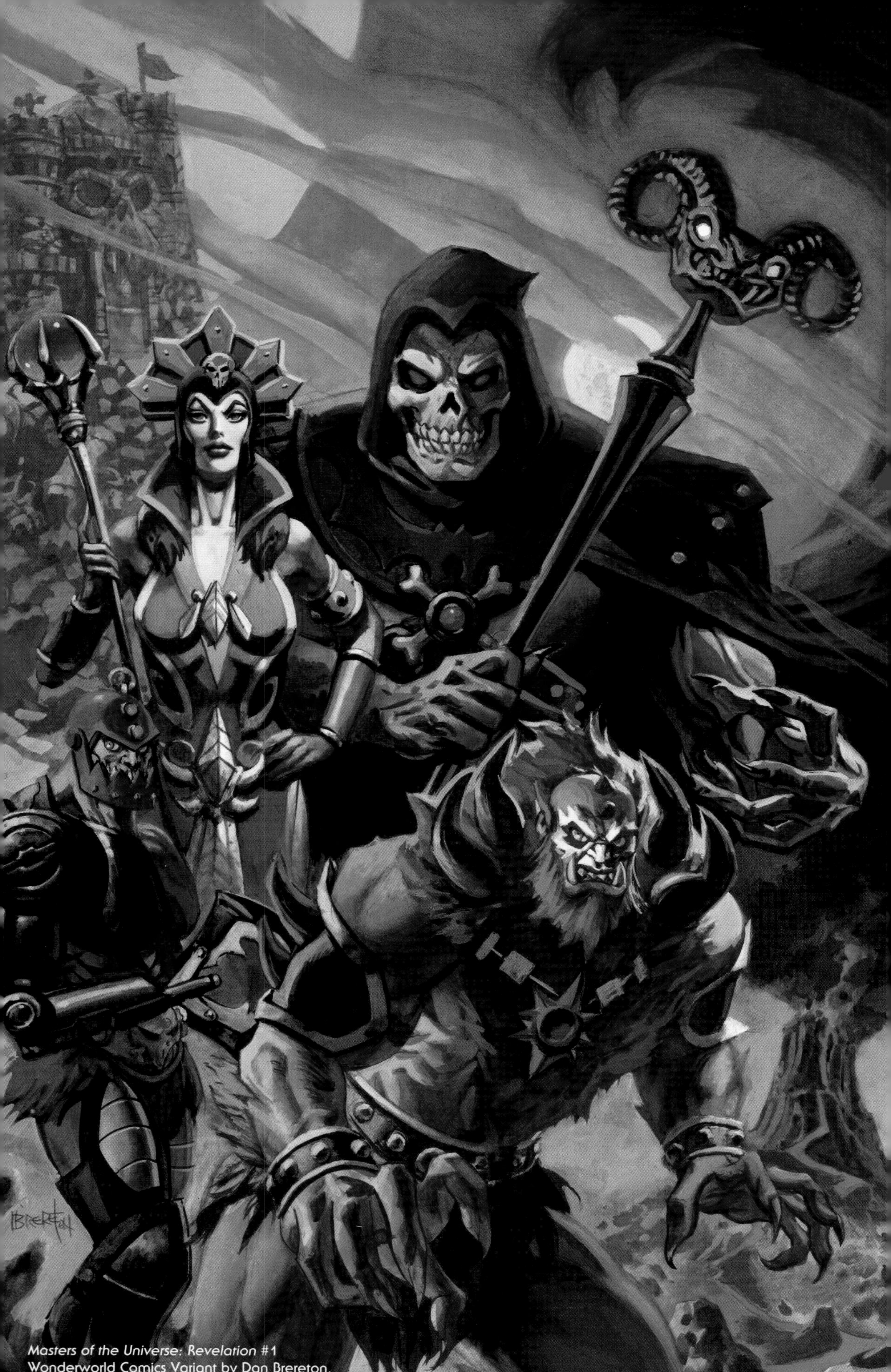

Masters of the Universe: Revelation #1
Wonderworld Comics Variant by Dan Brereton.

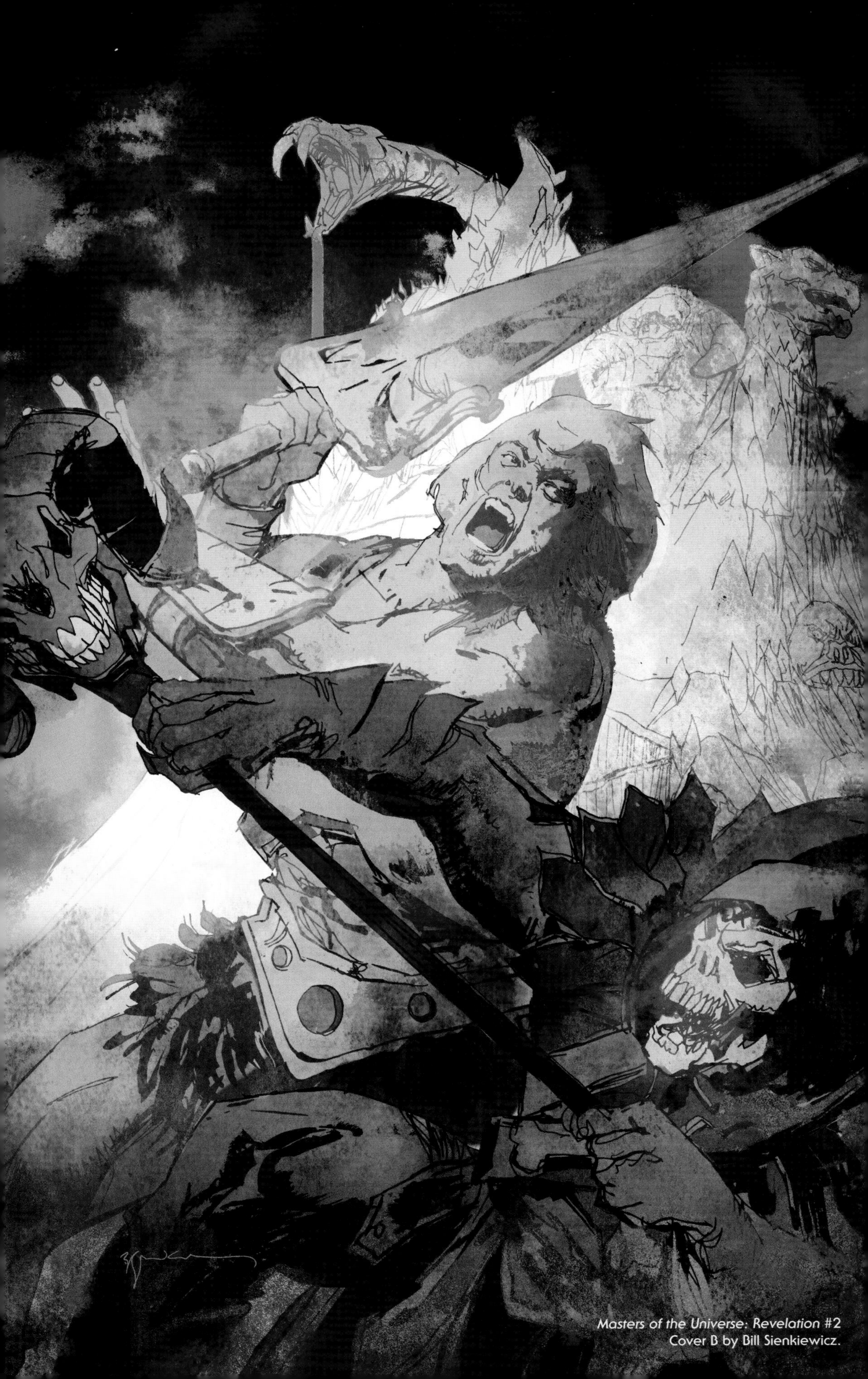

Masters of the Universe: Revelation #2
Cover B by Bill Sienkiewicz.

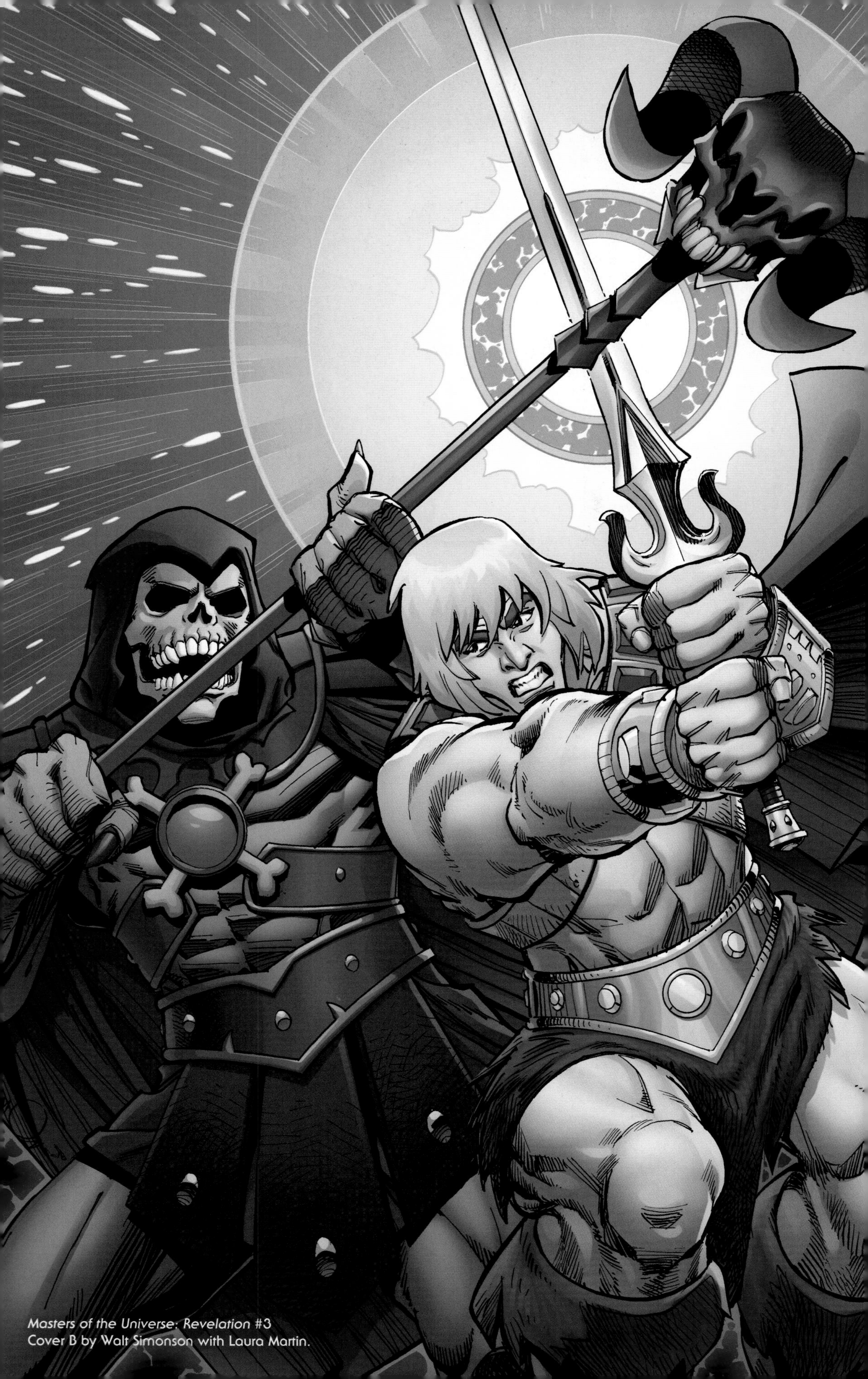

Masters of the Universe: Revelation #3
Cover B by Walt Simonson with Laura Martin.

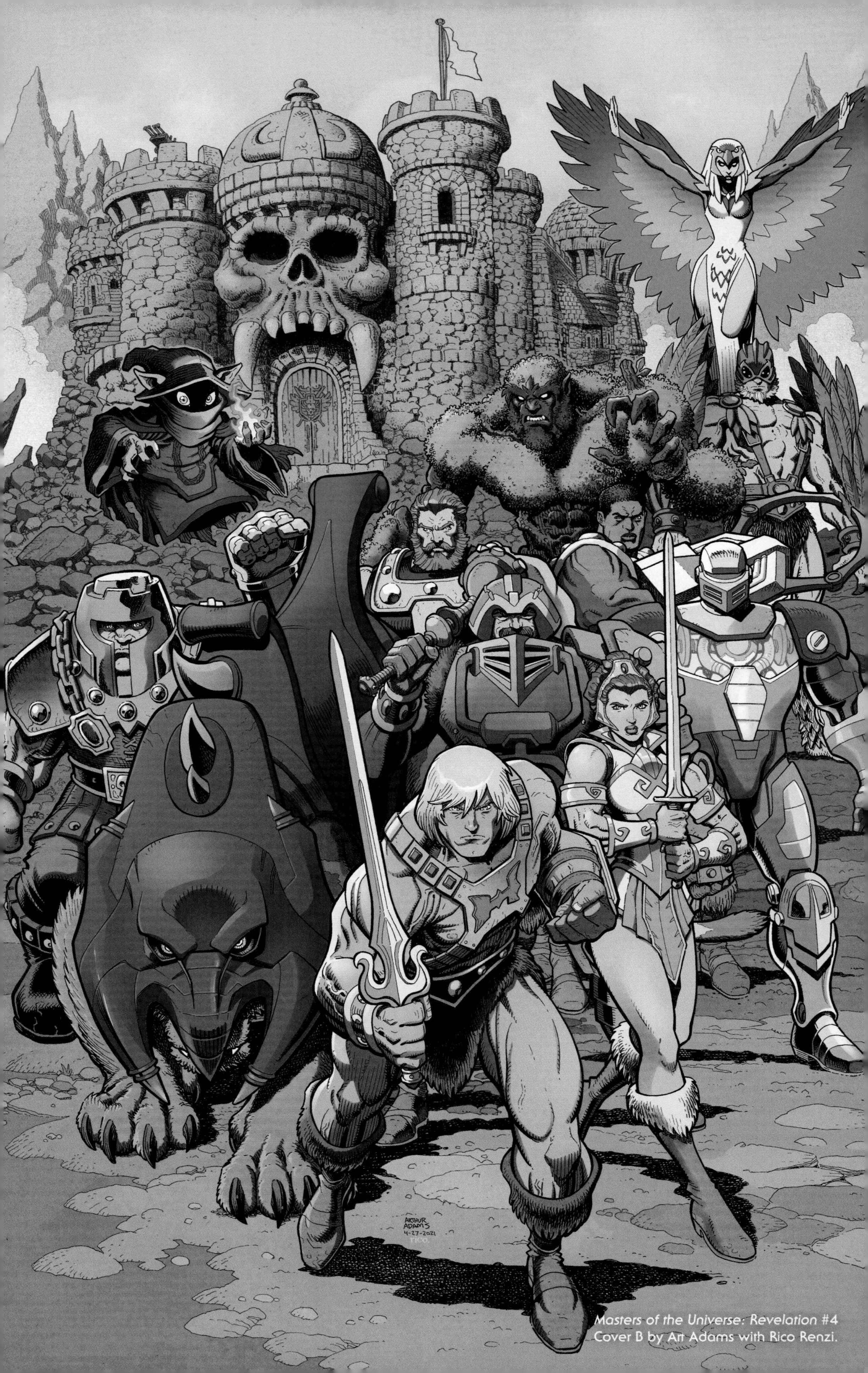
ARTHUR ADAMS 4-27-2021

Masters of the Universe: Revelation #4
Cover B by Art Adams with Rico Renzi.

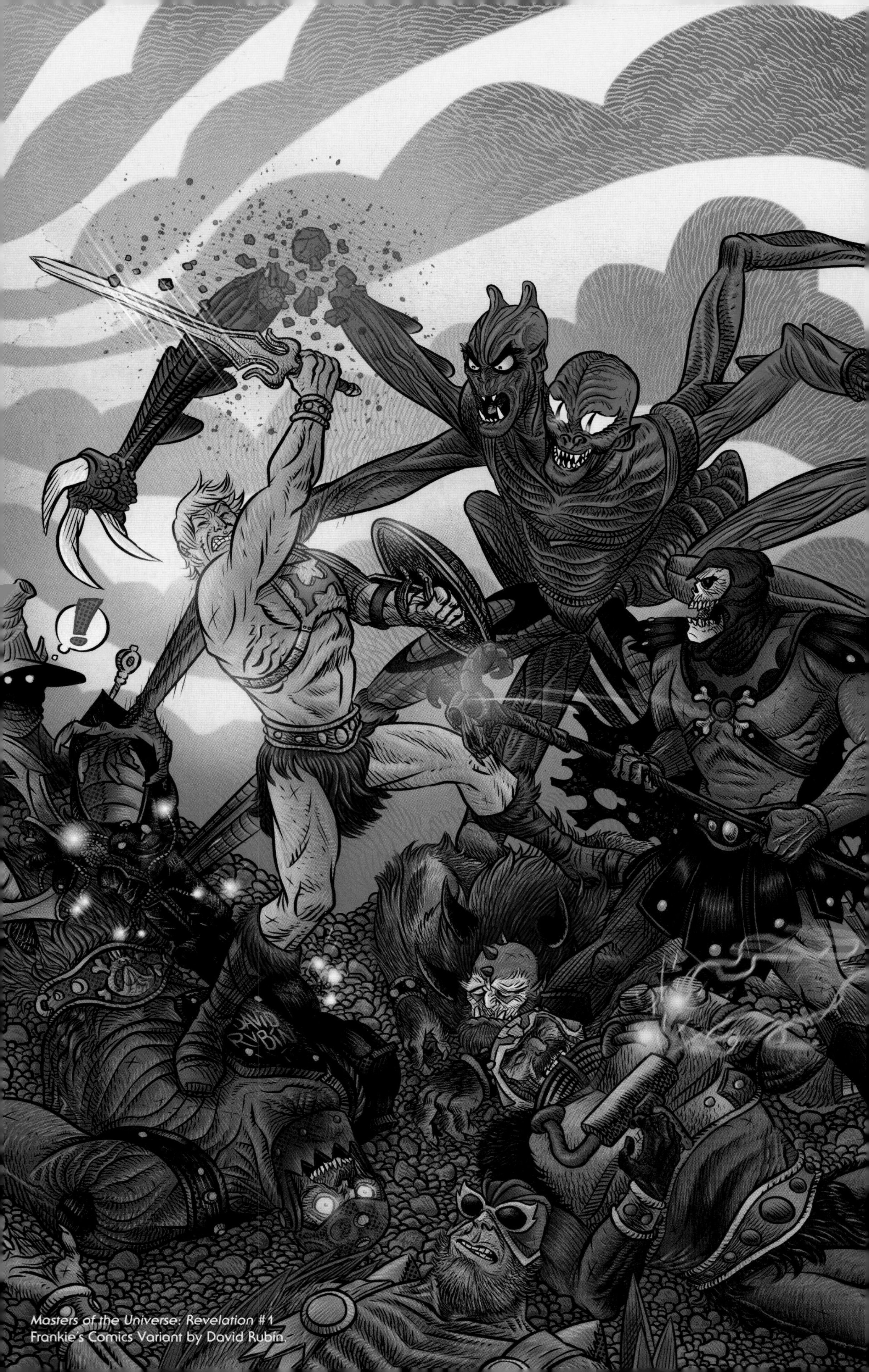

Masters of the Universe: Revelation #1
Frankie's Comics Variant by David Rubín.

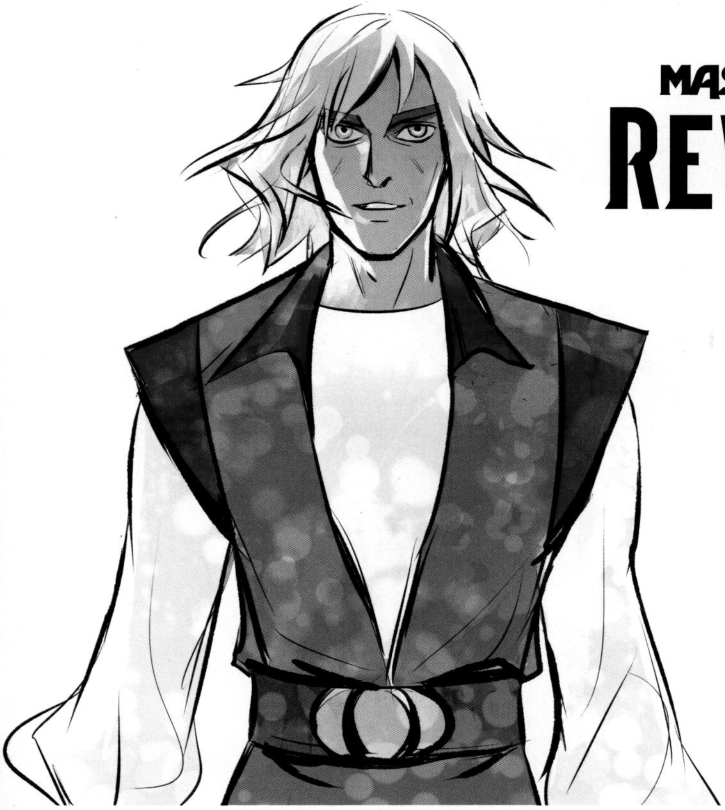

MASTERS OF THE UNIVERSE REVELATION™ SKETCHBOOK

All art by Mindy Lee, except where noted.

The following are art pieces, model sheets, and more by Mindy Lee and Rico Renzi, based off of the animation designs for the Netflix series.

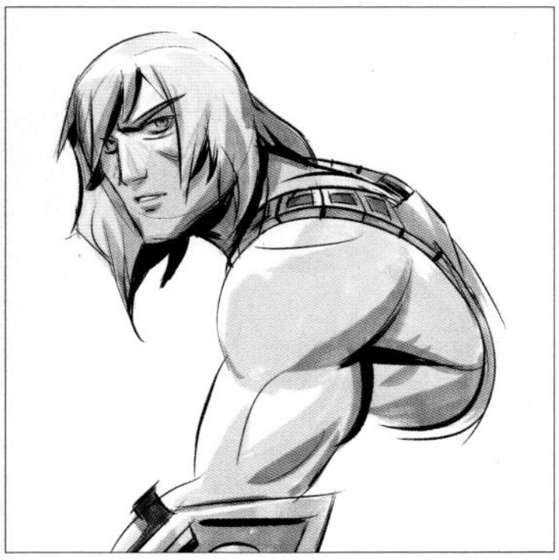

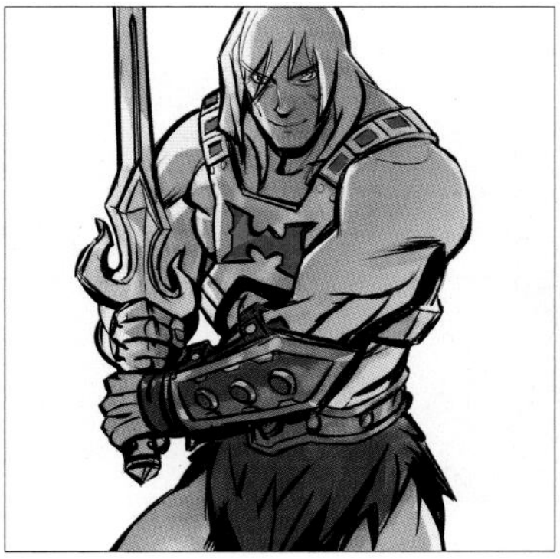

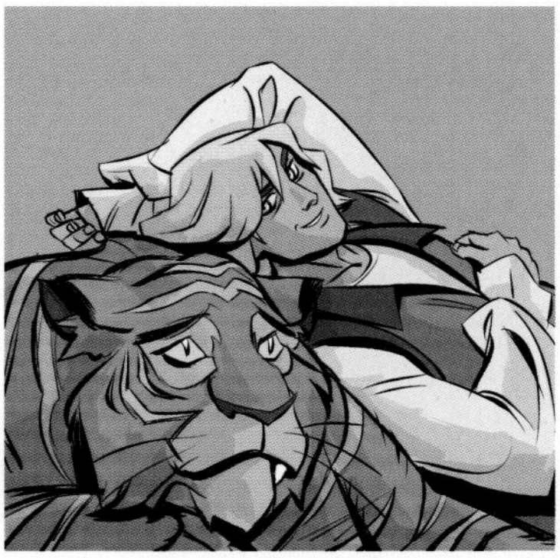

Line art by Mindy Lee. Colors by Rico Renzi.

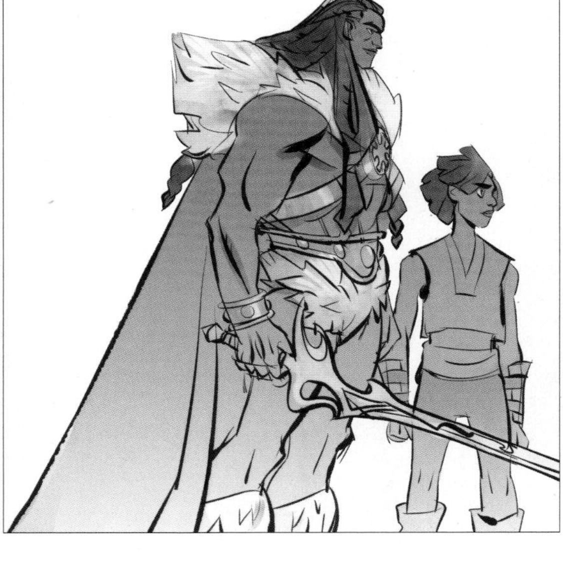

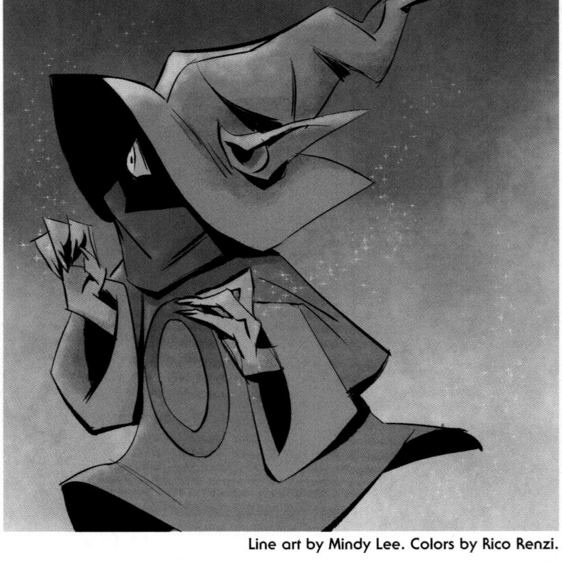

Line art by Mindy Lee. Colors by Rico Renzi.

Line art by Mindy Lee. Colors by Rico Renzi.

Line art by Mindy Lee. Colors by Rico Renzi.

Line art by Mindy Lee. Colors by Rico Renzi.

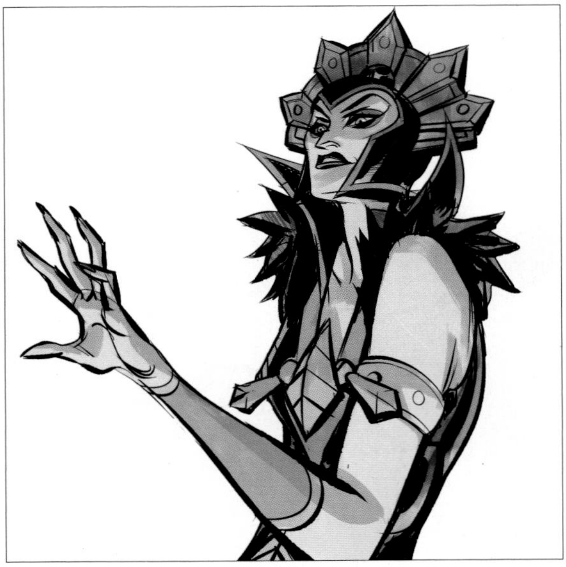

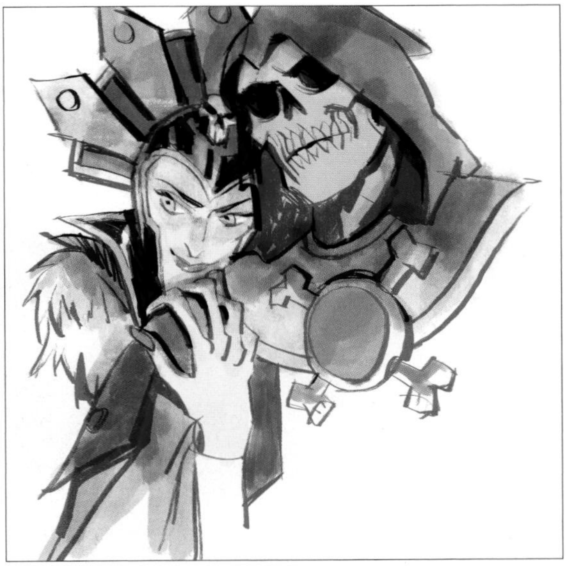

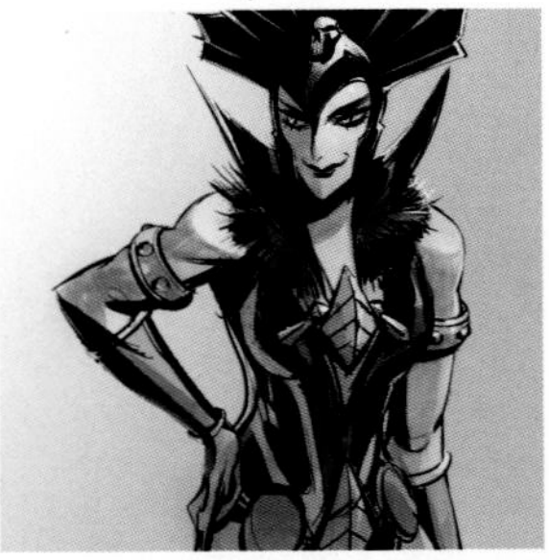

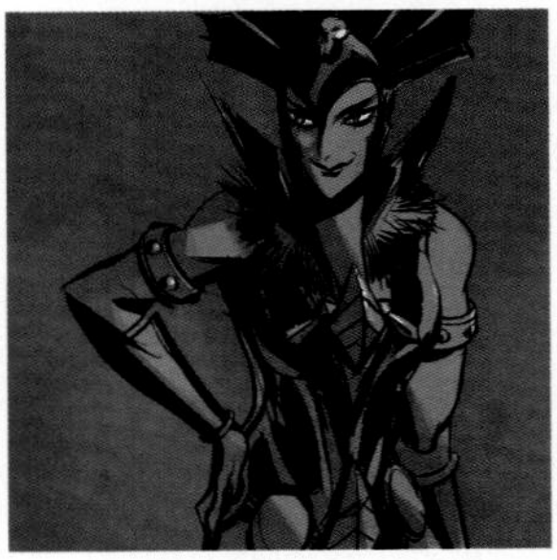

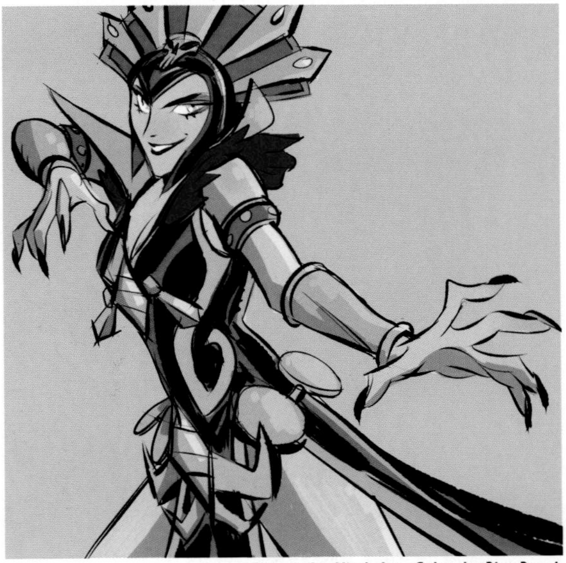

Line art by Mindy Lee. Colors by Rico Renzi.

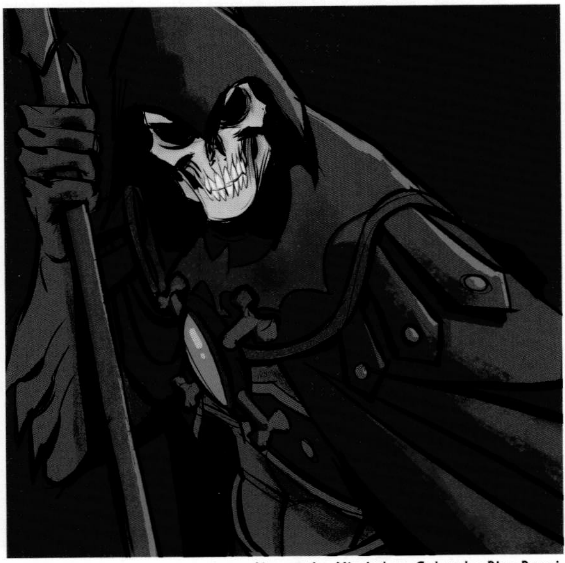

Line art by Mindy Lee. Colors by Rico Renzi.

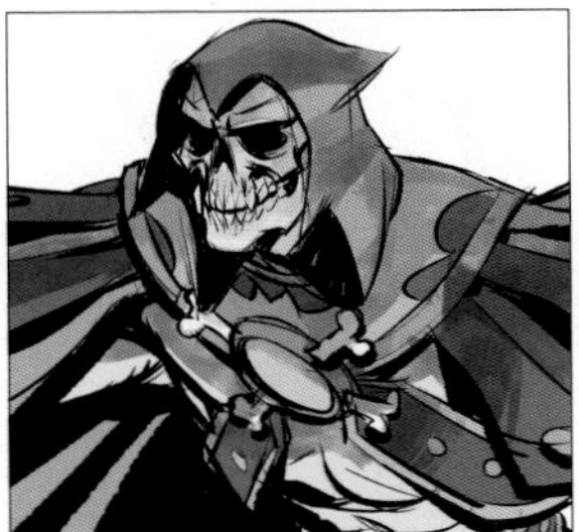

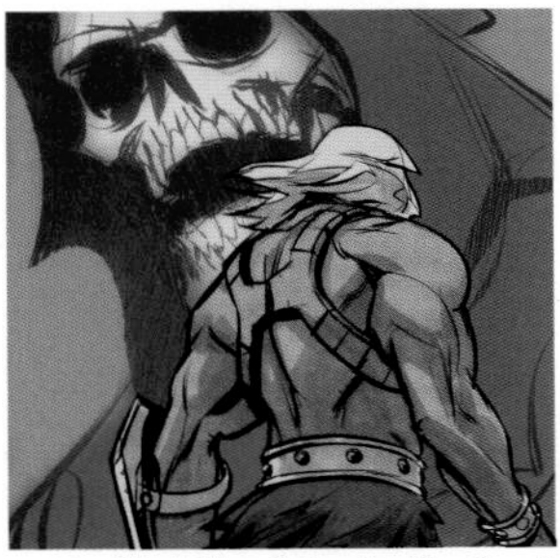

Line art by Mindy Lee. Colors by Rico Renzi.

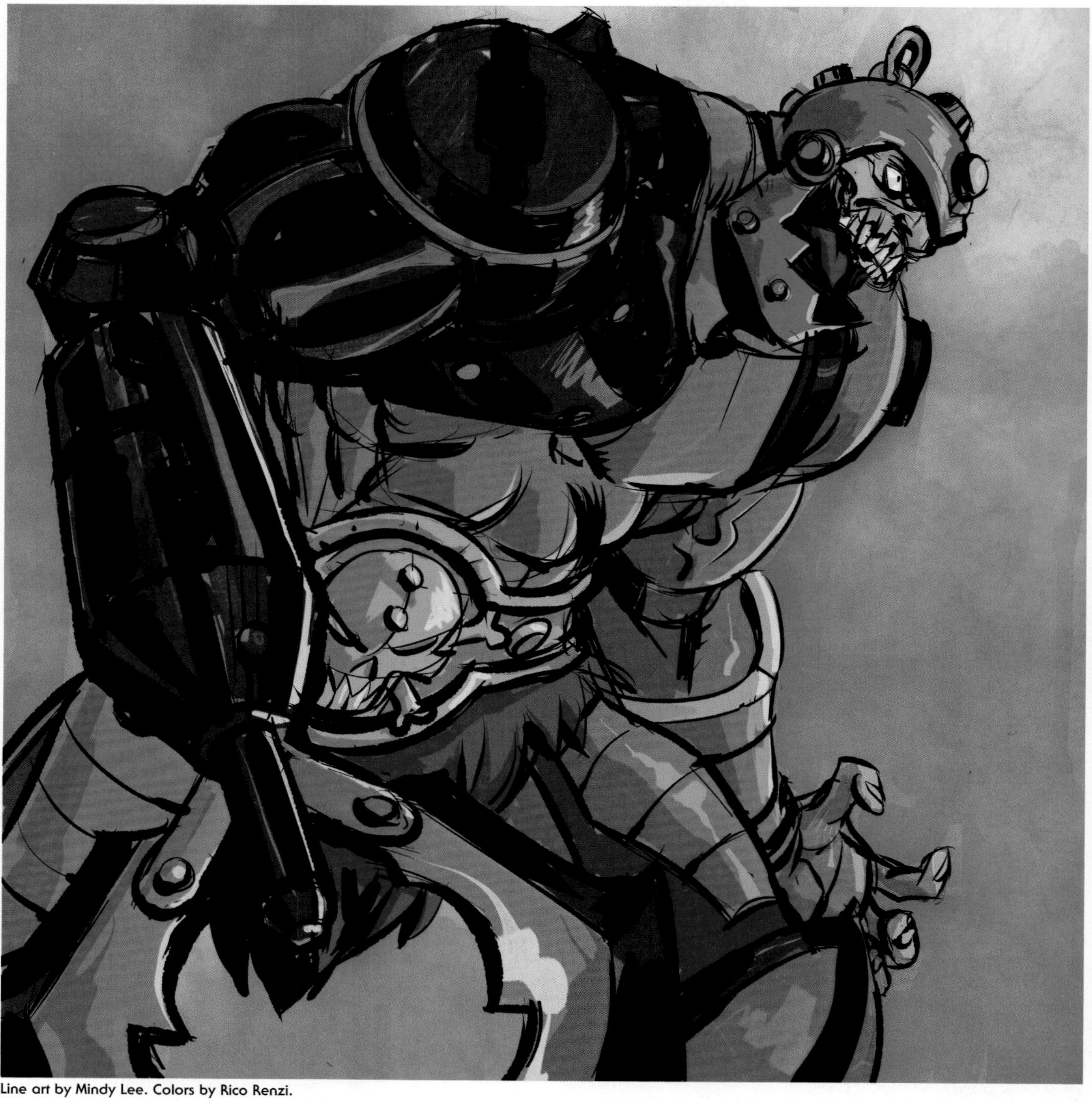

Line art by Mindy Lee. Colors by Rico Renzi.

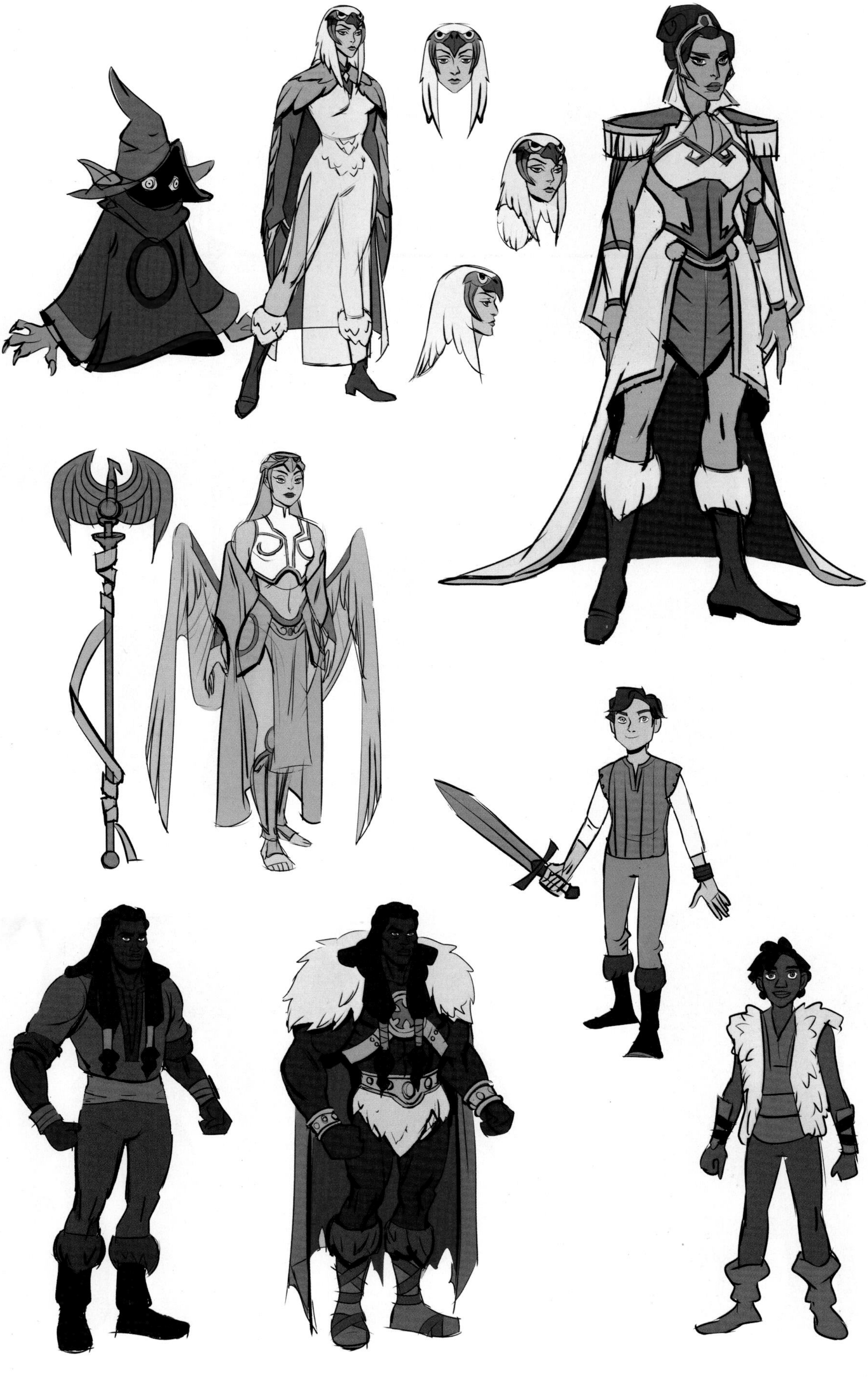

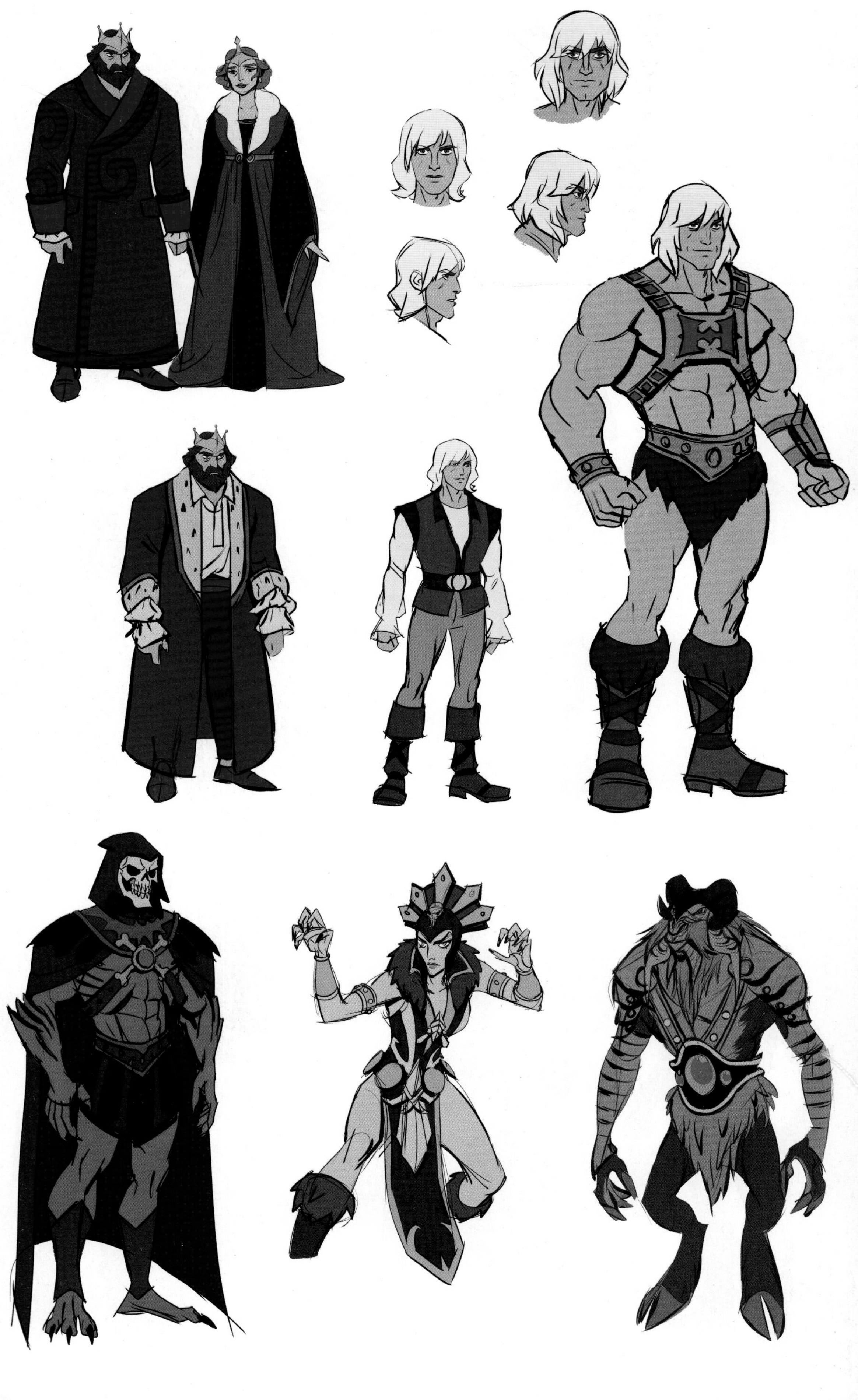